The Flatbush Journal of Jewish Law and Thought

Volume 11 / Spring 2011

A publication of
Hakirah, Inc.
www.Hakirah.org

Ḥakirah

The Flatbush Journal of Jewish Law and Thought

Volume 11 / Spring 2011

Introduction

The role of the *mesorah* in a rapidly changing world and the definition of what constitutes divergence from that *mesorah* are the central concept that dominates this edition of *Ḥakirah*. A recent controversy over the permissibility of female rabbis met with universal condemnation from all branches of Orthodoxy. The statement issued by the Modern Orthodox Rabbinical Council of America (RCA) reads, "Due to our ...commitment to sacred continuity... we cannot accept either the ordination of women or the recognition of women as members of the Orthodox rabbinate." Two of our articles deal with this issue that threatens to separate Modern Orthodoxy from the rest of Torah Jewry. Both articles agree with the condemnations, and a leading *posek* and *Rosh Yeshiva* explains in a brief *teshuva* why it is outside of halakhah and contrary to Jewish *hashkafah*. *Ḥakirah* also presents an article written by two prominent rabbis within the Modern Orthodox community (a member of RCA's BDA and the online editor of Tradition) in which they express their personal view that this exclusion is certainly valid but is based solely on the halakhic process, and question whether a consensus of Rabbanim could ever change this law. This stance contrasts with the *teshuva* and the statement of Agudath Israel, which includes the sentence "These developments represent a radical and dangerous departure from Jewish tradition and the *mesoras haTorah*, and must be condemned in the strongest terms. Any congregation with a woman in a rabbinical position of any sort cannot be considered Orthodox."

Articles in the *Talmud Torah* section and one Hebrew article deal with what may appear to be novel approaches to Talmudic analysis. In *Rava as Mara de-Aṯra in Maḥoza* the author looks at the positions of Rava as a whole and in his historical context to discern unified *shittot*. In another article, *Reconciling Divergent Estimates in Property Assessment Cases*, the authors propose a solution rooted in modern mathematical theory that seems to differ from the *Gemara* to explain a difficult statement of a Tanna. A Hebrew article takes a modern approach to look at how the structuring of a *sugya* impacts on halakhah. *Completing Creation* apparently interprets the Mishnah of the Ten Things Created *Bain HaShmashot* in an untraditional way. But in every case the authors show that their methodology is consistent with that of the *rishonim* and well within the guidelines of our *mesorah*.

The *History of Halakhah* section has three articles dealing with the accuracy of our *mesorah*. The kashrut of birds depends on a specific *mesorah* on the individual species. *Clarifying Why the Muscovy Duck is Kosher: A Factually Accurate Response* gives the history of the halakhic rulings on this bird, and discusses a recent controversy that arose because of misinformation with regard to the facts. *Aleinu: Obligation to Fix the World or the Text?* shows that a very strong case can be made that the original version of Aleinu read לתכן עולם (=**to establish the world** under God's sovereignty), and not לתקן עולם (=**to perfect/improve the world** under God's sovereignty), thus demonstrating that the concept of תקון עולם has no connection to the *Aleinu* prayer. *Methodologies Used by Poskim for Determining the Orientation of the Synagogue* traces how for centuries actual observations were done by the Rabbis trained in astronomy to find the direction of Yerushalayim.

In our *Jewish Thought* section, *Chimeras and the Limits of Casuistry in Jewish Bioethics* deals with the issue of cloning and seeks to analyze how an issue created by modern technology, upon which no *mesorah* could exist, should be dealt with in halakhah. *A Proposal to Improve Rabbinic Decision-Making for Serious Medical Problems* in our *Community* section suggests a new approach to ensure that the *baalei mesorah* are up to date on the latest medical knowledge—which in turn leads to a discussion on whether they should be involved in this area at all. An article on *pidyon shevuyim* questions whether recent calls for communal action to work for the release of Jews in modern prisons really conform to what *Ḥazal* qualified as the important mitzvah of redeeming captives.

The Mystical Spirituality of Rabbi Joseph B. Soloveitchik discusses the analytical and spiritual sides of Rav Soloveichick and suggests that they may be attributed to his paternal and maternal *mesorah*.

In our *Forum* section the issue of how to read Rambam's philosophical works centers on whether his thought represents the *mesorah* of *Ḥazal* or was itself an innovation. Thus our halakhic *mesorah* faces challenges from two directions, from those who feel that Jewish law must adapt as society "progresses" and from others who deny even the legitimacy of the fundamentals of our *masoretic* faith.

One thing remains certain, as Agudath Israel said in its statement on women rabbis, that at some point those taking a specific position that cannot be reconciled with our *mesorah* "cannot be considered Orthodox."

Special thanks to all those who worked hard to make this edition of *Ḥakirah* a reality, including Nina Ackerman Indig, Ari Bornstein and Eliyahu Krakowski who helped proofread and copyedit the English articles; and Heshy Roz for participating in the review process of many of the submitted manuscripts. Thanks also to Ronny Hersh for his constant encouragement and support; Tuvia Ganz for cover design and production; and Chaim Lam for the design and maintenance of our web page, www.Hakirah.org.

As always, it is our continuing hope that the articles in this journal will stimulate thought, study and discussion, and inspire other members of the public to contribute their own insights on topics that are close to their hearts. ☙

LETTERS TO THE EDITOR

Halakhic Will

THE BETH DIN DECISION in "Drafting a Halakhic Will" (*Ḥakirah* volume 10, pp. 73–99, the "Decision") raises several issues I hope R. Warburg can clarify.

1. The Beth Din decision compelling R. Reuben Singer to share the inheritance of his father, R. Simeon, with his sisters and their husbands was based on the application of *kibbud* or *morah av* [Decision at 88.] Yet it is clear-cut *halakha* that neither *kibbud* nor *morah av* applies where the father commands his son to transgress Torah law (*Shulḥan Arukh Yoreh Deah* 240:15). If R. Levy's will was indeed invalid, as the Beth Din found [pp. 86-87], is not the Beth Din's holding tantamount to requiring R. Reuben to transgress the Torah requirement that R. Reuben be the sole inheritor? *Cf. Sdei Ḥemed, maarekhet mem,* at the end of *klal* 219 (*mitzva lekayeim divrei hamet* inapplicable *b'makom issur*). At the very least, would not R. Reuben have a good *kim li* claim against the application by the Beth Din of *kibbud* or *morah av* here?

2. The Beth Din acted to spare R. Simeon *kalone,* embarrassment [Decision at 88]. The Beth Din argues that "*morah* resonates in the words of R. Simeon Levy" and notes "the decedent's concern for his own dignity and the paramount significance of avoiding '*kalone avihem,*' embarrassment to the parties' father in the distribution of his assets... " [*id.*]. As proof, the Beth Din quotes the deceased's own words from his *will* as follows: "... And by utilizing every possible expression of appeal, I request there shall be no difference of opinion on any matter or matters, but that everything shall be peaceful and unanimous, for this is my dignity, the dignity of the family and the dignity of your mother" [*id.*]. Yet it would seem that the Beth Din itself is guilty of embarrassing R. Simeon by deciding that, despite his best efforts to write and effectuate a valid *will* (especially his efforts with regard to the addendum that apparently was drafted and made effective under the auspices of a *rav*, Rabbi Israel [*id.* at 77]), the *will* was ineffective under *hilkhot shtarot,* the laws of *halakhic* documents, in transferring assets to

his daughters, non-Torah heirs. [*Id.* at 86.] It is only by coercing the parties to comply with the *mitzvot* of *kibbud* and *morah av* through enforcement of the signed arbitration agreement, the *shtar borerut,* that the Beth Din finds itself "propelled... to affirm this document, the wishes of R. Simeon Levy, and transfer the assets as set down in the *will*" [*id.* at 88 and note 36]. Essentially, by holding that the *will* was invalidly created, the Beth Din itself seemingly embarrassed R. Simeon by making him blameworthy of being *matneh al mah shekatuv baTorah,* making a stipulation that is contrary to what is enjoined by the Torah (an act that renders the stipulation invalid).

More important, the Beth Din's quote from the *will* is selective, as the Beth Din left out the critical sentence preceding the provision upon which it relies. That sentence reads: "In the event there will be any differences of opinion amongst my sons and daughters on any matter that relates to the estate, then I authorize Rabbi Reuben to decide on every significant or insignificant matter; he and his determination should be followed" [Decision at 98]. In light of that unequivocal directive, does not the Beth Din's *psak,* which contravenes R. Reuben's conclusion that his sisters were not entitled to the inheritance based on Torah law, leave R. Reuben in the position of failing to fulfill his father's wishes that he, and not others (perhaps even including a third party such as the Beth Din), be the final arbiter of disputes? Does not the Beth Din's *psak* result in a blatant disregard of the express wishes of R. Simeon and thus itself cause a failure in *kibbud* and *morah av* on R. Reuben's and his siblings' part?

3. The Beth Din warns the parties that they may not accept an award from the secular court, in which the daughters filed their own suit, if it is in excess of the award mandated by the Beth Din [Decision at 92]. Yet, according to the late Dayan Grunfeld in his English *sefer*, *The Jewish Law of Inheritance* (Targum Press 1987) at 71, R. Moshe Feinstein, *zt"l,* "maintains that a testament made by a Jewish person according to the law of the land [*dina demalchuta*], whilst he was in good health, is valid in Jewish religious law..." Thus, Rav Moshe apparently holds that "a testament, the dispositions of which will be put into effect by the authorities of the country [i.e., probate court], does not need a *kinyan* as one could not imagine a more effective *kinyan* than

this. Hence, since a *kinyan* is not necessary, the legatees can uphold their right also against persons who are the proper heirs by Torah law" [Grunfeld at 72 translating *Iggerot Moshe, Eban haEzer*, vol. I, ch. 104].

Under the circumstances, might the Beth Din have been better off awaiting a decision from the probate court before rendering its *psak?* More likely than not, as evidenced by the restraining order that it apparently granted the daughters [Decision at 76], the probate court ultimately would have reached the same decision that the Beth Din did, namely to grant R. Simeon's wishes evident from the face of the will [*cf.*, *id.* at 85-86], that his daughters and their husbands share in the inheritance. Arguably, the Beth Din might simply have been able to rely on Rav Moshe that no *kinyan* was necessary and thus uphold R. Simeon's efforts in implementing and validating his *will*. Such a decision would have spared R. Simeon the embarrassment of a finding to the contrary, and would have avoided imposing a *psak* upon R. Reuben based on *kibbud* and *morah av* notions, which, as discussed above, arguably are inapplicable here.

Having said all this, I recognize that neither this nor any other Beth Din may wish to rely on Rav Moshe—whose apparent approach in upholding otherwise *halakhically* invalid *wills* through application of *dina demalchuta dina* in probate proceedings is rather novel—especially to the extent that such reliance cedes the Beth Din's own authority in independently adjudicating probate disputes outside of secular court. Nonetheless, Rav Moshe's approach is a *limud zekhut* for those whose wills, such as R. Simeon's, lack a proper *kinyan* or might otherwise fall short under strict *halakhic* scrutiny.

R. Warburg's elucidation on the points that I respectfully have raised, and particularly as to why Rav Moshe's *shitah* is not more universally accepted and was totally ignored by the Beth Din, would be much appreciated and instructive.

Yitzchak Kasdan
Silver Spring, MD

A. Yehuda Warburg responds:

In reply to Mr. Kasdan, Esq.'s, insightful comments:

1. Mr. Kasdan is correct in stating that *kibud av* is inapplicable if such behavior contradicts the norms of halakha. However, compliance with the wish of a

testator is the fulfillment of *kibbud av* and one need not construe that his intent was to nullify the Biblical laws of *yerusha* and deprive his sons of their inheritance. Secondly, given that his sons received a portion of the *yerusha*, there was no nullification of the Biblical laws of *yerusha*. See *Mishpat ha-Yerusha*, p. 478.

2. The assumption of the author is that the *psak din* addressed the halakhic shortcomings of the will in terms of *hilkhot shtarot* and *mitzvah lekayeim divrei hamet*. As such, by the beth din's discussion of this matter we embarrassed the testator. Nothing could be further from the truth.

As was pointed out in the introduction of the essay, this article was "inspired" by a *psak din* rather than offering a rendition of the *psak din*. In fact, my colleagues and I specifically stated in the *psak din* that we will not address the will from the point of *hilkhot shtarot* etc., and we proceeded to address the matter solely on the basis of respecting the testator's wishes.

The second assumption of the author is that we blatantly disregarded the testator's express wishes by usurping the role of the son who was to be the final arbiter of any and all differences among his siblings. Again, nothing could be further from the truth.

As our introduction to the essay notes, some facts have been deleted from our presentation. In fact, Rabbi Reuben tried to resolve with his other siblings (and he had more than 2 siblings) the matter of the equitable distribution of the family assets. However, for numerous reasons his negotiations reaped no fruits. Moreover, both R. Reuben and this panel understood that his designated role did not include rendering a decision that ran afoul of the clear and unambiguous wishes of R. Simeon, i.e. divide up my estate equally between my children. It was only when "his back was against the wall" and he could no longer maintain peace among his siblings that he enlisted the Beth Din's assistance.

3. There are four reasons that most halakhic authorities refuse to subscribe to R. Feinstein's opinion and endorse the execution of a civil will. Firstly, in the context of monetary affairs, the operative principle is "an individual may stipulate contrary to what is written in the Torah." One of the exceptions to this rule is matters of *yerusha*. Given that the Torah labels these halakhot as "*ḥukat mishpat*," loosely translated immutable law, it

falls in the category of *issurim*, i.e., ritual halakhah, and therefore one is proscribed from executing such arrangements. Hence, the execution of a civil will is in violation of an *issur*.

Secondly, pursuant to Shakh's posture (*HM* 7:13-14 note 39), normative halakha will recognize only matters of *dina demalkhuta* that are reflective of halakhic norms. Given that the execution of a secular will is in violation of halakha, one cannot accept this method as a halakhically bona fide avenue for estate planning. Though R. Feinstein endorses the view of Rema, *ad locum,* who disagrees with the Shakh, nevertheless, normative halakhah rejects Rema's view.

Thirdly, there is an accepted rule "*ein kinyan leaḥar mitta*," loosely translated that one cannot acquire assets after death. Any assets that an inheritor acquires must be transferred prior to the testator's death. Consequently, a *matnat bari* is effective since the assets are transferred to the heirs prior to the demise of the testator. As such, given that in a civil will, assets are being transferred after death, such a mechanism is halakhically ineffective.

Finally, and this reason is rarely mentioned when discussing R. Feinstein's position: In offering a validation of a civil will, R. Feinstein states (among other rationales)that one does not require a *kinyan* given that "this is the best form of *gemirat da'ath*," loosely translated as firm resolve to conclude an agreement. In other words, by executing such a document one demonstrates the firm resolve of the testator to transfer his assets. And given that one of the central ingredients of the halakhot of *kinyannim* is *gemirat da'at,* a civil will ought to be recognized. Implicit in his position is that one can transfer assets based on *gemirat da'at* without the implementation of a *kinyan*. Though one can find some support for such a conclusion, many *poskim* reject such a position.

Rav Kook

I ENJOY *Ḥakirah* very much and look forward to reading the stimulating articles. Therefore, I was disappointed by the following:

In the article entitled "Two Controversies involving Rav Kook" by Chaim Landerer in *Ḥakirah* Volume 10 (Summer 2010), there are two serious errors.

On p. 245, fn. 6, the author mentions that Rav Kook wanted to attend the funeral of Rav Sonnenfeld but was dissuaded by

Rav Tzi Pesach Frank. The source for this 'anecdotal incident' is the book *Imrei Shefer* p. 261. However, if one looks in the actual source, one sees that the one who was dissuading Rav Kook was not Rav Zvi Pesach Frank but Rav Kook's own son, Rav Zvi Yehuda Kook.

The implication is obvious, as a son would obviously be more protective of his father than others.

Secondly, in fn. 7 on p. 245, the author again cites as his source *Sefer Imrei Shefer* p. 370; this again is perplexing as the book ends on p. 360.

Your attention to this matter would be very much appreciated.

Ron Yitzchok Eisenman
Congregation Ahavas Israel
Passaic, NJ

Chaim Landerer responds:

My thanks to Rabbi Eisenman for bringing these two issues to my attention.

1. There is indeed an earlier issue of *Imrei Shefer* that has R' Tzvi Yehuda dissuading his father from attending the funeral. This was changed in later editions to R' Tzvi Pesach Frank. Prof. Marc Shapiro was kind enough to contact Yitzchak Dadon, the author of *Imrei Shefer*, on my behalf. Dadon explained that when he heard R. Avraham tell the story he didn't hear him properly. Dadon is Sephardi and not so attuned to the Yiddish accent. R. Avraham told the story about R. Zvi Pesach, and Dadon thought when he said R. Zvi—not clearly hearing the second word—that R' Avraham was referring to R. Zvi Yehudah. When the book was published, two separate people came to him and told him that he misheard, and that R. Avraham was in fact speaking of R. Zvi Pesach Frank.

2. This was indeed a typographical error on my part. The correct page number is 350.

ᘓ

Instructions for Contributors

Ḥakirah, The Flatbush Journal of Jewish Law and Thought, publishes original, interesting, well-researched and well-organized manuscripts that provide new or profound insights into areas of Jewish *halakhah* and *hashkafah.*

Manuscripts should be sent by fax to (718) 534 – 3142, and an electronic copy should follow to HakirahFlatbush@msn.com. Short references—for example, to a Biblical verse or to a page within the Talmud—should be embedded directly into the text of the manuscript. Longer references should be inserted electronically as footnotes, rather than endnotes. The preferred word-processing program is Microsoft Word.

The author's name should not appear on the manuscript, as it is the Journal's policy to forward the articles for evaluation without disclosing the author's identity. On a separate cover sheet include your name, a short bio, an abstract of your article, your telephone number, fax number, and e-mail address.

After reviewing and accepting your manuscript, we are likely to request clarification of certain points. A revised electronic copy of your manuscript will then be required.

To encourage a wide variety of contributors, the Journal accepts articles employing the Hebrew transliteration style of either *Encyclopedia Judaica* or *ArtScroll.* If you have no preference we suggest that you follow the pronunciation rules used by the *Encyclopedia Judaica.* Words in languages other than English should always be italicized, unless the foreign words have become part of the English language.

For more information about writing an article for *Ḥakirah* see <www.Hakirah.org\HakirahGuideToWriting.pdf>.

Recent Statements by Agudath Israel and The Rabbinical Council of America Regarding Women Rabbis

To place the following two articles, regarding the ordination of women as rabbis, in perspective we present, in chronological order, the following statements issued by Agudath Israel and The Rabbinical Council of America. Ed.

Statement of the Moetzes Gedolei HaTorah of America (10 Adar 5770) [February 25, 2010][1]

Rabbi Avi Weiss has conferred "semikha" upon a woman, has made her an Assistant Rabbi at the Hebrew Institute of Riverdale where she carries out certain traditional rabbinical functions, and has now given her the title of "Rabbah" (formerly "Maharat"). He has stated that the change in title is designed to "make it clear that Sara Hurwitz is a full member of our rabbinic staff, a rabbi with the additional quality of a distinct woman's voice."

These developments represent a radical and dangerous departure from Jewish tradition and the mesoras haTorah, and must be condemned in the strongest terms. Any congregation with a woman in a rabbinical position of any sort cannot be considered Orthodox.

Moetzes Gedolei HaTorah of America

Rabbi Simcha Bunim Ehrenfeld
Rabbi Yitzchok Feigelstock
Rabbi Dovid Feinstein
Rabbi Aharon Feldman
Rabbi Yosef Harari-Raful
Rabbi Shmuel Kamenetsky
Rabbi Aryeh Malkiel Kotler
Rabbi Avrohom Chaim Levin
Rabbi Yaakov Perlow
Rabbi Aaron Schechter

---

1 See <http://torahmusings. com/2010/02/moetzes-condemns-ordination-of-women/>.

March 9, 2010, 23 Adar, 5770: Upon consultation with its rabbinic leadership, Agudath Israel of America issued the following statement today:[2]

The leadership of the Rabbinical Council of America and Rabbi Avi Weiss have apparently reached agreement that Rabbi Weiss would no longer confer the title of "Rabba" upon graduates of his women's seminary, but rather the title "Maharat."

This superficial move does not in any way change the position of the Moetzes Gedolei HaTorah that placing women in traditional rabbinic positions departs from the Jewish mesorah, and that any congregation with a woman in such a position cannot call itself Orthodox.

That the leadership of a respected rabbinical organization seems to have capitulated to Rabbi Weiss' enterprise is deeply dismaying. We trust that this capitulation does not represent the perspective of the principled majority of the organization's member rabbis.

Upon consultation with its rabbinic leadership, Agudath Israel of America issued the following statement today: [March 11, 2010][3]

Hamodia reports that Rabbi Shmuel Goldin, First Vice-President of the Rabbinical Council of America, has clarified that the RCA "in no way endorses the title '*maharat*' or the '*maharat*' program under the direction of Rabbi Avi Weiss."

Rabbi Goldin further quotes RCA President Rabbi Moshe Kletenik as having stated that ordination of women "is a breach of our *Mesorah* and is unacceptable practice in Orthodoxy," and that "it is also unacceptable for an Orthodox synagogue to have a woman on its rabbinical staff."

Agudath Israel warmly welcomes the clarification and commends the RCA leaders for their forthright and principled words.

---

2 See <https://www.5tjt.com/international-news/6388-a-statement-from-agutath-yisrael-of-america>.

3 See <http://www.cross-currents.com/archives/2010/03/11/agudath-israel-commends-rca-leaders/#ixzz1Axuo RUKb>.

May we all continue to stand guard to protect the integrity of our *Mesorah*.

Resolution on Women's Communal Roles in Orthodox Jewish Life Adopted Without Dissent by the 51st Convention of The Rabbinical Council of America. [April 27, 2010] [4]

1) The flowering of Torah study and teaching by God-fearing Orthodox women in recent decades stands as a significant achievement. The Rabbinical Council of America is gratified that our chaverim have played a prominent role in facilitating these accomplishments.

2) We members of the Rabbinical Council of America see as our sacred and joyful duty the practice and transmission of Judaism in all of its extraordinary, multifaceted depth and richness – halakhah, hashkafah, tradition and historical memory.

3) In light of the opportunity created by advanced women's learning, the Rabbinical Council of America encourages a diversity of halakhically and communally appropriate professional opportunities for learned, committed women, in the service of our collective mission to preserve and transmit our heritage. Due to our aforesaid commitment to sacred continuity, however, we cannot accept either the ordination of women or the recognition of women as members of the Orthodox rabbinate, regardless of the title.

4) Young Orthodox women are now being reared, educated, and inspired by mothers, teachers and mentors who are themselves beneficiaries of advanced women's Torah education. As members of the new generation rise to positions of influence and stature, we pray that they will contribute to an ever-broadening and ever-deepening wellspring of talmud Torah, *yir'at Shamayim*, and *dikduk be-mitzvot*. ☙

4 See <http://www.rabbis.org/news/article.cfm?id=105551>.

Women Rabbis?

By: HERSHEL SCHACHTER

I

In the printed notes of Rav Soloveitchik's *shiurim* on *Shulchan Aruch, Yoreh De'ah*,[1] prepared for publication by Rabbi Eliyakim Koenigsberg, in the very first essay, the Rav is quoted as having said that a woman may not serve as a rabbi. The Tanna'im understood the *pasuk* in Chumash as implying that women may not be appointed to the position of King.[2] The Talmud points out[3] that the repetition of the verb in the *pasuk* "*som tasim alecha melech*"[4] implies that this principle applies not only to the position of King, but to all positions of *serarah* and authority. Hence it would follow[5] that a woman may not be appointed president of a synagogue or as rabbi, since these are also positions of *serarah*.[6] The reason the Rav brought up this topic in the beginning of *Yoreh De'ah* is because the Rama[7] quotes the practice of not appointing a woman as the town

1 "שיעורי הרב על עניני שחיטה מליחה בשר וחלב ותערובות" (2005 Mesorah, OU).

2 שום תשים עליך מלך – מלך ולא מלכה (ספרי קנז) והשוה גמ' ברכות (מט.) מלכות אינה בנשים. ודין זה הובא ברמב"ם פ"א ה"ה ממלכים.

3 יבמות (מה:).

4 דברים יז:טו.

5 הרמב"ם פ"א ממלכים ה"ה מצרף ביחד שתי דרשות אלו וכותב להלכה שאין למנות אשה לשום שררה. וכנראה שכן היתה גרסתו בספרו הנ"ל (וכפי המופיע בפי' המיוחס להראב"ד שמה), האיש ממנים פרנס על הצבור אבל לא האשה. ותגובת רבנו על מינוי גולדה מאיר לראש הממשלה, עי' ס' נפש הרב (עמ' צ'-צ"א). ובענין שררה לנשים עי' עוד שרידי אש ח"ג (סי' ק"ה).

6 עי' רמ"א ליו"ד סוף סי' רמ"ה ובהגר"א שמה ס"ק ל"ח שתפסו בפשיטות שרבנות בקהילה גדרה כשררה. וכן תפס בפשיטות בתשו' אבני נזר חיו"ד (סי' שי"ב), ובתשו' שרידי אש ח"ב סי' פ"ט.

7 יורה דעה סי' א' ס"א.

Rabbi Hershel Schachter is *Rosh Kollel* in RIETS' Marcos and Adina Katz Kollel and occupies Yeshiva University's Nathan and Vivian Fink Distinguished Professorial Chair in Talmud.

shochet. The Beis Yosef quotes the Kol Bo who seems to say[8] that although a woman may *shecht* privately, she may not be appointed as the town *shochet*. If indeed this was the intention of the Kol Bo it could be understood that this appointment would constitute a form of *serarah*. Indeed in Europe before the war, the town *shochet* was, in a certain sense, the assistant rabbi. The *shochet* knew sections of *Shulchan Aruch, Yoreh De'ah*, and often when the rabbi would be on vacation, the *shochet* would *paskin* the *she'eilos*.

The idea behind this halachah is the principle of *tznius*. People make a mistake in thinking that *tznius* only applies to the proper form of dress for women. That is only one aspect of *tznius*. The basic principle of *tznius* is that Hashem is described by the prophet Isaiah as a *Keil Mistater*, "a G-d who concealed Himself."[9] In fact, he does such a good job at hiding, many don't even realize that He is really there. Hashem created all men *B'Tzelem Elokim*, and *Bnai Yisrael* with an even deeper degree of this *Tzelem Elokim*—known as *Banim LaMakom*. In *Parashas Ki Savo,*[10] the Torah commands all Jews *ve'halachta bidrachav*, to imitate Hashem by going in His ways. The idea behind the mitzvah is not to pretend that we are someone that we are not, but rather to preserve the *Tzelem Elokim* that we already possess. The very next *pasuk* in the Torah continues, *ve'ra'u kol amei ha'aretz,* and all the nations of the world will realize that we have succeeded in preserving our *Tzelem Elokim*, then *ve'yar'u mi'meka*, they will learn from us how to act in a fashion of *yir'as Shamayim*.[11] They too possess a *Tzelem Elokim*, and they too have the ability to preserve their *Tzelem Elokim*. The Chumash is pointing out here by *ve'ra'u kol amei ha'aretz*, the idea that was spelled out later by the prophet Isaiah, that one of the roles of the Jewish people is to serve as "a light unto the other nations" (*or la'goyim*).[12]

Included in the mitzvah to go in the ways of Hashem and thereby preserve our *Tzelem Elokim* is the concept of a *Keil Mistater*.

8 בית יוסף ריש טור יו"ד.

9 ישעיה מה:טו.

10 דברים כח:ט.

11 עיי"ש בס' אדרת אליהו (בשם הגר"א). See my essay in *Rav Chesed: Essays in Honor of Rabbi Dr. Haskel Lookstein* vol. 2 p. 203.

12 ישעיה מט:ו.

We too must therefore strive to be anonymous and maintain strict privacy. We know that Hashem did reveal Himself on rare occasions. This is known as *Gilui Shechinah*. So on occasion we are all called upon to do things in a demonstrative fashion and in a public forum. We must have a government with a king, a governor and a mayor. We need a *shaliach tzibur* to lead us in *tefillah*; we need a rabbi. But even then we recommend that whenever possible, only the men should compromise on *tznius* and take on these public positions. Women are always encouraged to avoid compromising on their privacy. The Midrash[13] comments on the fact that the first *luchos*, which were given with great publicity and fanfare, were broken; they suffered from an *ayin hara*. The second *luchos*, which were given in a very quiet and private fashion (*b'tznius*), were not broken. The moral of the story is that it is always best to strive for *tznius*.

We have a very old *minhag* to break a glass under the *chuppah*. According to the Tashbatz (a *talmid* of the Maharam miRottenberg), the *minhagim* of the wedding are based on *Maamad Har Sinai* which was, so to speak, the wedding between Hashem and Klal Yisrael. The Maharshal suggests[14] that the breaking of the glass under the *chuppah* is to commemorate the smashing of the *luchos*. What is the significance of commemorating the breaking of the *luchos* at our weddings? Rav Soloveitchik suggested that perhaps this is to serve as a warning to the young couple that they should be careful to maintain *tznius* in their lives. When *tznius* is lost, sometimes this might lead to utter *churban*.[15]

II

From the interpretation of the *pesukim* in *Parashas Mishpatim*,[16] the *Chachamim* of the Talmud[17] have established that at least for a *din Torah* in the area of *gezeilos ve'chavalos*, a Bais Din consisting of three *semuchim* (ordained rabbis) is required. Usually we have a

13 תנחומא על הפסוק פסל לך. ועי' מפניני הרב (עמ' שפ"ו – שפ"ז).

14 ביש"ש פ"א דכתובות סי' י"ז.

15 השוה ס' דברי הרב (עמ' רכ"ט).

16 שמות (כב:ז,ח).

17 סנהדרין (ג:).

rule[18] that one who is disqualified to serve as an *eid* in a *din Torah* is likewise disqualified to serve as a *dayan*. The Mishnah[19] has established that women are disqualified to serve as witnesses in a *din Torah*. The combination of these two principles has led the majority of the Baalei HaTosafos to believe that women are disqualified from serving as *dayanim*. Tosafos[20] record a minority position that a woman may serve as a *dayan*.

Biblically, to qualify as a *dayan*, one must have *semichah*. Obviously this minority opinion of Tosafos feels that a woman may have *semichah*. However, this opinion has been outvoted centuries ago, and the accepted view in *Shulchan Aruch* (*Choshen Mishpat*, Chapter 7, no. 4) is that a woman may not function as a *dayan*.

About fifteen hundred years ago, the Biblical institution of *semichah* was discontinued. *Semichah* can only be conferred in Eretz Yisrael,[21] and for many years the non-Jewish government in Eretz Yisrael attempted to prevent the rabbis from conferring *semichah*. The Talmud records[22] the *mesirus nefesh* of the Tanna, Rabbi Yehuda ben Bava, in publicly conferring *semichah* on several of his students, knowing in advance that he would be put to death for so doing. He obviously felt that this issue belonged in the category of mitzvos where we declare *yehareg v'al ya'avor*;[23] we encourage one to give up his life in order to secure the continuation of the chain of *semichah* from the days of Moshe Rabbeinu. The *Shulchan Aruch* states[24] that today's *semichah* is not really the biblical ordination spoken of by the halachah, but merely an "imitation *semichah*" in fulfillment of the rabbinic law instituted by the later rabbis that no one should *paskin* any *halachos* unless authorized to do so by his *rebbe*. It is for this reason that in Europe many referred to today's *semichah* as "*heter hora'ah*" (permission to *paskin*).

Years ago, when the Jewish Theological Seminary was considering ordaining women, Rabbi Shaul Lieberman expressed his ex-

---

18 נדה (מט:).

19 שבועות (ל.).

20 תוס' ב"ק (טו.) ד"ה אשר.

21 סנהדרין (יד.).

22 סנהדרין (יג: - יד.).

23 עי' כסף משנה ריש פ"ה מהל' יסה"ת.

24 רמ"א ליו"ד סי' רמ"ב סי"ד וש"ך שמה ס"ק כ"ב.

treme disapproval. He quoted *Rishonim* that the modern "imitation *semichah*" is, in a certain sense, a carryover from the *semichah* of old, and since the accepted view is that women may not serve as *dayanim*, and the *semichah* of old was for the purpose of enabling one to function as a *dayan*, it would follow that the real biblical *semichah* was never conferred on women.[25] And likewise, the modern imitation *semichah*, being a carryover from the *semichah* of old, cannot be conferred on women.

Based on the interpretation of the *Torah she'Be'al Peh*, the *pesukim* tell us that we may not appoint a *ger* to serve as King or in any capacity of *serarah*, as, for example, to serve as a rabbi of a community, or (as mentioned by the Talmud)[26] as president of a labor union. A *ger* may not serve as a *dayan* in a *din Torah* involving a Yisrael, but may serve as a *dayan* in a *din Torah* involving other *geirim*.[27] Obviously it is possible to confer *semichah* on a *ger*, otherwise he would not even be able to serve as a *dayan* for a case involving other *geirim*. Although a *ger* may not serve as a rabbi in a *kehillah* of Yisraelim, we still allow *geirim* to join the *semichah* program in the Yeshiva and to receive *semichah* upon successful completion of their studies, because years ago real *semichah* was sometimes conferred on *geirim*. Women, however, never received real *semichah*. Therefore, according to the *Rishonim* quoted by Rabbi Lieberman, today's "imitation *semichah*," being a carryover from the biblical *semichah* of old, ought not to be granted to women.[28] ☙

---

25 See Marc B. Shapiro, *Saul Lieberman and the Orthodox* (University of Scranton Press, 2006) p. 37 in the Hebrew section.

26 קדושין (עו:).

27 יבמות (קב.).

28 ולהרחבת הדברים עי' עוד מש"כ במאמרי ב <http://www.torahweb.org/torah/2004/parsha/rsch_dvorim2.html>.

Orthodox Women Rabbis? Tentative Thoughts that Distinguish Between the Timely and the Timeless

By: MICHAEL J. BROYDE and SHLOMO M. BRODY[1]

I. Introduction: Unity without Uniformity, Diversity without Divisiveness

In the second half of the twentieth century, the halakhic community has confronted several new intellectual challenges to the structure of Jewish law. Painting with a broad brush, these include: The reestablishment of the State of Israel with all of its unique halakhic dilemmas; the welcoming of Jews as equal citizens into the open Western democracies of the United States, Canada, and many other nations; the rise of new and powerful technologies as part of daily life; and the changing social status of women in the world.

Orthodox Judaism has not responded to any of these developments with a unified approach. Before we focus on the issue of women, it is worth briefly reviewing the first three topics. The reestablishment of the State of Israel has produced diverse responses, ranging from Rabbi Tzvi Yehuda Kook's advocacy of messianic

---

[1] We thank the dozens of *poskim*, rabbis, and lay leaders who provided valuable comments to earlier drafts of this article, which has been significantly revised and expanded since its original presentation and limited distribution at the April 2010 Rabbinical Council of America (RCA) convention.

Michael J. Broyde is a Professor of Law at Emory University School of Law, was the Founding Rabbi of the Young Israel in Atlanta, and is a Dayan in the Beth Din of America.
Shlomo M. Brody teaches at Yeshivat Hakotel, serves as the online editor of *Tradition* and its *Text & Texture* blog, and writes the *Ask the Rabbi* column for *The Jerusalem Post*.

Zionism to the Satmar Rebbe's full-blown rejection of the State as the devil's work. Most of Orthodoxy falls comfortably between these poles, and we recognize the entire spectrum as part of the Orthodox halakhic community. The welcoming of Jews as equal citizens in America has produced a similar diversity, from Rabbi Menashe Klein's denial that *dina demalkhuta dina* applies in America to Rabbi Joseph Soloveitchik's claim that it is a sin to purchase products from people who do not pay sales tax. Again, most of Orthodoxy resides between these poles. While more subtle, the same diversity exists with regard to approaches and attitudes to technology. Ranging from the contrary analyses of Rabbi Shlomo Zalman Auerbach and the Chazon Ish of the prohibition to use electricity on Shabbat, to larger questions regarding medical ethics and other technological advances, the Orthodox community lives with a diversity of very different approaches.

Many of these disagreements remain passionate and unfortunately sometimes hostile, to the point where some disputants have dismissed their interlocutors as beyond the pale of Orthodox Judaism. Most Orthodox Jews, however, continue to recognize their disputants as acting within the framework of halakhic Judaism, even if they deem the opposing position to be in error. While occasionally an attitude of complete intolerance toward other positions may be correct (the dangerous anti-Zionist activities of certain members of the *Neturei Karta* come to mind), we think that the more expansive demarcation of Orthodox opinions, in almost all circumstances, remains the better approach.

Until the reestablishment of a Sanhedrin, we need to achieve unity and not uniformity, enabling diversity without divisiveness. This is the appropriate historical lesson of the terrible schism within European Orthodox Jewry in the nineteenth and early twentieth centuries. The vicious fights between religious groups (Ḥasidim versus Mitnagdim, Zionists versus anti-Zionists) and the many polemical disputes about the details of ritual life (sermons in the vernacular, the placement of the *bimah*, *sheḥittah* knives) strike one, with the wisdom of hindsight, as unwise. The fratricidal fighting did not help our community or Judaism as a whole, and appears particularly misguided in light of how we have come over time to live with these differences. This has been made possible, in part, because we have learned which areas we can and cannot fully cooperate together, but largely because we recognize that there are different acceptable Orthodox responses to modernity. As such, much work is done together in *kashrut*, *gittin* (divorce documents) and *batei din* (judicial courts)—areas in which reciprocal recognition of *ne'emanut* (fealty to halakhah) are essential—even as our different rabbinic and synagogue organizations advocate varying Orthodox ideologies and agendas.

This same motto of "unity without uniformity, diversity without divisiveness" should also apply to the range of opinions regarding women's issues, and in particular, the role of women as students and teachers of Torah. Clearly, there exists a wide spectrum of opinions on this matter, ranging from Rabbi Soloveitchik's opinion that Talmud study ought to be a routine part of women's education, to Rabbi Teitelbaum's approach that women may only be taught the Written Torah without even Rashi's commentary. Many others fall out between these two poles, again recognizing that all remain a part of the Orthodox community.

Recently, the Orthodox community came perilously close to fissuring over the decision by Rabbi Avi Weiss to grant the title Rabba (the feminine of the Hebrew term Rav, or Rabbi) to a woman who he felt was deserving of this title. The fissure was partially averted, at least temporarily, by Rabbi Weiss's decision to cease granting such titles in the future, but his actions have thrust the larger issue of women clergy onto the public stage.

In the coming pages, we attempt to offer a framework for understanding the legal and meta-halakhic factors that shape the divisive debate over women rabbis. We hope that our study will foster dialogue and generate greater clarity of the relevant issues, even as we acknowledge that different opinions will remain.

It is important to emphasize that serious halakhic questions with major ideological and sociological implications require sensitive and nuanced analysis. In particular, we aim to avoid polemics and theatrics, and instead carefully define all of the relevant issues. The first step always entails delineating questions of technical halakhah, and only then addressing the significant elements relating to more global values, the "spirit of the law," "public policy," and "intra-communal politics." Given that halakhah forms the backbone of our behavior, we cannot risk distorting or misrepresenting the Torah by conflating the different elements, as they all remain independently significant considerations within the halakhic process. We thus divide this essay into two sections: technical halakhic questions and meta-halakhic considerations.

II. Technical Halakhic Questions

A. Eligibility to Receive Semikhah

What is *semikhah* (ordination) and may it be given to women? The contemporary notion of formal ordination, which first appears in fourteenth-century halakhic literature, does not authorize the same judicial activities as classic *semikhah* of Mosaic origins given exclusively in Eretz Yisrael in the Talmudic and pre-Talmudic eras.[2] Rather, as Rabbi Yitzḥak ben Sheshet (Rivash 271) delineated and Rabbi Moshe Isserles (Rama) codified (*Darkhei Moshe* and *YD* 242:14), *semikhah* grants license by a teacher to a student to issue rulings on matters of Jewish law. It thus certifies the knowledge of the recipient of the degree, and further warrants him to issue halakhic rulings even within the locale of his teacher.[3] While Rivash believed that it was not necessary to receive such *semikhah* following the death of one's teacher, R' David ben Ḥayyim HaKohen (Shu"t Radach 18:10) and others always required it to prevent unqualified people from issuing *hora'ah*. This *semikhah* was not necessary to teach Torah or to explicate basic or decided matters of halakhah (*YD* 242:8-9).[4]

---

2 Confusion regarding this matter led some Sephardic figures to criticize their Ashkenazic colleagues for issuing *semikhah*, which in its classic form, cannot be issued outside the land of Israel. See, for example, the 6th chapter of *Naḥalat Avot*, Rabbi Yitzḥak Abarbanel's commentary to *Pirkei Avot*.

3 In this respect, Rivash adds, the student literally becomes his own master (or "rav"), since he is no longer subject to the limits of his teacher's jurisdiction.

4 It should be noted that the licensing given through *semikhah* was not a form of necessary investiture that granted powers invested by God, so to speak. As such, someone who decided not to accept *semikhah*, out of modesty or piety, could still perform functions like weddings and *gittin* (*YD* 242:14). Conversely, even if one had *semikhah*, but did not have the

Three different theories emerged regarding eligibility for contemporary *semikhah*. The first and simplest view, drawing the logical conclusion from the above depiction of *semikhah* and adopted by Rama in both the *Darkhei Moshe* and *Shulḥan Arukh*, concludes that anyone is eligible to receive *semikhah* when their teacher certifies they have acquired requisite knowledge and licenses them to issue halakhic rulings. The scope of this license may be limited to certain areas of law (depending on the student's actual knowledge and qualifications) and may be granted to one who is ineligible to receive Mosaic ordination that was present in Talmudic times. As such, basic contemporary *semikhah* is based on one's knowledge and competence to answer questions of law.[5]

A second approach, taken by Rama in his responsa (24), contends that modern ordination should adopt the standards of the classical Mosaic ordination, and therefore one should not ordain anyone who could not receive the classical *semikhah* of Talmudic times.[6] The criteria for classic *musmakhim* (recipients of ordination)

---

proper knowledge to perform certain functions, the standing of this individual's actions could be called into question.

5 This system, of course, may lead to situations of abuse, since two *musmakhim* with vastly different degrees of knowledge and qualifications may share the same title. Indeed, throughout the generations, some have protested the abuse of the title rabbi by those who issue rulings on matters on which they are not sufficiently qualified. See, for example, *Yam Shel Shlomo, Bava Kamma* 8:58. This may have particularly dire consequences in cases relating to personal status (such as *gittin*), and therefore Rama adds that one must be particularly careful that only rabbis competent in this complex area of law should engage in *gittin*. Nonetheless, the basic concept of *semikhah* remains the same for all. One frequently sees this manifested today by yeshivot that issue separate *semikhot*, one for *yoreh yoreh* and the other for *yadin yadin*. Each *semikhah* testifies to the successful completion of a distinct course of study, and licenses the recipient accordingly. Similarly, the Israeli Chief Rabbinate issues different *semikhot* for judges, neighborhood rabbis, and city rabbis, in addition to their basic *yoreh yoreh* certification.

6 Rama cites concerns that those ineligible to perform certain tasks will not be able to garner proper communal respect. Rabbi Moshe Sofer, *Ḥatam Sofer EH* 2:94, also adopts this position, albeit for a different concern, that out of self-pity or ignorance, the rabbi will ultimately err and end up per-

included that they be eligible to perform all judicial functions of the Sanhedrin, even if their particular ordination only permitted them to do limited tasks (*Mishneh Torah, Hilkhot Sanhedrin* 4:8-10). Women are thus not eligible for contemporary ordination in this view, since they cannot fulfill all duties performed by recipients of Mosaic ordination.

A third approach argues that for various cultural and legal reasons, different limitations were imposed on who could receive *semikhah*. For example, debates were held whether a minimum age was required to receive *semikhah*, or if it should be issued only at one's wedding. A more prominent issue related to competition and the licensing of someone to practice in an area where other rabbis presently served. Some *semikhot*, for example, authorized a person to establish their own yeshiva, despite the presence of others previously established.[7]

Similar issues relating to synagogue rabbis are highlighted by Rabbi Yehiel Michel Epstein in his *Arukh Ha-Shulḥan* (*Yoreh Deah* 242:29). After affirmatively citing the Rama, he adds:

> In our times and for many previous generations, each city chooses its official rabbi (*rav muvhak*) to issue legal rulings (*psak*) and to adjudicate (*lehorot ve-ladun*), and he is considered the official rabbi for the entire city and its surrounding areas. No one else has permission in this area, even if they have achieved requirements to issue rulings on Jewish law and adjudicate (*higgia le-hora'ah lehorot*), unless the city rabbi grants him permission by giving him ordination so that he can be chosen as the rabbi of any given community (*kehillah*). But without

---

forming tasks ineligible to him. He does provide a *limud zekhut*, however, for those who followed different standards of *semikhah* eligibility.

7 On the history of modern *semikhah*, including the various cultural and legal debates involved in these ordinations, see Mordechai Breuer, "*Ha-Semikhah Ha-Ashkenazit*," *Zion* 33 (5728), p. 15–46 (also reprinted in his collection of articles, *Assif: Mi-Pri Et Ve-Et*, Rimonim Publishers, 1999). On the concept of *heter hora'ah*, see Rabbi Dr. Yaakov Blidstein, "*Heter Hora'ah Be-Mishnat Ha-Rambam U-Mashmuato Ha-Ḥevratit*," in his *Iyyunim Be-Maḥshevet Ha-Halakhah Ve-Ha-Aggadah*, Ben Gurion University Press, p. 103–113, and the sources cited in *Encyclopedia Talmudit*, "*Hora'ah*" (vol. 8), p. 486–494.

such ordination, it is prohibited to be a (synagogue) rabbi or resolver of questions (*moreh tzedek*) and this has been the practice for generations. Heaven forbid: one should not deviate! This is currently the central matter of ordination. It is getting permission and an attestation that one has reached the stage where one can issue ruling on matters of Jewish law.

The context of the statement clearly applies to a situation in which a locale has a bona fide community rabbi (*mara de-atra*). The larger issue of authorization (*reshut)* is less relevant in many contemporary situations since multiple rabbis can function within a given area. Nonetheless, *Arukh Ha-Shulḥan* understands that one conception of *semikhah* authorizes—and therefore necessitates one to be eligible for—the position of synagogue rabbi. That is to say, the licensing given to anyone who has received this ordination is that they have received the social sanction to lead a *kehillah*, and not just issue rulings of Jewish law (*hora'ah*).[8] Rabbi Yehiel Y. Weinberg further attests that the meaning of standard *semikhah* or *heter hora'ah* was to authorize a person to serve in a rabbinic position (*rav*, *dayan*, or *moreh tzedek*).[9]

One might conclude that whether women may be ordained as rabbis depends, in part, on the dispute between these three different conceptions of *semikhah.* In his responsum, Rama limits *semikhah* to those men who could theoretically perform all tasks filled by members of the Sanhendrin. In the *Shulḥan Arukh*, however, he rules that anyone sufficiently knowledgeable to answer questions of Jewish law may be given *semikhah.* For the *Arukh Ha-Shulḥan* and others this would only be so if he were additionally eligible to do the jobs customarily performed by those with *semikhah*, such as serving as a synagogue rabbi.

---

8 However, all agree that ordination is not required to teach Torah, either to adults or children, neither as a matter of logic nor as a matter of historical practice.

9 See the 4th volume of *Seridei Esh*, p. 138, Mosad Harav Kook edition (1969). In some recent reprints of *Shu"t Seridei Esh*, as well as the Bar Ilan CD version, the non-responsa essays have been removed. See also his essay in *Lifrakim* (new edition) in which he depicts the roles necessary to serve as a contemporary rabbi.

Different *poskim*, we suspect, would resolve this technical dispute of halakhah differently, as each position is supported by other authorities and historical practices.[10] Any *semikhah* issued to women would have to resolve this issue and explicitly delineate the nature of its ordination.

B. The Issue of *Serarah*

Independent of the official licensing and title one receives from *semikhah*, a separate issue is whether women may perform certain rabbinic tasks or hold offices that constitute positions of *serarah*. The concept of *serarah* emerges from the Talmudic and halakhic discussions that exclude women and converts from being appointed as monarchs and serving as judges (*dayanim*).[11] In the *midrash halakhah* that excludes women from the monarchy, Ḥazal use the term to describe the fear *(eimah)* that the monarch instills upon his subjects.[12] An exact definition of the restricted positions, nonetheless, remains somewhat elusive. Rabbi Moshe Feinstein, in his responsum that permitted women to serve as supervisors for kashrut agencies, defined it as any position in which someone has discretio-

---

10 This dispute might be reflected in the fact that a few yeshivot only issue *semikhah* that includes both *yoreh yoreh* and *yadin yadin* licensing, thereby licensing their graduates to perform almost all rabbinic tasks (with the exception of issuing *gittin*). Most *yeshivot*, such as RIETS, as well as the Israeli Chief Rabbinate, however, issue a basic *heter hora'ah*, primarily based on *Orakh Ḥayyim* and *Yoreh De'ah*, while granting other *semikhot* to graduates who have achieved more advanced training. Other *yeshivot* regularly issue something colloquially known as "*Rav u-Manhig semikhah*," which is mostly an honorific title. In some *yeshivot* it was issued on condition that one not engage in *psak halakhah*, yet in other *yeshivot* it authorized one to serve as a religious authority, with bearers of these certificates frequently adopting rabbinic positions. (Rabbi Weinberg states that in the Hildesheimer Seminary in Berlin, this *semikhah* was issued only to certify one's qualifications as a teacher, but not to issue *hora'ah*. This certification helped garner the proper respect necessary to teach, while preventing those unqualified from issuing *hora'ah*.)

11 See, for example, *Yevamot* 45b, *Shevu'ot* 30a, *Kiddushin* 76b, and *Yevamot* 102a.

12 *Sifri Devarim* 17:15, #157.

nary, coercive powers to impose obligations or responsibilities against someone's will.[13] In his responsum that permitted women and converts to serve as communal leaders and *poskei halakhah,* Rabbi Eliyahu Bakshi Doron, the former Israeli Sephardic chief rabbi, defined the forbidden job as a position in which the authority of their decisions stems from their appointment to a position of power (*shilton*), as opposed to their knowledge and wisdom (*yo'etz*).[14]

As Rav Moshe and others have noted, Rambam (*MT Melakhim* 1:5) understands the prohibition of women serving as a monarch as a prohibition of women functioning in all communal roles.[15] The *Sefer Ha-Ḥinuch* (497), on the other hand, explicitly limits the prohibition for women to the realm of monarchy, even as he extends it more broadly in its application to *gerim* (498).

More significantly, independent of the definition and scope of *serarah*, many medieval authorities (and according to Rav Moshe,

---

13 *Iggerot Moshe YD* 2:44–5. This definition flows from *Shakh YD* 269:15.

14 *Shu"t Binyan Av* 1:65.

15 The contested source of Rambam's ruling has garnered much discussion, since many editions of the Sifri only exclude women from the monarchy, even as research has shown several manuscripts that include textual variants to the Sifri which justify Rambam's position. See, most recently, Aliza Bazak "*Dayyanut nashim: nitu'aḥ mekorot ha-din u-behinatan be-dayyanut u-be-serarah*" in *Lihyot Ishah Yehudiyah* (Vol. 3, 2005), ed. T. Cohen and A. Lavi, p. 89–98. (While this article focuses specifically on women serving as judges, it also discusses the larger issue of women holding positions of *serarah*). It is therefore surprising that Rabbi Daniel Sperber, in his responsum (online at <http://yeshivatmaharat.org/resources-0>) to justify the ordination of a woman, simply rejects Rambam's position, because, in his words, "Later authorities stated that they know no source for this opinion (R. Moshe Feinstein, *Iggerot Moshe, Yoreh de'ah*, vol. 2, 44–45), and that it is "a rejected ruling "(R. Ben-Zion Meir Hai Uziel, *Mishpetei Uziel*, vol. 3, *Ḥoshen Mishpat* 6)." Yet they, of course, did not have access to these manuscripts, and it is precisely Rabbi Sperber himself, in his very erudite work, *Netivot Pesikah* (Reuven Mass, 2008), who has most forcefully argued for the use of manuscript research in halakhic decision making. In any case, it remains undeniable that this was Rambam's position, which was also held, in part, by the Ritva (see below).

the majority) contend that communal acceptance would grant women the license to hold positions of authority in regard to political power and legal matters. The context of these statements is a discussion about the prophetess Devorah's extended reign as a "*shofetet*," normally translated as a judge. The Talmudic commentators are bothered by the possibility of how she could function as a judge, since the Talmud seems to prohibit women from that role.[16] One common answer affirmed that she functioned as a judge, which was allowed on the basis of a well-established rule that litigants can agree (*kabbalah*) to be judged by those normally forbidden from this position.[17]

16 This is the widespread understanding of *Yerushalmi Shevu'ot* 4:7 and *Bavli Shevu'ot* 30a, which was ultimately codified in halakhah, *Ḥoshen Mishpat* 7:4. See *Tosafot Niddah* 50a d.h. *kol* (cited by Ritva *Kiddushin* 35a d.h. *veha* and Rashba *Bava Kamma* 15a d.h. *asher*) for a different opinion. Cf. *Kohelet Rabbah, Parasha* 2. *Tosafot Niddah* alternatively cites a position that Devorah was an entirely unique circumstance because she was chosen by God. Cf. *Tosafot Bava Kamma* 15a d.h. *asher*, *Tosafot Yevamot* 45b d.h. *keivan*, and Radbaz *Hilkhot Melakhim* 1:5.

17 Normally, such acceptance of judges is done on an *ad hoc* basis. *Sefer Ha-Ḥinuch* (#87) however, posits the possibility that the communal leaders appointed Devorah to this position, firmly establishing her position as a judge, usually held for an indefinite time period. This would explain the duration of her service. The issue of indefinite or permanent *kabbalah* for judicial positions has greatly engaged *poskim* who sought to understand how the converts Shmaya and Avtalyon could be appointed *Nasi* and *Av Bet Din*. Rabbi Chaim Benvenisti, *Knesset Ha-Gedolah*, *Haghot Bet Yosef* CM 7:1, asserts that the *kabbalah* of all Klal Yisrael works to appoint a *ger* as *Av Bet Din* or *Nasi*. This position was challenged by Rabbi Yonatan Eybeschutz, *Tumim* CM 7:1, and Rabbi Yeḥezkel Landau, *Doresh Le-Zion* #3. Alternatively, Rabbi Yitḥak ben Asher (*Riv"a Al Ha-Torah*, *Parshat Mishpatim*, citing Rabbi Moshe of Coucy) and Rabbi Shimon Duran (Tashbetz, *Magen Avot* 1:10) assert that *gerim* are not *pasul* for such positions if they are the most qualified for the job. This might constitute a definitive exception to the *serarah* rule. (Cf. *Midrash Eliyahu Rabbah*, 10, d.h. *u-Devorah Ishah Neviah*, where the *midrash* notes that Devorah was chosen as the *shofetet* over Pinḥas ben Elazar, and then further elaborates that all people—Jews and non-Jews, men and women, free-people and slaves—are blessed with the divine spirit according to the merits of their actions.) Alternatively, Rabbi Meir Dan Plotzki, *Ḥemdat Yisrael*, *mitzvah* 362, un-

Others, however, answered that while she could not function as an official judge, she could teach the relevant laws for the disputed case.[18] The judges could then simply act on her halakhic wisdom. Yet many *rishonim*, including Ramban, Rashba, and Ritva, alternatively asserted that the term *shofetet* means that she served as a political authority.[19] This was not prohibited to her under the terms of *serarah,* since the people decided to follow her authority.

In other words, the autonomous choice of people to accept in practice someone's authority, be it political or intellectual (and possibly judicial), precludes their power from constituting *serarah.* It is on this basis, for example, that a number of *poskim* in Israel have permitted women to hold office in the democratically-elected Knesset, despite the power of these positions. Similarly, many American rabbis have permitted women to be elected as presidents of their

---

derstands that their greater qualifications naturally led to their assumption of leadership roles, as opposed to a (forbidden) formal appointment. Rabbi Ḥayyim David Azulai (Ḥid"a), *Birkei Yosef ḤM* 7:6, while initially citing the opinion of the Knesset Ha-Gedolah, ultimately adopts the opinion of the Tashbetz and seems to conclude that *kabbalah* does not work for *gerim* to assume positions of *serarah.* He also mentions the alternative position, advocated by the Maharal (*Avot* 1:10), that Shmaya and Avtalyon were mere descendants of converts, but not actual *gerim.*

18 *Tosafot Niddah* 50a, *Ḥinuch* 87. On this notion, see *Hilkhot Dayanim im Halakhah Pesukah*, Machon Harry Fischel, p. 94–95, and Rabbi Joseph B. Soloveitchik, *Reshimat Shiurim: Shevu'ot-Nedarim,* ed. Rabbi H. Reichman, vol. II, p. 4.

19 Ramban *Shevu'ot* 30a d.h. *matni*, Rashba 30a d.h. *ve-lo nashim*, Ritva 30a d.h. *matni.* The latter source is particularly significant since he, like Rambam, explicitly states that the prohibition of *serarah* encompasses all communal positions, but contends that communal acceptance precludes this from being a *minui* of *serarah* and other *mesimot.* It appears that communal acceptance (*nohagin bah ke-din malkah* or *nohagin al pi-hah*) is seemingly differentiated by many *rishonim* with the *kabbalah* done in judiciary cases, which may be governed by different limitations, as noted above. Yet some *aḥaronim* seem to equate the two factors. It should be noted that Rabbi Ben-Zion Uzziel, *Shu"t Mishpatei Uziel*, vol. 4, *ḤM* #6 and others believed that even Rambam would allow women to fill positions when they have received communal acceptance. This interpretation, however, is far from universally accepted.

synagogues and schools.[20] Rabbis, who are almost universally elected and selected by their synagogues or schools, work under a limited employment contract, and do not inherit their office,[21] are logically also covered by this license.

---

20 The major reasons cited by the lenient *poskim* are one or many of the following factors traditionally found in the liberal democratic process: 1) the officer is elected by the public, 2) the power is either limited or shared with others, 3) the position is held for a limited time period, and 4) officers cannot automatically bequeath this power to their heirs. For different perspectives of these issues relating to *serarah*, see Rabbi J. David Bleich, "Women on Synagogue Boards," *Tradition* 15:4 (Spring 1976), (reprinted in his *Contemporary Halakhic Problems*, Vol 2, Ktav Publishing House, 1983, p.254-267) and more recently, Rabbi Aryeh Frimer, "Women in Communal Positions: Shul Presidents," *Text & Texture* (2 June 2010), <http://text.rcarabbis.org /?p=931>, which is an edited transcript of an oral presentation based on his Hebrew article, Aryeh A. Frimer, *"Nashim beTafkidim Tsiburiyyim beIdan haModerni"* in *Afikei Yehudah—Rabbi Yehuda Gershuni zt'l Memorial Volume,* ed. R. Itamar Warhaftig, Ariel Press: Jerusalem, 5765 (2005), pp. 330-354. These articles, of course, discuss positions shaped by many issues, and not just the concept of *serarah*. Additional discussion may be found in Prof. Menachem Elon, *Ma'amad Ha-Ishah*, Hakibbutz Hameuchad Publishing House (2005), pp. 51–100. See also Rabbi Dr. Ariel Pikard, *"Ma'amad Ha-Nokhri Be-Medinat Yisrael Be-Pesikat Rabbanei Ha-Tzionut Ha-Datit,"* *Reshit* 1 (2009), p. 187–208, which discusses non-Jews filling positions of power within the State of Israel.

21 This point is significant, since in addition to its indefinite duration, one of the classic characterizations of positions of *serarah* is that it includes the rights to bequeath the position to inheritors (much like the monarchy). See Rambam *Hilkhot Melakhim* 1:7, *Shu"t Ḥatam Sofer OḤ* 12–13, *Shu"t Avnei Nezer* 312, and the discussion in *Encyclopedia Talmudit*, "*Chezkat Serarah*" (vol. 14) p. 346–373. This was a historically accepted practice in many locales with regard to the rabbinate, even as it was highly disputed and certainly not universal. On this topic, see Rabbi Ephraim Weinberger, "*Yerushah Ba-Rabanut*" in *Ba-Tzomet Ha-Torah Ve-Hamedinah,* vol. 1 (Tzomet Institute) p. 294-300 (republished in his *Yad Ephraim*, *siman* 2). For a recent historical survey, including a detailed bibliography, see Shaul Stampfer, *Families, Rabbis, and Education: Traditional Jewish Society in Nineteenth-Century Eastern Europe,* Littman Library (2010), chapter 14. In such circumstances, rabbinic positions might indeed constitute *serarah*. However, in most communities today, there is no definitive inheritance right for children in rabbinic positions. See the position of R' Weinberg-

Of course, one might argue that if we rule like Rambam and furthermore do not adopt the concept of communal acceptance, then those limited by the strictures of *serarah* could not receive *semikhah* and serve in any rabbinic positions. This, however, is not the established practice, since very few, if any, yeshivot exclude male *gerim* from receiving *semikhah* and functioning as rabbis.[22]

---

er, as well as *Arukh Ha-Shulḥan* 245:29, who affirm the legitimacy of this practice. It should be further noted that the controversial historical practice of purchasing one's position from either the community or the previous rabbi is no longer practiced today, a factor that was also occasionally cited as contributing to a *serarah* position.

22 In the course of writing this essay, we spoke with a senior administrator at a universally respected yeshiva that regularly issues *yoreh yoreh yadin yadin semikhah.* He told us that his yeshiva planned to issue this distinguished *semikhah* to a student who was a *ger*, as a sign of his accomplishment in learning, even as he would be instructed that he could not serve as a *dayan*. He would, however, be allowed to serve in the shul rabbinate, a position which the yeshiva deemed not as *serarah,* but rather as "*avdus*" (servitude), because of the nature of the communal service and pressures. One historical precedent for such a stand may be found in Rabbi Yitzḥak (ben Avraham) Graanboom (d. 1809), author of *Zera Yitzḥak* (Amsterdam 1789) on *Pirkei Avot.* A convert, he served as a rabbi of multiple congregations in Amsterdam, and was for an interim period the Chief Rabbi of Amsterdam. See Dan Rabinowitz, "The Chief Rabbi of Amsterdam: A Jewish Convert," *The Seforim Blog* (6 Dec 2006), accessible at <http://seforim.blogspot.com/2006/12/chief-rabbi-of-amsterdam-jewish-convert.html>.

It is reasonable to argue that contemporary shul rabbis in modern America do not possess coercive powers over their congregants, who can easily leave the institution but cannot be easily barred from membership, at least by the rabbi alone, and whose behavior cannot be easily regulated. One European reader has noted to us that the lack of *serarah* in the American rabbinate—as indicated by both their lack of coercive powers as well as their partial subservience to the whims of the synagogue board—remains problematic, as rabbis do not feel sufficiently empowered or protected to perform their duties with dignity and integrity. Indeed, in certain cases, this lack of *serarah* can be harmful and even malicious, as evidenced by the 2010 RCA Convention resolution to assist pulpit rabbis in difficult employment situations. Nonetheless, we believe that even as the rabbinate is entitled to greater respect and discretionary power, this does not change the fact that the hiring, contract, and powers of rabbis are sub-

This is despite the fact that the full scope of *serarah* restrictions more definitively applies to them, and they cannot serve as *dayanim* or in rabbinic positions of compulsory authority.[23]

This halakhic tradition seems to reflect the understanding that many rabbinic duties—with the definite exception of acting as a standing rabbinic court judge—do not constitute *serarah*. This is especially so in situations where rabbis are elected to that position and are subject to restraints of other governing bodies. As such, it remains unpersuasive to bar women, on the basis of the *serarah* ar-

ject to checks and balances imposed by the community. In any case, however one understands this specific rabbinic position, the larger issue of giving women *semikhah* and allowing them to fill *some* rabbinic positions remains the same.

23 Even if one would understand a certain position to constitute *serarah*, such as a synagogue rabbi, that does not necessarily preclude a *ger* from serving, in function if not in title, in that position. See *Teshuvot Ve-Hanhagot* 3:305, where Rabbi Moshe Sternbuch, *shlit"a*, permits appointing someone else with the official title of shul rabbi, and letting a *ger* act in practice as the *posek*, even with a title of *moreh tzedek* or assistant rabbi. This goes beyond the statement of Rav Moshe Feinstein, who asserted that even according to those who believe a *kashrut mashgiaḥ* is a position of *serarah* forbidden to women, a female could be a kashrut supervisor since the ultimate authority rested with the (male) head of the kashrut agency. Alternatively, Rabbi Eliezer Waldenberg, *Tzitz Eliezer* 19:47-8, suggests that even according to those who do not accept the concept of *kabalah* for positions of *serarah*, a *ger* could be included within a group of people serving in a certain position, if the community accepted his appointment to this committee. This would seem to be especially true if the person was deemed as the most qualified to serve in a certain position, which was cited by many *rishonim* and *poskim* as a mitigating factor to override the *serarah* limitations to *gerim*, as noted by Rabbi Waldenberg and others. In any case, everyone agrees that many positions currently filled by rabbis do not constitute *serarah*, and as such, *gerim* may receive *semikhah*. Parenthetically, we expect the number of *gerim* with *semikhah* will greatly increase in the coming generations, as many children will undergo Orthodox conversion because their mother originally did not receive a halakhic conversion.

gument alone, from receiving *semikhah*, when the long-time halakhic tradition has not applied that standard to *gerim*.[24]

Indeed, it is worth noting that one position in the Jewish community which seems to contain some form of coercive powers is the one communal position that is most likely to be held by women: Head of School. A school principal has powers to discipline students and hire and fire staff, amongst their other duties of determining curriculum and shaping school policy. Nonetheless, our communities regularly hire women for these positions, and this is because the nature of their hiring, plus the checks and balances im-

---

[24] On this point, it is worthwhile to investigate the writings of Rabbi Moshe Feinstein with regard to *serarah*. In his most thorough treatment on the topic, written about a widow who wanted to succeed her husband as a *mashgiḥah kashrut* (*Iggerot Moshe YD* II:44), Rav Moshe asserted that according to most *rishonim*, women are not excluded from most communal positions, in contrast with the position of Rambam. Rav Moshe, who makes clear that he would like to allow, if possible, the widow to receive this livelihood, then argues that we can construe the position to be permissible for all women, even according to Rambam, if she serves under a rabbinic kashrut administrator. In the next responsa (II:45), Rabbi Meir Amsel correctly noted that according to Rav Moshe's understanding of the *sugya*, the majority halakhic position would allow women to serve as Israel's prime minister or as a shul president. Rav Moshe affirmed that this was the case, but asserted that we do not have to worry about such a proposition, since *frum* people under the guidance of a rabbi would not act accordingly, and would rule like Rambam. He then asserts that we should follow Rambam, unless there is some case of need (such as with the widow). In other words, Rav Moshe understood that according to the majority of *rishonim*, *serarah* would not prohibit a woman from acting in a communal position, but that we should not *pasken* like this position unless there was such a need (as in the case of a widow, or if the alternative candidates for a communal position were less observant or supportive of religious tenets). In his next *teshuva* on *serarah*, with regard to appointing a *ger* to the position of Rosh Yeshiva (*Iggerot Moshe* 4:26), Rav Moshe stated that there was a need to be *mekil* in light of the *mitzvah* of *ve-ahavtem et ha-ger*. It seems clear that Rav Moshe believes that *serarah* alone is not an insurmountable problem should there be a perceived need for women (or converts) to fulfill such positions. Of course, all things being equal, Rav Moshe clearly believed that women should not fill such positions, presumably for other reasons mentioned in this paper.

posed upon them by their boards, prevents this position from constituting *serarah*.[25] As such, we believe that a compelling case can be made that the halakhic principle of *serarah* alone does not preclude women from receiving *semikhah* and fulfilling rabbinic roles practiced by rabbis in America today.

C. Concerns of Women as Decisors of Jewish Law and Modesty Matters

Two other technical questions remain. The first is "Can women issue decisions of Jewish law?" It seems clear from a number of halakhic sources that there is no limitation on women issuing decisions of Jewish law *(psak halakhah)* in matters for which they are sufficiently trained. This point, stated in both the *Sefer Ha-Ḥinukh* (77, 152) and *Minḥat Ḥinukh* (78:9), is also implied in many of the sources (cited above) regarding Devorah. This remains the clear ruling in recent halakhic compendiums, from rabbinic works like *Encyclopedia Talmudit* (vol. 8, p. 494), *Hilkhot Dayanim im Halakhah Pesukah* (7:4, p. 95) and Dayan Masud Elchadad's *Minḥat Asher* (*Ḥoshen Mishpat*, vol. 1, p.14) to halakhic handbooks such as Rabbi David Auerbach's *Halikhot Beitah* (28:8). Of course, if we want to have such women, we will need to train them, but that is exactly the issue at hand. Normative halakhah allows a woman who is competent in Jewish law to issue decisions on matters of halakhah.[26]

In their role as communal leaders, teachers, and *ba'alot hora'ah*, women will almost inevitably be found in the public limelight. In general, the virtue of *tzni'ut* (modesty) encompasses a significant

---

25 This point is made explicitly by Rabbi Aryeh Leib Grosnass, *Shu"t Lev Aryeh* 2:21. Rabbi Moshe Feinstein, as noted above, similarly contends that a *ger* can serve as a Rosh Yeshiva because their administrative powers do not constitute *serarah*.

26 We think it is not insignificant that in the rare historic circumstances when women did achieve the requisite level of knowledge or expertise in halakhah, they did engage in halakhic discourse. See, for example, the sources cited in *Halikhot Bat Yisrael* 9:7. See also Shlomo Ashkenazi, *Nashim Lomdaniyot: Sekirah Historit* and Shoshana Pantel Zolty, *'And Your Children Shall Be Learned': Women and The Study of Torah in Jewish Law and History*, Jason Aronson Press, 1993.

element to many laws, and our community must vigilantly maintain this value. Many of these laws are objective and timeless, applicable in any era or context. Yet it is important to note that some matters of *tzni'ut* remain subject to time and context, as attested to by the *gemara* and confirmed in *Tosafot, Pitḥei Teshuvah*, and many other sources.[27] In broader society, women regularly work with men, and serve as professors, lawyers, doctors, and other professionals with highly public roles, and this is not seen as immodest behavior. In Orthodox communities in which women work in these jobs, it seems inconsistent to contend that women cannot fulfill such roles in the context of serving the community.[28] This is particularly true within the non-Hasidic community, where, for example, many regularly address the OU and RCA conventions while others give *shiurim* and lectures in many synagogues. Of course, in communities where women are not allowed to hold such jobs, such communal behavior might be deemed inappropriate or forbidden.[29]

---

27 *Tosafot Kiddushin* 81a d.h. *hakol le-shem shamayim, Pitḥei Teshuva EH* 21:3. For example, in the early 20th century, *poskim* debated the right of women to vote, with many arguing that it was immodest. Today, all *poskim* permit it and recognize it as perfectly appropriate behavior. Similarly, women regularly serve as school teachers, even though this position is explicitly prohibited to them in the *Shulḥan Arukh* (*YD* 245:21), lest it lead to inappropriate interaction with their students' fathers. For other examples of this larger phenomenon, see *Tzitz Eliezer* 9:50 and *Yabia Omer OḤ* 6:13.

28 A similar point was already made by Rabbi Yitzchak Herzog in *Teḥukah le-Yisrael al-pi ha-Torah*, vol. 1, p. 98-99 and Rabbi Ben-Zion Uziel, *Mishpatei Uziel* 4 CH 6 d.h. *ha-halakhah ve-ha-musariyut*. Some have further contended that it might be more appropriate for fellow women to address certain halakhic and pastoral questions relating to women, such as the area of *Hilkhot Niddah*.

29 One reader of an earlier draft contended that it would be inappropriate for women to hold rabbinic positions because they would not receive the requisite respect required for the office. As codified in Rambam *Hilkhot Melakhim* 1:6, this was a reason why people who had occupied socially-denigrated positions (such as a barber, tanner, or bathhouse caretaker) could not become king. (Indeed, *Arukh Ha-Shulḥan He-Atid, Hilkhot Melakhim* 71:9 cites Rambam's position and suggests that the prohibition of

III. Meta-Halakhic Considerations

We believe that the technical halakhic questions regarding women rabbis remain debatable, but that ultimately a reasonable case can be made that it is not forbidden to issue qualified women *semikhah* and let them perform many rabbinic functions. Yet this does not necessarily make it appropriate or advisable in the current context. As with all cases of changes in normative halakhic practice, one needs to weigh and address other meta-halakhic or non-halakhic issues. This calculation plays a central role in determining whether we should deviate from traditional practice and begin to ordain women.

A. Some Thoughts on the Mesorah

Many have invoked "mesorah" or traditional practice to explain why ordaining women is prohibited. While we agree that ordaining women as rabbis would certainly be a profound departure from the traditional practice, it is important to delineate the different definitions and roles the concept of *mesorah* plays within halakhah.

In one sense, *mesorah* refers to specific halakhic traditions relating to subject matters which, by their nature, were difficult to codify in words. Examples of such phenomena include the *trop* (musical notes) for Torah reading or the identity of kosher birds. A *mesorah* remains necessary in these cases to transmit the relevant laws. In such cases, these traditional practices become binding, absent some contrary halakhic argument.

Another example of such a phenomenon applies to cases in which a certain position has taken root in practice, even as the technical halakhah might point in a different direction. Under some circumstances, for example, the community might follow a *mesorah* to practice leniently on a given matter, even as many halakhic

---

serarah for *gerim* and women was to ensure that the position of king receives the greatest of respect.) This assessment, based on sociology and not sources, would seemingly lead to the conclusion that the positions of Israeli Prime Minister or Chief Justice, British Prime Minister, or United States Secretary of State, have become lessened in the public's eyes because they are or were held by women. We believe this to be incorrect, and do not see why genuinely qualified women would garner less respect or tarnish the stature of the rabbinate.

sources might rule stringently. At other times, contemporary practice might refrain from performing certain behaviors, even as the sources explicitly permit them.

A well-known example of the latter phenomenon (because it is found within the first paragraph of *Yoreh De'ah*) includes women serving as ritual slaughters (*shoḥetot*). The *mishna* explicitly permits women to slaughter animals, a position which is codified by Rabbi Yosef Karo in *Shulḥan Arukh* (*YD* 1:1), against those medieval authorities who claimed that women should not perform this function for ancillary reasons (such as concerns for fainting). The Rama, however, following the position of the *Agur*, contends that we do not allow women *shoḥetot*, since this has become the common practice. The logic of this position—that which we have not seen should not be done—is disputed by Rabbi Yosef Karo in his *Bet Yosef*, who contended that the fact that something has not yet occurred does not imply any impropriety in doing it. Accordingly, a contemporary practice to refrain from a certain action only becomes authoritative if we have a *mesorah* that *poskim* specifically addressed this question and forbid the behavior.

Shakh (*YD* 1:1 and *ḤM* 37:38), however, defends Rama, and citing a *teshuvah* of the Maharik, contends that we do not need a *mesorah* of a prohibitive *psak* to assert that the absence of certain behavior proves that this was halakhically-required abstinence. We do, however, require it to be the type of question which would have regularly arisen, for if it would have been a permitted behavior, then someone would have acted accordingly on some occasion.[30] Since the need for meat arises regularly, and the laws of *sheḥittah* (in those times) were a matter of day-to-day practice, Shakh contends that we would have seen women slaughterers had they been allowed to fulfill that function. Regarding the dispute on the different defi-

---

30 See *Maḥatzit Ha-Shekel* to *Shakh YD* 1:1 who confirms this straightforward reading of the Shakh. In the case of *sheḥittah*, one presumes that the reason to prohibit women from slaughtering stemmed from ancillary concerns, such as concerns for fainting, an issue raised in numerous halakhic sources. Parenthetically, it appears that in a few Sephardic communities, women continued to serve as slaughterers. See, for example, Rabbi Ḥayim David Azulai (Ḥid"a), *Birkei Yosef* YD 1:4.

nitions of *mesorah*, different *poskim* may take varying positions, with some siding with R' Yosef Karo and others following the Shakh.[31]

31 Rabbi Aryeh Frimer has suggested that Rabbi Joseph B. Soloveitchik, based on his explanation of this Rama in his *Yoreh De'ah shiurim*, as well as other rulings of his regarding women in leadership rules, would forbid women from serving as rabbis. See "The View of Rav Joseph B. Soloveitchik on the Ordination of Women," *Text & Texture* (26 June 2010), <http://text.rcarabbis.org/?p=958>. We think this view is insufficiently proven as the view of Rabbi Soloveitchik, for the following reasons: A) Firstly, it should be emphasized that the Rav made his statements regarding *minui kahal* in *iyyun shiurim*, based solely on Rambam, and never gave a specific *psak* regarding women as rabbis. B) Secondly, Rabbi Soloveitchik's well-known view, practiced *le-ma'aseh*, was to give *semikhah* to converts, even as it has been reported that he felt they should not take on synagogue pulpits. In other words, *semikhah* can be given to someone, even if the proscriptions of *serarah* may limit their rabbinic activities. C) Rabbi Frimer's conjecture is partly based on a statement of Rabbi Soloveitchik in his *Yoreh De'ah shiurim* which suggested that women were excluded from communal positions beyond those prohibited to *gerim*. This remains counter-intuitive, however, since for many rishonim like the *Sefer Ha-Ḥinuch*, the exclusion of *gerim* from positions of *serarah* is more definitive than it is for women, as noted above, and further remains inconclusive in the writings of Rambam, who in fact seems to understand the proscriptions regarding a woman to derive from the more explicit Biblical statements regarding a *ger*. Of course, the Rav was speaking in an *iyyun* context, exclusively using Rambam to explain a difficult Rama, and was not specifically asked *le-ma'aseh* if women could receive *semikhah* or work in rabbinic positions. D) It further remains possible that Rabbi Soloveitchik could have permitted women to receive *semikhah*, and not function as synagogue rabbis, a view that Rabbi Frimer simply dismisses, even as it was exactly the view of the Rav with regard to converts. E) Furthermore, in a statement in *Ḥamesh Derashot* p. 122 fn. 9 (a source not cited by Rabbi Frimer), the Rav distinguishes the appointment of a shul rabbi from the selection of a member of a Sanhedrin or *bet din*. The latter—classic beholders of *serarah* positions—are chosen by a limited group and specialize in *hora'ah, din*, and *harbatzat Torah*. The former, however, also serve as a communal leader and representative—a *parnas*—and therefore requires the consent of the entire community, based on R' Yitzḥak's statement in *Berakhot* 55a. (Cf. *Nefesh Ha-Rav*, ed. Rabbi Herschel Schachter, p. 267, where the Rav is quoted as telling an embattled shul rabbi that he is not entitled to his position if the community does not

Be that is it may, we believe this dispute is not germane to our question for two important reasons. Firstly, even according to Shakh, the belief that contemporary practice proves halakhic propriety only applies to cases in which an issue would have regularly arisen, and therefore the abstinence from such behavior proves that *poskim* believed it was prohibited. Given the lack of formal education for women, the question of women rabbis, quite simply, did not arise on a regular basis. There is no basis for a *mesorah* which would assert that women were regularly qualified to serve as rabbis, but did not do so for some halakhic reason. This seems to be proven by the fact that in the vast literature written from the fourteenth century onward regarding the nature of *semikhah*, the issue of women *musmakhot* simply does not arise, even as they do discuss the propriety of ordaining a qualified minor. As such, we do not find it compelling to claim that women cannot receive *semikhah* or serve as rabbis based on this notion of *mesorah*.

---

want his services.) This might indicate that the Rav understood that even though the rabbinate constitutes a *parnas*, it has imposed upon it certain limitations that prevent it from becoming a *serarah* position. The statement in *Ḥamesh Derashot* might derive from a well-trodden position in rabbinic literature that the rabbinate represents *keter Torah* and cannot constitute lordship. See, for example, *Shu"t Ḥatam Sofer OḤ* 12, where he posits the right to *yerushah* could exist in many communal positions like a *sofer* or a *shoter*, but not in positions of *kedushah*. For further sources, see *Encyclopedia Talmudit*, "*Ḥezkat Serarah*," cited earlier, and the sources cited on p. 542 of the source index to the Frankel edition of Rambam's *Hilkhot Melakhim* 1:7 d.h. *marbitz Torah*. Hence, it remains possible that the prohibition of *serarah* might exclude a woman from serving as a synagogue president but not as its rabbi. (This, parenthetically, was reported to us as to have been the view of Rav Ahron Soloveichik, who believed that a shul president constituted *serarah*, but a shul rabbi did not. We were told that he felt this way because contemporary *shul* presidents possess greater discretionary power than the rabbi.)

In any case, as Rabbi Frimer notes, other *poskim* certainly may (and did) disagree with the Rav's positions on each particular matter. In fact, many of the Rav's most devoted students have departed from his *psak* regarding women as shul presidents, because they understand the relevant sources, and the described position and social context, differently today.

Secondly, as a general rule, contemporary needs will trump this notion of *mesorah* in cases when no technical issue prohibits engaging in a certain behavior. There is no doubt that certain practices remain immutable within Orthodox Jewish law. For example, neither a great rabbi nor a panel of great rabbis could announce, "Given the needs of the time, pork now becomes permanently kosher," or, "From now on, Shabbat will be observed on Sunday." That authority is simply not present in Orthodox Jewish law. Such is not the case with practices established by tradition alone. When the Orthodox community, its leaders, and its *poskim* feel that circumstances have changed and that the needs of a time are such, any practice that is permitted as a matter of technical Jewish law receives halakhic mandate, even if it has never been done within the Orthodox community.[32] That is exactly what occurred a century ago with the expansion of women's Torah education. It is precisely this innovation that has led to the new possibility of female clergy and provides an appropriate conceptual framework to understand the relevant meta-halakhic issues.

---

32 In this regard, see *Shu"t Noda Be-Yehudah Tanina OḤ* 18 (R' Yeḥezkel Landau on 12 windows in a shul) and *Shu"t Orakh Mishpat*, *OḤ* 112 (R' Abraham Isaac Kook on the consumption of sesame oil on Pesach), who affirm that matters which have not been traditionally practiced, but are *mutar* according to law, are absolutely permissible once deemed necessary. This point, which we believe is readily apparent to all students of halakhah, is made by Professor Eliav Shochetman in his trenchant critique of women's *aliyot*. He notes that as opposed to the latter case, in which there is an explicit prohibition listed in the *gemara* and *poskim*, many other recent innovations in female ritual practice, such as bat mitzvah celebrations, received the approbation of many *poskim* precisely because they felt there was no technical *assur* and that such innovation was mandated, even as it went against traditional practice. See Eliav Shochetman, "*Aliyot Nashim La-Torah*," *Sinai* 135-136 (5765), p. 338-343. This section of the article was unfortunately not included within its recent translation in the book, *Women and Men in Communal Prayer: Halakhic Perspectives*, ed. Chaim Trachtman, Ktav Publishing House, 2010.

B. Continued Changes in Talmud Torah for Women

Rabbi Yisrael Meir Kagan, the Ḥafetz Ḥayyim, felt very strongly that the tradition (*mesorah*) of not teaching women Torah from texts had to change.[33] Based on this premise, *poskim* debated throughout the 20th century what this study should entail, and in particular, if it should encompass intense study of *Torah she-Be'al Peh*. Some believed that women's education must include Talmud study, others limited this to the intellectual elite, while others discouraged this study and some prohibited it. The question of what changes should be made, and at what rate, remains an open conversation, and therefore women learning torah on a serious level is certainly far from a universal practice. As with other hotly-debated issues, holders of the various positions remain members of the broader Orthodox community. Different communities adopt diverse models, each with its own strengths and weaknesses.

The pressing question today is whether to retain the status quo, or if women who have received intense Talmudic training should have new outlets to utilize their knowledge and skills. This

---

33 As he explicitly notes in his *Likutei Halakhot, Sotah* 20b (emphasis added):

> It seems that all of this [prohibition against women learning Torah] applies only to times past when all daughters lived in their fathers' home and tradition was very strong, assuring that children would pursue their parents' path, as it says, "Ask your father and he shall tell you." On that basis we could claim that a daughter needn't learn Torah but merely rely on proper parental guidance. **But nowadays, in our iniquity, as parental tradition has been seriously weakened and women, moreover, regularly study secular subjects, it is certainly a great mitzvah to teach them** Ḥumash, Prophets and Writings, and rabbinic ethics, such as *Pirkei Avot, Menorat Hamaor*, and the like, **so as to validate our sacred belief; otherwise they may stray totally from God's path and transgress the basic tenets of religion, God forbid.**

The *Ḥafetz Ḥayyim* recognized that a change in the way women are educated is needed when confronting modernity. Indeed, simply contrast the above statement with Rabbi Yeḥiel M. Epstein's observation (*Arukh Ha-Shulḥan YD* 246:19) in the 1880s, "Since the beginning of time, we have the practice not to teach women from a book, and we never heard of such a practice. Rather, for the laws that one needs to know, a woman teaches her daughter or daughter-in-law."

represents a natural question within our heritage that believes in *lilmod u-le-lamed,* to learn and to teach. Moreover, one must ponder whether the community could benefit from the additional resources afforded by a cadre of learned and talented women. These are important questions to ask, and as we attempt to keep Torah meaningful in the contemporary context, we must act with great forethought, acknowledging that any changes in the *mesorah* must develop carefully.

To take root, these changes need to become accepted and validated by a significant spectrum of the community. In Israel, the recently-developed positions of *yoatzot halakhah* (advisers in *hilkhot niddah*) and *toanot rabbaniyot* (rabbinical court advocates), created with the endorsement of a series of *poskim* and *gedolim*, have achieved much initial success and growing acceptance. The former position has now been introduced into the American Orthodox community, while other synagogues begin to experiment with female community scholars. In this early stage, the concept of women rabbis has certainly not received broad acceptance, and any further developments should only evolve after continued dialogue with *poskim*, rabbinic and lay leaders, and the community of learned women.

C. Slow and Careful Changes Take Root over Time

Second, the nuanced hesitations expressed by Rabbi Norman Lamm, *shlit"a*, requires serious thought. He states:

> There are certain things that are acceptable only in the long run. I approve of the idea of increasing the role of women in religious life and think it is an important one... Just imagine: we have taken women who have good brains, good characters, and good personalities and devoted their lives to Hitler's 3 K's: *Kinder* (children), *Küche* (kitchen), and *Kirche* (church)! Women are not just good for these three things. There are enough individual cases that are exceptions to allow you to learn *min ha-perat el ha-kelal* (from the specific case to the general category). It is just not true that they cannot think straight—they can. We have crooked ideas if we think otherwise.

> At the same time, things have to be done gradually. To have a woman learn Gemara a generation or two ago like women learn Gemara today would have been too revolutionary. But with time, things change; time answers a lot of questions, erodes discomfort, and helps. So my answer, when I was asked by a reporter about what I think about women rabbis, was, basically: "It's going too fast." I did not say it was wrong, I did not say it was right. It just has not paced itself properly. I was criticized, of course. People asked, "You mean that *al pi din* they're allowed to become rabbis?" My response: "I don't know—are you sure they're not allowed to?"[34]

We should take note of Rabbi Lamm's reservations and hesitations regarding the future and recognize that the pace of change is central to achieving a positive outcome, whatever that might be. His nuanced formulation addresses well the question of change in *minhag Yisrael. Minhag Yisrael* does evolve over time, and it certainly has changed considerably in the last century with regard to women's general and religious education. Slow and careful change facilitates greater insight, feedback, and development, and could be a good motto for Orthodoxy in this area.[35]

D. Practical Issues that Must be Resolved

One element of this process would entail contemplating whether the many complex practical issues associated with women rabbis

---

34 Interview with Rabbi Dr. Norman Lamm, *YU Commentator*, Feb 12, 2010. It can be read at: <http://www.yucommentator.com/kol-hamevaser/an-interview-with-rabbi-dr-norman-lamm-1.1127268>. To a certain extent, a similar sentiment was expressed in the early 1950s by Rabbi Yeḥiel Yaakov Weinberg, *Seridei Esh* 1:139 (new edition), on the topic of women's suffrage and rights to serve as elected communal officials. After very briefly noting the different halakhic arguments, he refrains from taking a stand, contending that 1) time will determine the matter, and 2) that the halakhic argumentation is secondary to "deeper" issues at stake.

35 In this regard, let us share a witticism of one of our teachers: "Change in Orthodoxy is a lot like orthodontics. To move teeth, you have to apply small amounts of pressure over great periods of time. Lots of pressure over small periods of time do not move teeth but break them. So too with the Orthodox community. Slow change produces positive developments, while large movements break us apart."

remain resolvable—and if the potential solutions are worthwhile steps. Even if one were to basically agree that as a matter of technical halakhah, women can serve as rabbis—in the sense that they may teach Torah in various settings, provide guidance on Jewish theology to individuals and groups, perform certain roles of emotional and pastoral care, answer questions of Jewish law on many matters which they are trained, and, from these tasks, ultimately function as communal figures and leaders—certain practical issues must be addressed. Many rabbinic job descriptions entail serving in functions prohibited to women as a matter of Jewish law, including being the *ḥazzan* or *ba'al kore*, serving on a bet din, and many other matters. A great deal of clarification as to what a rabbi is empowered to do by their *semikhah*, and expected to do in a given position, would be needed before women rabbis could be considered.[36] Of course, the most important practical change needed to even consider the possibility of women rabbis is the creation of women's seminaries that focus intensely on providing a top-flight multi-year talmud and halakhah curriculum. Most rabbis in training learn in yeshiva for the better part of a decade nearly full-time before *semikhah*, and there is no program like that for women anywhere in the world now. Indeed, we recognize that it took women nearly a century to climb to the top echelons of American law (a discipline less broad or complex than halakhah) and the same long journey is likely present here as well. On the other hand, long journeys start with small steps.

To prevent confusion and mishaps that will lead to violations of halakhah, the exact delineations of these roles would require understanding within both scholarly circles and the broader public.[37] This

---

36 Another issue to be examined is how the issues of *serarah* and authority differ in various communities with different rabbinic organizational structures, such as England, continental Europe, the United States and Israel. While the power of *kabbalah*, as well as internal checks and balances of power, may be able to surmount all of these issues, they nonetheless must be fully explored.

37 For example, it would need to be clear that despite the fact that the rabbi is the tenth person in the room, she cannot make the *minyan*, or serve as the *ḥazzan* despite the fact that others in the room have inferior Hebrew skills. While these halakhot remain obvious in today's environment, they might become sociologically awkward (and therefore liable to violation)

is not easily or quickly achieved. Toward this goal, we might need different titles and ordinations for men and women clergy. In England, for example, different members of the Orthodox rabbinate go by distinctly different titles, reflecting different roles, functions and rights: Reverend, Minister, Rabbi, and Dayan. This model may be worthy of being adapted for these issues and adopted in different locales.

E. Non-Orthodox Movements?

Others add another cautionary factor into this calculus. Given the broader phenomenon of non-halakhic egalitarianism with liberal Judaism, the introduction of women as rabbis might appear as a concession to non-Orthodox movements. As such, they claim, we ought to prohibit this development, even if in a different cultural context it would be permissible.

This very real world calculus—focusing not on the halakhic reality, but rather on the perception of reality—is important to consider. If one were to decide to employ this reasoning, of course, it would be important to recognize and stress that the underlying activity is not really prohibited, and that the ruling serves as a prophylactic tool to address the needs of the generation. Otherwise, we would run the risk of distorting the halakhic tradition for polemical purposes.

In the end, however, we do not think this concern should play the deciding role for three reasons. First and foremost, as a general principle, we believe that the spiritual needs of women and the attempt to resolve these types of issues should trump fears of sectarian triumphalism. As Rabbi Aharon Lichtenstein *shlit"a* has recently argued, with his characteristic wisdom:

---

when the woman is the congregation's spiritual leader. Indeed, it was this consideration that led the *Ḥatam Sofer*, cited above, to forbid giving *semikhah* to anyone not eligible to perform all duties of Sanhedrin members. While some rabbis play a less fundamental role in performing these functions, there remains no question that many regularly perform such rituals and all are expected to be able to do so. As such, the halakhic parameters and communal expectations would have to be greatly clarified to prevent halakhic violations.

> Serious and responsible *poskim*, impeccably committed and with catholicity of Torah knowledge, should, I believe, give greater weight than in recent generations has been assigned, to the dispensation of *la'asot naḥat ruaḥ lenashim*[38] cited in the Gemara and in *Shulḥan Arukh* as the basis for permitting what might otherwise have been proscribed.

Second, this is especially true in our case, since we are uncertain if the issue of ordaining women stems from non-Orthodox origins. It is quite reasonable, as Rabbi Lamm observed, this is simply a logical conclusion of the policy supporting women's immersion in Talmud study. Many pious Orthodox women, fully dedicated to halakhah, genuinely desire to use their knowledge toward serving the community. As a general rule, we should not thwart the genuine religious desires of some simply because others may have nebulous motivations for a similar goal.

Moreover, we believe that the threat of sectarian triumphalism with regard to halakhic matters has greatly abated. In early generations, one might have plausibly worried that different changes could be perceived as acceptance of the claims of non-Orthodox movements. That applied in eras when Orthodoxy was embattled, and the non-Orthodox movements tried to justify themselves through halakhic discourse. Today, even as it continues to face significant challenges and dilemmas, Orthodoxy is thriving, and the non-Orthodox movements are no longer perceived as competing or threatening alternative halakhic societies. As such, our community will understand that changes made with some form of consensus of the Orthodox community and its *poskim* represent genuine and legitimate halakhic activity.

We do believe, however, that within the more liberal segments of Orthodoxy today, there exists a nascent movement to try to push the envelope toward greater egalitarianism in the prayer setting and create halakhic change in other areas, with or without rabbinic approbation. In recent years, this sector has published articles to justify, and sometimes implemented in practice, amongst other proposals: women's *aliyot*; the allowance for unmarried women to

---

[38] *Ḥagigah* 16b. Loosely translated, "To give spiritual satisfaction to women."

go to the *mikveh*; the unjustified nullification of marriages without a *get;* and the abolishment of the seven "clean days" of *niddah.* While each of these cases adopts various degrees of radicalism and halakhic plausibility, they all reflect frustration with, and occasionally animosity toward, traditional halakhic norms and contemporary rabbinic leadership, and they have the potential to recklessly break the bonds of Orthodoxy.

The appropriate response to this phenomenon, however, is not to launch polemical halakhic rejoinders or to engage in overly sensationalistic rhetoric. Defensive, reactionary responses, lacking both direction and nuance, will only inflame the situation. Rather, we must display responsible halakhic leadership by openly tackling each issue, separately and transparently, with care to distinguish and address technical halakhic arguments and meta-halakhic considerations. This process maintains halakhic integrity without compromising traditional values, and is the only way that we can address contemporary needs while maintaining full fidelity to the Torah and the *mesorah.*

F. The Breakdown of Gender Distinctions within Judaism

Others have expressed concern that the ordination of women will lead to the breakdown of all gender distinctions found within the Torah, halakhah and the *mesorah.* This has been raised by a number of people who are generally sympathetic to other developments regarding the role of women in halakhic ritual and Jewish public life.[39]

---

39 In the above cited interview, Rabbi Lamm expressed a general sketch of this concern. He stated,

> "Do I think having women rabbis is a good thing? I do not know. I am, however, concerned that, before long, we will find ourselves overly feminized, and I would not want to see that happen. Women will begin complaining about why they cannot be *Kohanot* and *dukhen.* I can name 100 different *halakhot* that just do not work with women—for instance, a woman cannot be an *ed kiddushin* (a witness for betrothal)... When it comes down to it, I am a believer that there are differences between men and women that should be reflected in halakhic practice."

If we understand this concern correctly, we may break it down into halakhic and sociological considerations. The halakhic argument, it would seem, fears a slippery-slope situation, in which the ordination of Orthodox women rabbis leads to a barrage of other changes not mandated by halakhah, all in the name of egalitarianism. We definitively oppose such a non-halakhic movement, and believe that anyone who would advocate such an agenda will find themselves excluded from the community of those committed to halakhah.

Each halakhic issue should be individually and appropriately addressed. Sometimes changes are permissible and a good idea, other times they remain *assur*, and many proposals fall into a grey area.[40] One should not simply address all issues relating to women under the heading of "*Hilkhot Feminism*" (in a positive or negative sense).

See also the remarks of Rabbi Gidon Rothstein in two essays on *Text & Texture*: "Women and the Splitting of Modern Orthodoxy: Confronting the Underlying Issues" <http://text. rcarabbis.org/?p=769> and "The Component Issues of a Traditional Jewish Womanhood <http://text.rcarabbis.org/?p=804>.

Indeed, many have understood the entire notion of *serarah* as stemming from the need to differentiate roles between men and women. See, however, the contrary position of Rabbi Ḥayyim David Halevi, *Teḥumin* 10, p. 121, who states that the law is a *gezerat ha-katuv*. He bases this on the position, adopted by Rabbi Yeḥezkel Landau, *Noda Be-Yehuda Kamma*, *ḤM* 1 and pondered by *Minḥat Ḥinuch* 497:2, that *serarah* only prohibits the action of a formal anointment (*hakhtarah*), but not their assumption of powers by inheritance. Since a woman might be able to inherit a position, but not receive the initial formal appointment, gender differentiation seems an insufficient explanation for the law. (The position that women may inherit *serarah* is explicitly rejected by Rabbi Yechiel M. Tuchizinsky, *Ha-Ishah Al-Pi Torat Yisrael*, p. 50-51. For further sources on the inheritance of women to *serarah* positions, see p. 540 of the source index to the Frankel edition of Rambam's *Hilkhot Melakhim* 1:5.)

40 For example, something might be technically *mutar* but a bad idea for other reasons. Alternatively, one might make a plausible halakhic argument for a change, but the contrary read of the sources remains more compelling. Likewise, something might only have the support of a *da'at yachid* in the sources, but *gedolei Yisrael* might believe that the times dictate following this opinion. All of these models, well established within the history of halakhah, apply to all realms of halakhic discourse.

The ordination of women certainly is not the first issue that has been raised regarding the role of women in the last century, nor will it be the last. Yet as long as we remain within the framework of the established halakhic process, led by our *poskim* in consultation with our rabbinic and lay leadership, we believe that this will prevent the distortion of halakhah and the destruction of communal unity.

Alternatively, some contend that on a sociological level, the ordination of women will lead to the distancing of men from the synagogue and communal leadership. The evidence for such a claim stems from recent studies of the non-Orthodox movements which find that as these movements adopt egalitarian norms and special programming aimed to attracting women, men have become less engaged in communal and religious life.[41] It remains difficult to gauge the exact nature of this threat. It is important to note, however, that if we continue to work within the framework of the established halakhic process, we will not find ourselves anywhere close to the full-fledged non-halakhic egalitarianism advocated by non-Orthodox movements. We cannot imagine a situation in which gender distinctions will not forever remain with the Orthodox community. Moreover, while this issue may require caution and further thought, it should not prevent us from addressing the issues that already distance (for one reason or another) many women (and men) from an Orthodox halakhic lifestyle.

IV. Concluding Thoughts: A Path Forward

We believe that any requisite amount of consensus needed within Orthodoxy for ordaining women is far from being present. The law has thus not changed. Yet one of this article's central intellectual endeavors is to assert that when seeking to determine whether certain practices are timely or timeless, one must distinguish between the unchanged and the unchangeable.

41 See Sylvia Barack Fishman and Daniel Parmer, *Matrilineal Ascent / Patrilineal Descent: The Gender Imbalance in American Jewish Life*, Hadassah-Brandeis Institute, 2008. The study is available online at <http://www.brandeis.edu/hbi/pubs/Gender_Monograph_5aug08_Complete.pdf>.

Especially if one follows the position of the Rama on *semikhah* found within his *teshuvot*, and Rambam's position on *serarah,* one may reasonably argue that women cannot serve as Orthodox rabbis because of technical halakhic argumentation. We believe, however, that a reasonable argument may be made that no technical halakhic issues prohibit Orthodox women from serving as rabbis, or at least receiving some other form of ordination as Orthodox clergy. Nonetheless, this halakhic question does not require immediate resolution. A host of others concerns—relating to *mesorah,* practical rabbinics, communal unity, and unpredictable sociological consequences—leads us to favoring slow and non-radical development on this issue as some form of consensus develops and emerges.

We have tried to present a framework for thinking about the halakhic and meta-halakhic issues involved in this issue, so that our community can try to develop some form of consensus on this issue over a period of time. This is the responsible approach on this matter, given the complexity of the total picture and the importance of the institution of the rabbinate to Orthodox life.

Some will not like this conclusion because they will maintain, "If this is plausibly *mutar* on a technical level, we should proceed at full speed." Others will not like it because it did not conclude, on whatever basis, that "Giving *semikhah* to women is categorically *assur*." Both approaches are not a proper vision of how Jewish law ought to work. Halakhah, like life, is frequently nuanced and complex, and is not always well encapsulated merely by words like *ḥayav* or *assur*.[42] This is such a case, and it is important to strive to be wise, acting with foresight and vision, as well as insight and probity. Simple solutions to complex problems are always easy to find, but they are rarely correct.

The responsible handling of these issues will help ensure Orthodox unity even as we respect our diversity. We should not fall prey to the errors made in previous eras and allow our lack of

---

42 Hence, halakhic literature has phrases like "*ain ruaḥ ḥakhamim noḥa hamenu*" or "*mutar aval eino rauy*" or "*reshut aval eino ḥayav*."

uniformity to become overly divisive. Orthodox women rabbis should not be a schism issue between the various groups within Orthodoxy. All the communities need to take small steps toward fulfilling their vision, and not giant steps that rip us apart as a broad community of people bonded by halakhah.[43] Over the last half-century the role of women within the halakhic community has vastly changed, and yet thankfully, all those committed to halakhah remain within the broader tent of Orthodoxy. Slow and steady movement is wise, as is civil discourse, coordinated interaction, and dialogue between all members of the Orthodox community.

Support for women learning gemara is wide and deep within a segment of the Orthodox community, deriving from the clear and direct leadership of Rabbi Joseph B. Soloveitchik, *zt"l*, as well as many other *gedolim* both in America and in Israel. We support this for the community that needs and wants it, and believe that women's (and men's) learning deserves even more communal encouragement and institutional support. Pious women involved in intense study should receive access to all realms of Torah knowledge by the best educators and *talmidei ḥakhamim*, and receive proper training to serve the community. Even without a rabbinic title, genuinely deserving women should receive appropriate *kavod ha-Torah*, and be included in all communal matters for which they are qualified to contribute, including those areas not related to "women's issues."

---

43 Based on this, we believe the unprecedented decision to ordain a woman with the title rabba was justly criticized since it was not supported by a major halakhic authority, did not develop with appropriate communal coordination, and did not address the major issues raised by such a change. We further believe that it would have been much better—for the sake of the halakhic process as well as the long-term growth of women's participation in Torah and mitzvot—for the title to be forsaken for now by its sole user. The continued use of this title will only continue to serve as a distraction from the central issues that must be appropriately addressed regarding women's leadership roles. We believe that this could be rectified through a self-sacrificing action for the sake of communal unity, women's scholarship, and the halakhic process, following the model of Rabbi Yehoshua (*Rosh HaShanah* 25a).

Given that there does not appear a panel of Torah giants to endorse the immediate and far-reaching change of giving *semikhah* to women, those who support increasing women's leadership roles should return to the path of incremental development on which Orthodoxy has been traveling until recently. Women should sit and study for increasingly long periods of time, write serious scholarship in Torah, develop as inspiring spiritual personas, and lead torah institutions, in function if not in form. In short, they should build the Orthodox community brick by brick, and see what happens over time. The passage of time, as Rabbi Lamm observes, solves many problems. We endorse this approach. ☙

Rava as Mara de-Aṯra in Maḥoza

By: YAAKOV ELMAN

We tend to talk in collectives: Ḥazal—*hakhameinu zikhronam li-verakhah*, "our Sages, blessed be their memory," "the Sages"—plural, the *nevi'im*, the Tannaim, the Amoraim, the Rishonim and Aḥaronim, but on another level we are—or should be—aware that each one of our Sages was himself a treasure-house of Torah, and had *shittoṯ* and *darkei limmud* of his own, some of which he had in common with other members of his yeshiva or *beiṯ midrash*. We are also aware of the fact that our Sages' words were spoken with great precision and express concepts and principles that are internally consistent. We all know that the Ramban has certain *shittoṯ* that differ from those of the Rambam, for example, and this is true in areas of Halakhah, Aggadah and *hashqafah*. The Gemara already notes that that is true of the Tannaim, and, to some extent, it does the same for the Amoraim (see below). If we want to understand the Rambam *ki-peshuto*, we cannot mix the Ramban's kabbalistic teachings with the Rambam's Aristotelian ones, (even though some kabbalists have done so, as in *Sefer Shomer Emunim* which depicts the Rambam as a kabbalist).

In *Paḥad Yitzḥak*, *Hanukah*, *ma'amar* 3, Rav Yitzḥak Hutner זצוק"ל,[1] wrote as follows:

> מרובה היא מדת הבלטת כוחה של תורה שבעל פה המתגלה במחלוקת הדעות, מאשר במקום הסכמת הדעות. כי הלא בהך דאלו ואלו דברי אלוקים חיים כלול הוא היסוד כי גם השיטה הנידחית מהלכה דעת תורה היא, אם רק נאמרה לפי גדרי

[1] R. Yitzḥak Hutner, *Paḥad Yitzḥak: Quntras Ve-Zot Hanukah*, Brooklyn, 5624, p. 18.

Yaakov Elman, a long-time resident of Flatbush, is Professor of Judaic Studies at Yeshiva University and an associate of Harvard's Center for Jewish Studies. He has authored or edited eight volumes, and dozens of articles on Jewish Biblical exegesis, intellectual history and ḥasidic thought.

המשא ומתן של תורה שבעל פה. והיינו משום דתורה ניתנה על דעתם של חכמי התורה (לשונו של הרמב"ן) ואם יעמדו למנין אחר כך ויכריעו כהדעת הנידחית, מכאן ואילך תשתנה ההלכה אליבא דאמת. (יעוין אור ישראל פרק ל' בהערה[2]) ונמצא כי מחלוקתם של חכמי תורה מגלה את כוחה של תורה שבעל פה הרבה יותר מאשר הסכמתם. מלחמתה של תורה איננה אופן אחד בין האופנים של דברי תורה, אלא שמלחמתה של תורה היא יצירה חיובית של ערכי תורה חדשים, שאין למצא דוגמתם בדברי תורה סתם.

> Our perception of the power of *Torah she-be'al Peh* as revealed through disagreements is greater than when there is agreement. For within the principle that "these and those are the Word of the Living G-d" is included the essential principle that even the *shittah* that is rejected as practical halakhah is nevertheless a Torah view, when it is expressed according to the norms of the discourse of *Torah she-be'al Peh*. This is because the Torah was given by the *da'aṯ* of the Sages of the Torah (as enunciated by the Ramban). And if they then vote and decide according to the rejected view, the halakhah then changes in a true sense (*aliba' de-emeṯ*). (See *Or Yisrael*, chapter 30 in a note.) The result is that in disagreement the power of *Torah she-be'al Peh* is revealed to a greater extent than by [the Sages'] agreement. The "war of Torah" (*milḥamtah shel Torah*—Torah debate) is thus not merely one mode of *divrei Torah* among others, but rather "the war of Torah" is a positive creation of new Torah values, whose like is not to be found in ordinary words of Torah [where there is no disagreement].

At first glance, this seems contradictory, but it is no more contradictory than the *ma'amar* that Rav Hutner זצוק"ל quotes: "these and those are the Words of the Living G-d"—even when they disagree. The reason is that the Torah is the model, the blueprint of the universe, with all its contradictions and contrary tendencies. Each legitimate Torah view has its own *ḥeleq* of truth, even when, for practical purposes, we must decide in favor of another one in the here and now. And, here, as elsewhere, the *first* level of understanding is the *peshat* level, the level of "plain meaning," which requires understanding each view in its context. And since every *memra* was uttered by a Tanna or Amora, the first level of meaning is what that *memra* meant to the one who enunciated it. Thus for example, at the beginning of Pesahim R. Huna and R. Yehudah seem to disag-

---

2 In the index to *Paḥad Yitzḥak*: *Ramban al ha-Torah* to Devarim 17:11.

ree whether in that mishnah the mishnaic word *or* means "light", or is a euphemism for "darkness." The Gemara however concludes that there is no disagreement: R. Huna, who defined it as *noghei* ("light") was employing the word as it was used in Sura, where it was used as a euphemism for "darkness." On a very basic level, understanding an individual Amora's mode of speaking, his characteristic turns of expression, etc., is indispensable to Torah study.

In a statement repeated several times in Shas, Rava emphasizes the importance of an individual's input in Torah study, that is, the process of *making Torah one's own.* Let us look at AZ 19a, where this appears in the context of Rava's '*musar shmuess*' regarding Talmud Torah.

> אמר רבא: לעולם ילמוד אדם תורה במקום שלבו חפץ, שנאמר: כי אם בתורת ה' חפצו.
> ואמר רבא: בתחילה נקראת על שמו של הקב"ה ולבסוף נקראת על שמו, שנאמר: בתורת ה' חפצו ובתורתו יהגה יומם ולילה. ואמר רבא: לעולם ילמד אדם תורה ואח"כ יהגה, שנאמר: בתורת ה', והדר ובתורתו יהגה.

> Rava said: One should always study that part of the Torah which is his heart's desire, as it is said, "But whose desire is in the Torah of the Lord [Psalms 1:2]." Rava also said: At the beginning [of this verse] the Torah is assigned to the Holy One, blessed be He, but at the end it is called by his name, for it is said, "Whose desire is in the Torah of *the Lord* and in *his* [own] Torah does he meditate day and night" (Joshua 1:8) [That is, first it is called *Toras Hashem*, and then it is called *his* Torah—the Torah of the one who studies it]. Rava also said the following: One should always study the Torah first [i.e., memorize it] and meditate on it afterwards, as it is said: " . . . the Torah of the Lord," and then, "and in his [own] Torah he meditates."

In other words, our task in studying Torah, if we merit it, is to put our own *individual stamp on Hashem's Torah by filtering it through our own understanding, as limited as that may be.* The souls of Kelal Yisrael were all at *Mattan Torah*, and we each have our own portion of Torah assigned to us. Of course, that understanding, even if part of our 'self' contributes to it, must reflect true Torah values and modes of thought and argument. Clearly, this individual stamp on Torah learning applies to the Amoraim; after all, Rava was first and foremost addressing his own colleagues, who were Amoraim. Thus, we should expect that each Amora has his own individual understanding of various issues, and when they differ, seemingly isolated differences might be understood as expressions of a more general outlook.

Of course, most of the time the texts of *Torah she-be'al Peh*—the Mishnah, the Tosefta, the Bavli, the Yerushalmi—provide the names of those Tannaim or Amoraim who hold a certain view, (and in doing so bring redemption to the world.) But even in those cases where these *sefarim* don't cite the name of the authority holding a particular view, Hazal go out of their way to track it down. This is particularly significant, since, at least in the case of the Mishnah, it was Rebbe who omitted the name of the Tanna in order to indicate that the Halakhah followed his view, and, as we know, the Gemara often notes that a particular mishnah does not follow the view of a particular Tanna. Thus, it is important to identify views that are not dominant—*halakhah le-maaseh*!

By ignoring the differences, the individual nature of each *de'ah* and *shittah*, we lose an important aspect of Torah. In the following essay I hope to provide a useful example of what can be learned when we follow Rava's teachings *as a unit*. In this light we can understand why the authoritative compilation of *Torah she-be'al Peh*—the Talmud Bavli—investigates the question of whose view a particular mishnah reflects no fewer than 232 times, and the Yerushalmi does the same no fewer than 72 times. Why was this important? Because each view has a reason behind it, reasons based on principles that are held by one Tanna or another, and it is important to understand not only the particular view in a mishnah, but also to understand how mishnahs are linked by consistently held principles. This is true even when that view is not the majority view. Thus, the Gemara notes that R. Meir is concerned about minority occurrences some 16 times, and refers to that opinion another four times.[3] Again, the Gemara attempts to determine the opinion of various Tannaim on the matter of *bererah*, the retrospective determination of reality.[4] When a question is asked that mixes opinions,

3 Yev 61b, 119a, Git 2b, AZ 34b, 40b (2x), Ḥul 6a, 11b, 86a, Bek 19b, 20a, 20b, 42b, Nid 31b, 48a (2x); see also Yeb 67b (3x) and Qid 3b.

4 See Git 25a, Eruv 37b, Beẓ 37b, BQ 69a.

the Bavli asks: *gavra agavra qa ramiṯ?*—are you throwing together opinions of different Amoraim? Such a procedure has no validity! Each Sage's teaching is consistent in his own terms, but not necessarily when combined with another Sage's.

At times the Gemara also traces the reasons for Amoraic opinions, as it does in the case of *asmakhta* in matters of commercial law. But, on the whole, it only began the task of providing the links between the various Amoraic statements. In the case of Rava, who is mentioned 3,800 times in the Bavli, the observation that *ve-azda Rava le-ta'ameih*—that his opinion in one place follows his *shittah* in another—appears only 13 times in Shas.[5] In other words, the process of showing Rava's consistency in his *memroṯ* was only at its start when the Bavli was closed. In this respect, as in many others, the Rishonim (and especially the Baalei Tosafoṯ, see below) continued the task. The expression *azda R. Peloni le-ta'ameih*, is used some 60 times in all, and another 28 times if more than one Tanna or Amora is involved,[6] but only 30 times in relation to Babylonian Amoraim: thirteen times for Rava, twelve times in relation to Shmuel,[7] once each for Rabbah (Ket 34b) and R. Ḥisda (Qid 63b), twice for R. Nahman (BM 26a, Hul 25b), and, finally, once for R. Ashi (Shab 100b). Three of these observations concern Amoraim closely associated with Rava: R. Ḥisda, his teacher and eventual father-in-law, R. Nahman, his *rebbe muvhak*, and Samuel, who was, at least to some extent, R. Naḥman's teacher (see BM 16b). This is not surprising since these Amoraim are among the most influential in Shas. But, as we noted regarding R. Meir, the *baalei ha-Shas* are concerned about this issue even when the *man de-amar* is not necessarily of that level of prominence—it is a consistent concern. The Gemara notes the consistency of the views of Tannaim with the ex-

5 Ber 36b, Shab 5b, 80a, 124b, Pes 6a, 30a, 110a, Beẓ 8b, Ḥag 22a, Git 84b, BB 56a, Sanh 74b, Ḥul 81a.

6 Shab 38a, 125b, Eruv 87b, Pes 29a, 93a, RH 11b, Yom 40a, Beẓ 40a, Yev 62a, 72b, Ket 34b, Git 47b, Qid 80a, BQ 48a, 51b, 77b, BB 65a, Mak 91, 15b, Shev 20a, Zev 9b, Men 92a, 109a, Ḥul 39a, 69b, 81b, Bek 47a, Ker 6b.

7 Shab 116b, Eruv 49a, Pes 30a, 101a, Suk 34b, Yev 18b, 56a, Ket 100b, Git 24b, BB 42b, Ḥul 79a, Nid 25a.

pression *be-shittat* (22 times)[8] or *le-shittato* (5 times).[9] Although this is still far from systematic, enough examples of this *derekh* survive to demonstrate that the *ba'alei ha-Shas* considered this a legitimate way of understanding the words of the Tannaim and Amoraim.

Why is understanding the link between Amoraic opinions important? There are at least two reasons. Since the Torah's laws are not, *ḥas veshalom*, arbitrary or haphazard (even if, as in the case of *ḥuqqim*, the reason is hidden from us), understanding the link between Amoraic opinions allows us to see the reason behind their *shittot*. In most areas of Halakhah, we are encouraged to seek the reasons for every *din* because it is only by means of such study that one makes Torah one's own—it becomes part of one's being. If one does not understand something, it remains foreign—outside oneself.

Secondly, generally speaking, understanding a *memra ki-feshuto*—understanding it in its immediate *context*—is a key to understanding it in its multiple contexts, including that of *pesak*. In the end, when we deal with halakhic texts, we must understand the *memra* in the broader context of Halakhah, from Ḥumash and Shas through contemporary Poskim. But on the *peshat* level we seek to understand a particular *memra* in the context of the Amora's views and approaches, his *shittot*. Generally speaking, his *shittot* will be consistent not only within themselves, but also within the wider context of those of his *rebbes* and *talmidim*, that is, his *beit midrash*. In the case of the Babylonian Amoraim, this means understanding, say, R. Huna's *memrot* in terms of the views of his *rebbe*, Rav, and his talmidim, Rabbah b. R. Huna and R. Ḥisda. In the case of Rava, it means—when possible--tracing his views back to his *rebbes* R. Naḥman and R. Ḥisda, to R. Naḥman's *rebbes*, Rabbah b. Avuha and Shmuel, but also seeing the view of Rava's talmidim, R. Papa, R. Huna b. R. Yehoshua, R. Zevid, and others.

Of course, the ultimate *pesak* is not bound to the *peshat* of any one Amora, even when we decide according to his view. A *sugya* can combine the views of one Amora with the principles of another in order to apply the halakhah in question to various situations. It is

---

8 Eruv 86b, Pes 18a (2x), 53b, R.H. 30b, Suk 16b, 41a, Beẓ 27a, Meg 27b, Ket 40a, Zev 30a, 93a, Men 68b, 71b (3x), 72a, 102b, 103b, Ker 18a, Me'il. 13b.

9 Git 9b, 10b, Ḥul 74b, 92b (2x).

up to the *poskei ha-dor* to determine the relevant halakhah for their time. That is why *halakhah ke-batra'ei*, the halakhah follows the later opinion (within the limits of Masorah, of course). But if Talmud Torah is pursued with the proper *derekh*, or, more precisely, with one or more of the proper *derakhim*, then, as Rav Hutner זצוק"ל pointed out, the result is "a positive creation of new Torah values."

II

This concern for consistency remained with the Rishonim. A particularly instructive example, which will teach us something of the challenges that Rava himself faced in his own community, concerns Mordechai's reaction to Haman's demand that he bow down to him. According to Rava, both Mordechai and Haman were Persian officials in charge of the banqueting arrangements in Ahasueres' palace (Est 1:8, see Meg 12a). Despite his status, however, Haman became Mordechai's superior and he would have had to bow down to him, and this he refused to do. The reason for his refusal is not made clear in the Megillah. It appears from a discussion between Rava and Abaye that Haman claimed to be a god, and though no one really believed that he was one, Mordechai refused to honor him as one. However, as Tosafot pointed out, it is Rava himself who in Sanh 61b holds that one who performs an idolatrous act out of "love or fear" is *patur*. According to Rava, one transgresses the *issur* of *avodah zarah* only when one *accepts* the idol as one's god, but not when worshiping it out of fear. Abaye holds that the intention is irrelevant; what counts is the action. If so, ask Tosafot: why—according to Rava himself--did Mordechai not employ Rava's *heter* and bow down to Haman (see Tosafot Sanh 61b s.v. *Rava amar patur*)? Indeed, Rava himself notes that the Jews of Mordechai's time had complaints against Mordechai for arousing Haman's ire against them (Meg 12b-13a).

From the analysis in Sanh 61b it is apparent that Rava himself held that Haman made himself into a god (*de-ihu gufeih eloha*) but since he was worshiped out of fear, even this was not considered a violation of the prohibition of *avodah zarah* (*de-ilu Haman mi-yir'ah*). Moreover, Rava points out elsewhere that in his own time and place it was customary to provide clay braziers and bellows for

Zoroastrians (Sanh 74b) because the Halakhah takes cognizance of cases in which the idolater intends the Jew's cooperation for his own benefit, and not for the *avodah zarah* itself. Surely that was Haman's motive. We see from this that Rava's *heter* was not theoretical, but may have applied to conditions in his own time. Indeed, the Rishonim disagree on the exact circumstances under which such *heterim* may apply, and the Ran is particularly stringent on this issue.

In the end, though, Tosafoṯ conclude that the *issur* could not be contravened even according to Rava either because (a) Haman wore idols around his neck, or because (b) it was a matter of Kiddush Hashem. Unfortunately, since this midrash does not appear in the Bavli, we cannot prove that Rava was aware of this idea. Moreover, there was another consideration that Mordechai must have had: the danger to the further existence of Kelal Yisrael if Mordechai had yielded to Haman's demands! As noted above, Rava pointed out that Kelal Yisrael criticized Mordechai for his intransigence (Meg 12b-13a). In the end, Mordechai's position required that, as a *leader* of Kelal Yisrael, he could not permit himself to make use of Rava's *heter*, as a matter of Kiddush HaShem, as Tosafoṯ point out.

This is an enormously instructive case, not only for the reasons given, but also because Tosafoṯ here combined Rava's views in Halakhah *and* Aggadah; each is part of Rava's Torah, and to understand Rava in one area, we must understand him in both. In the following cases, we will examine Rava's views on aggadic topics that have halakhic consequences.

This in turn sheds light on a personal decision of Rava's. In Shab 116a the Gemara reports that various Amoraim disagreed as to whether they should attend an interdenominational discussion in a Bei Abidan. While Rashi (as quoted by Tosafoṯ in A.Z. 17a, see below) understands this phrase as referring to an idolatrous temple, Tosafoṯ suggest that it was merely a neutral place where discussions were held on various matters (see Tosafoṯ A.Z. 17a, s.v. *harḥeq me-aleha*), and presumably not a place for religious discussions—even though it is clear from the Gemara that there were *kisvei qodesh* kept there. Tosafoṯ conclude that the Bei Abidan was not a place of *minuṯ* (*meqom minuṯ mammash*) but rather a place where gentile scholars would gather to debate their laws (*nose'im ve-notenim be-*

dinim). Indeed, Rav would not go, Shmuel would, and a certain Mar b. Yosef went enthusiastically, while Rava excused himself because of the difficulty of reaching that particular Bei Abidan. It is noteworthy that Tosafot seem to have had a different *girsa* in *Shabbat*, since they note that R. *Naḥman* went and endangered himself. If this *girsa* is correct, it may have been the experience of his own *rebbe* that convinced Rava not to go to these debates, simply because of the dangers to which such attendance could lead. Despite all of this, however, it is noteworthy that *kitvei ha-qodesh* were kept there, indicating that there was some religious dimension to the discussions, and the fact that Rav could refuse to attend indicates that these were not medieval style "forced debates."

Nevertheless, Rava was careful to maintain good relations with the non-Jewish communities around him, and thus did not refuse outright, but pointed to a large palm tree in the way, which, even if uprooted as the government offered to do, would leave a large hole in the road leading up to the Bei Abidan. Indeed, his excuse is plausible, since we know that his rebbe, R. Nahman, travelled in a palanquin (presumably carried by four men) (Git 31b), and Rava himself (when he became a *dayyan* of the Resh Galuta?) would do so as well (B.M. 73b); as convenient as a palanquin was for the passenger, a large hole in the ground would have made passage difficult and dangerous. He would send Bar Sheshakh, apparently a pagan Babylonian, gifts even on idolatrous festivals, since he was certain that Bar Sheshakh was not himself an idolater (AZ 65a). He also maintained friendly relations with Issur the *Ger*, and even once based a *pesak* on information he had gotten from him (AZ 70a). In this connection it should be noted that Maḥoza, Rava's town, was a suburb of the Persian winter capital of Ctesiphon—it was right across the river, and as a consequence, many non-Jews lived there. Both the Jewish Resh Galuta and the Christian bishop of Ctesiphon resided in Maḥoza (called Kokhe by the Christians). We can understand then why there were many *gerim* in Maḥoza (Qid 73a), as opposed to Pumbedita and Mata Maḥasia, where R. Yehudah and R. Ashi observed that there were none (Ber 17b). The Maḥozan Jewish community was, for better or worse, much more open to outsiders than Pumbediṯa'.[10]

III

While relations with the government and non-Jews were full of potential dangers and pitfalls, Rava's need to deal with dissidents in his own community was no less delicate and complicated. As the Maharsha recognized, Rava's community also contained people who were skeptical of the authenticity of *Torah she-be'al Peh* and of rabbinic authority (*amei ha-aretz*; see Maharsha on Mak 22b s.v. *kammah tipsha'ei*, where he points to Sanh 99b-100a), and Rava had to deal with such people as well. As the Gemara testifies, he kept them in the community by responding to their arguments when necessary, but also by employing a certain ironic humor at times (Sanh 99b-100a), and veiled threats at other times (Shab 133b). It would seem that Rava succeeded, at least in his own lifetime, but it may be significant that none of his *talmidim* stayed in Maḥoza after his *petirah*; R. Nahman b. Yitzhak reestablished Pumbediṯa as a place of learning, R. Papa moved to Naresh, and Ravina apparently went to Maṯa Maḥasiya, a suburb of Sura. It may be that none of them felt able to take up the challenge of dealing with Maḥoza's Jewish community, or as one of *Ḥakirah's* editors suggests, they felt unable to deal with the royal court across the river—or both.

Three texts illustrate the situation he faced, one from Mak 22b, one from Sanh 99b-100a, one from Shab 23a, and, finally, one from Eruv 21b, respectively.

אמר רבא: כמה טפשאי שאר אינשי דקיימי מקמי ספר תורה ולא קיימי מקמי גברא רבה, דאילו בס"ת כתיב ארבעים, ואתו רבנן בצרו חדא.

10 For details, see Yaakov Elman, "Ma'aseh be-Shtei Ayaroṯ: Maḥoza u-Pumbediṯa Ke-Meyatzegoṯ Shtei Tarbuyoṯ Hilkhatiyyoṯ," *Torah li-Shemah: Meḥqarim be-Mada'ei ha-Yahaduṯ li-khvod Prof. Shamma Yehudah Friedman*, Jerusalem: Bar Ilan UP, 2007, pp. 3-38, and "The Socioeconomics of Babylonian Heresy," *Jewish Law Association Studies* XVII (2007), pp. 80-126.

Said Rava: How foolish are most people who rise [in respect] before a Torah scroll but not before a rabbinic scholar, for in a Torah scroll is written, "forty [strokes shall you give him and not more] (Deut 25:3)," and the Rabbis came and reduced it by one! [Thus they are due as much respect as a Torah scroll, if not more, since they control its interpretation, even when it goes against the plain meaning of the text.]

אפיקורוס כגון מאן?.... רבא אמר: כגון הני דבי בנימין אסיא , דאמרי: מאי אהני לן רבנן? מעולם [ק ע"א] לא שרו לן עורבא , ולא אסרו לן יונה. רבא, כי הוו מייתי טריפתא דבי בנימין קמיה, כי הוה חזי בה טעמא להיתירא, אמר להו: תחזו, דקא שרינא לכו עורבא. כי הוה חזי לה טעמא לאיסורא, אמר להו: תחזו דקא אסרנא לכו יונה

What is a heretic [of whom the Mishnah states that he will have no portion in the World to Come]? ...Said Rava: [These are] like those members of the household of Benjamin the Physician, who say: What use are the Rabbis to us? They never permitted the raven [which the Torah forbids], nor have they forbidden the dove [which the Torah allows; thus the Rabbis cannot undo what is written in the Torah]. When [members] of the household of Benjamin the Physician would bring a [question regarding the permissibility for consumption of animals] with a fatal organic defect [which are ordinarily forbidden] before Rava, when he saw a reason to be lenient, he would say to them: See, I have permitted the raven for you! And when he saw a reason to be strict, he would say to them: See, I have forbidden the dove to you!

אמר רב הונא: חצר שיש לה שני פתחים - צריכה שתי נרות. (ואמר) (מסורת הש"ס: [אמר]) רבא: לא אמרן אלא משתי רוחות, אבל מרוח אחת - לא צריך. מאי טעמא? אילימא משום חשדא, חשדא דמאן? אילימא חשדא דעלמא - אפילו ברוח אחת נמי ליבעי! אי חשדא דבני מתא - אפילו משתי רוחות נמי לא ליבעי - לעולם משום חשדא דבני מתא, וזימנין דמחלפי בהאי ולא חלפי בהאי, ואמרי: כי היכי דבהאי פיתחא לא אדליק, בהך פיתחא נמי לא אדליק.

Said R. Huna: A courtyard that has to entrances must have two [Hanukah] lamps. Rava said: This applies only [to a case where the entrances face] in two [different] directions, but it is not necessary [when it faces in only] one direction.

What is the reason? If we say [that this is] because suspicion [that one of the courtyard's inhabitants had not lit a Hanukah lamp]—who [harbors this] suspicion? If we say: the suspicion of outsiders (lit., "the world"), [R. Huna's] requirement should also apply even [to a case] of [entrance(s) in one direction]! If the suspicion of the inhabitants of the neighborhood (lit., "the people of the place"),

> and sometimes one may pass on one [street] and not the other, and say: Just as he did not light in this entrance, so too he did not light on [the other].

Why would people be suspicious that someone was negligent in lighting a Hanukah lamp? The mitzvah is not onerous or expensive, and it is attractive to children.

As we shall see, the reason seems to have been that there were people in Maḥoza who did not observe Hanuka on "religious" grounds; they felt that since it was not mentioned explicitly in the Torah or in Nakh (as Purim is), Ḥazal did not have the right to establish such a holiday. Perhaps also they felt that the Maccabee's victory should not be celebrated because their dynasty ended up by bringing the Roman's into Eretz Yisrael. In any case, they took it upon themselves to reject a mitzvah established by Ḥazal.

Rava had two answers for these "proto-Karaities."

First, in this environment, we can well understand why Rava shows a deep sensitivity to the theory and practice of midrash, especially *midrash halakhah.* He is one of only two Amoraim to whom the principle that "a verse does not depart from its plain sense" is attributed;[11] he was sharply attentive to the problem of *pesukim* for which *derashoṯ* were missing. In his work on midrash he learned from earlier Amoraim of Eretz Yisrael, some from his father-in-law-to-be, R. Ḥisda, and some of which he pioneered himself. While we have *aggadoṯ* in the name of earlier Babylonian Amoraim, aside from scattered *derashoṯ*, *midrash halakhah* seems not to have been of great interest in Bavel before Rava's time, and to a lesser extent, that of R. Ḥisda, his rebbe. This interest was carried on by his *talmidim.* Among those who are associated with the many discussions of rabbinic biblical exegesis attributed to Rava in the Bavli are R. Papa, R. Mesharshiah, and R. Zevid; these discussions were continued in the next generation by R. Papa's disciples in Naresh, eventually engen-

---

[11] Mar b. Ravina (Rabbana) of the third generation to R. Kahana in Shab 63a, and Rava in Yev 24a; the third occurrence, in Yev 11b, is anonymous.

dering those large exegetical *sugyoṯ* so typical of the Bavli (and so rare in the Yerushalmi).[12]

Rava also addressed the issue in a more direct way. The "household"—presumably, the sons, but perhaps even the grandsons—of Benjamin the Physician charged the rabbis with being essentially powerless, since they could not permit what the Torah forbad, and vice versa. Rava, presumably on another occasion, pointed to the Rabbis' power in limiting the forty stripes ordained by the Torah to 39. Elsewhere, Rava emphasizes the severity of violating rabbinic ordinances, even as against those of the Torah.

> דרש רבא: מאי דכתיב (קהלת י"ב) ויתר מהמה בני הזהר עשות ספרים הרבה וגו'. בני! הזהר בדברי סופרים יותר מדברי תורה. שדברי תורה יש בהן עשה ולא תעשה, ודברי סופרים - כל העובר על דברי סופרים חייב מיתה. שמא תאמר אם יש בהן ממש מפני מה לא נכתבו - אמר קרא עשות ספרים הרבה אין קץ. (קהלת י"ב)

> Rava expounded [presumably in public]: What [is the meaning of the verse] that is written, "And of more than these, my son, take heed, the making of many books" (Koh. 12:12)? My son, take heed of the words of the Scribes more than the words of the Torah, for the words of the Torah contain positive and negative commandments, while as for the words of the Scribes, whoever transgresses the words of the Scribes is worthy of death. Perhaps you will say that if they have substance to them, why were they not written down? The verse [therefore] says: "Of the making of books there is no end" (Eccl. 12:12).

Paradoxically, though ordinarily doubts regarding rabbinic decrees are decided leniently, Rava here wished to emphasize the greater severity of the violation of those decrees even as against biblical laws. In this way he emphasized the authority of Hazal in instituting those *takkanoṯ*. In an exchange with R. Nahman he raised the question of why the mishnah in BM 55a-b included a rabbinic decree (*demai*) along with biblical ones in listing those *mattanoṯ kehunah* for which a fine of a fifth was demanded. The answer: to strengthen the authority of those rabbinic decrees!

---

12 All of this is discussed in more detail in my "Rava ve-Darkei ha-Iyyun ha-Eretz Yisraeliyyot be-Midrash ha-Halakhah," in Y. Gafni, ed., Merkaz *u-Tefutzah: Eretz Yisrael veha-Tefutzoṯ bi-Ymei Bayiṯ Sheni, ha-Mishnah veha-Talmud*, Jerusalem: Merkaz Shazar, 2004, pp, 217-242.

משנה. חמשה חומשין הן, אלו הן: האוכל תרומה, ותרומת מעשר, ותרומת מעשר של דמאי, והחלה והבכורים - מוסיף חומש. והפודה נטע רבעי ומעשר שני שלו - מוסיף חומש. הפודה את הקדשו - מוסיף חומש, הנהנה שוה פרוטה מן ההקדש - מוסיף חומש, והגוזל את חבירו שוה פרוטה ונשבע לו - מוסיף חומש.

גמרא. אמר רבא: קשיא ליה לרבי אלעזר תרומת מעשר של דמאי: וכי עשו חכמים חיזוק לדבריהם כשל תורה? –
אמר רב נחמן אמר שמואל: הא מני - רבי מאיר היא, דאמר: עשו חכמים חיזוק לדבריהם כשל תורה. דתניא: המביא גט ממדינת הים, נתנו לה ולא אמר לה בפני נכתב ובפני נחתם - יוציא והולד ממזר, דברי רבי מאיר. וחכמים אומרים: אין הולד ממזר. כיצד יעשה? יטלנו ממנה, ויחזור ויתננו לה בפני שנים, ויאמר לה בפני נכתב ובפני נחתם.
ולרבי מאיר, משום דלא אמר לה בפני נכתב ובפני נחתם - יוציא והולד ממזר?
אין, רבי מאיר לטעמיה, דאמר רב המנונא משמיה דעולא, אומר היה רבי מאיר: כל המשנה ממטבע שטבעו חכמים בגיטין - יוציא והולד ממזר.

MISHNAH. [The addition of] a fifth [to the principal] is required in five cases: [i] one who eats *terumah*, the *terumah* of *ma'aser*, the *terumah* of *ma'aser* of *demai*, *ḥallah*, and the first fruits—must add a fifth; [ii] he who redeems the fourth year planting and his own *ma'aser sheni* adds a fifth; [iii] he who redeems his *heqdesh* adds a fifth; [iv] he who benefits from *heqdesh* the value of a *perutah* adds a fifth; and [v] he who robs his neighbor of a *perutah*'s worth and swears [falsely] to him concerning it must add a fifth.

GEMARA. Rava said: The *terumah* of the tithe of *demai* presented a difficulty to R. Eleazar: Did then the Sages set up protective measures for their enactments [that is, to the same degree of severity] as for those of the Torah?—
Said R. Naḥman in Samuel's name: The author of this [Mishnah] is R. Meir, who maintained: The Sages did set up protective measures for their enactments as for those of the Torah. For it has been taught: If one brought a divorce from countries overseas and delivered it to her [the wife] without declaring, 'It was written in my presence and signed in my presence,' he [=her next husband] must divorce her [too], and their offspring is a *mamzer*; this is R. Meir's view. But the Sages say: Their offspring is not a *mamzer*. What then shall he [the messenger] do? He must take it [the divorce] back from her, give it to her again in the presence of two witnesses and declare, 'It was written in my presence and signed in my presence.'
But according to R. Meir, [merely] because he did not declare to her, 'It was written in my presence and signed in my presence,' he must divorce her, and the child is a *mamzer*! —

> Yes. R. Meir is consistent with his view. For R. Hamnuna said on 'Ulla's authority: R. Meir used to say, Whenever one departs from the fixed procedure ordained by the Sages in case of divorce, he [her next husband] must give a divorce, whilst the offspring is a *mamzer*.

Here Rava addresses the same question, but in a halakhic mode: Do the Sages equate the punishment for violating one of their own enactments (*taqqanot*) in the same way that the Torah does? Do they make a *de-rabbanan* as severe as a *de-oraita*? And the answer is yes, they do, at least according to R. Meir, who will even declare a child a *mamzer* because his mother did not fulfill all the requirements—even the *de-rabbanan* requirements—of receiving a *get*. Thus, the problem of ensuring respect for rabbinic *taqqanot* was an issue that concerned both Rava and R. Nahman.

We should also note in passing that the Gemara hastens to identify the author of this Mishnah as R. Meir, and to coordinate this Mishnah's teachings with his other *shittot*.

In Eruvin, though, he had to deal with another challenge to rabbinic *taqqanot*: "if they [=the rabbinic decrees] are indeed valid (אם יש להן ממש), why are they not written down?" Once again, we hear echoes of the family of Doctor Benjamin—or their Mahozan neighbors, other "sharp ones" of Mahoza. Members of the non-rabbinic acculturated elite of Mahoza were open to the intellectual currents and theological controversies of the Sasanian Empire at its hub. The question of the authenticity and authority of non-written traditions was a burning issue in the wake of the self-styled prophet Mani's missionizing efforts for his new religion.[13]

Ideally, Rava's audience apparently thought, law should be written down; why then is the law of the Rabbis unwritten? Rava responds to this problem by quoting Kohelet 12:12 once again: "Of the making of books there is no end," that is, rabbinic law is too

---

13 See my discussion of this issue in "Middle Persian Culture and Babylonian Sages: Accommodation and Resistance in the Shaping of Rabbinic Legal Tradition," in Charlotte Elisheva Fonrobert and Martin S. Jaffe, eds., *Cambridge Companion to Rabbinic Literature*, Cambridge UP, 2007, pp. 165-197, esp. pp. 178-9.

voluminous to be written down. It is pertinent to recall at this point that the largest Middle Persian compilation known to us is the *Dēnkard*, a nine-volume Zoroastrian encyclopedia, which runs to about 169,000 words, and that dates from the ninth century. In contrast, the greatest compilation of Roman law, the second edition of Justinian's *Code* of 534, weighs in at about a million words and the Bavli runs to 1.8 million words. Based on the large fragment of Bavli Ḥulin from the Cairo Geniza identified by Marc Bregman and published by Shamma Friedman 15 years ago, which contained an average of 576 words per column, and assuming a Torah-scroll-sized scroll as standard, it would have taken about ten and a half scrolls of that size for 2,522 columns. But Justinian had the resources of the Roman Empire at his disposal. In Babylonia, even the government could not requisition such efforts. Even if we assume that Rava's "words of the Scribes" ran to only a third of the size of the Bavli at its close, this would have been beyond the capabilities of Babylonian scribes of the mid-fourth century. Aside from the technical problems, however, we must note that Rava's statement cannot be detached from the interreligious debates of the time. In one of these debates, the self-proclaimed "prophet" Mani claimed that his religion was superior to the state religion of Zoroastrianism since he had provided his followers with a written scripture, while the Zoroastrian bible, the Avesta, was still being transmitted orally. This argument was so persuasive that the Zoroastrian priests had to invent a new alphabet to write down the Avesta. Apparently some Jews accepted his argument and applied it to *Torah she-be'al Peh*—and Rava had to respond to them.[14]

Despite all this, Zoroastrians still held to the superiority of oral transmission of sacred texts. Mary Boyce, a major historian of Zoroastrianism, notes that three centuries after the Avesta was finally written down by the sixth century, oral transmission was still considered the superior mode: *zindag gōwišnīg saxwan az an ī pad nibišt mādagwardar hangērdan čimīg*—"it is reasonable to consider the liv-

[14] See my "Orality and the Redaction of the Babylonian Talmud," *Oral Tradition* 14/1 (1999) [published in 2000], pp. 52-99.

ing spoken word more important than the written."[15] And indeed, so did Ḥazal; R. Aharan ha-Kohen Sarjado, rosh yeshiva of the Pumbediṭa yeshiva in Baghdad, testifies that in his time, in the middle of the tenth century, the Bavli was still memorized by heart by most *talmidim* of his yeshiva.[16]

IV

Rava did more than preach. From many *memroṯ* transmitted in his name and in the name of his *talmidim*, we can see that Rava had already embarked on a systematic examination of *midrash halakhah*, an examination that stood him in good stead when confronted with the challenges of the household of Dr. Benjamin and the other "sharp-witted ones of Maḥoza."

For example, in Ḥulin 84a Rava is challenged by one Yaakov Mina'a (Was he Yaakov the Heretic or Jacob the Christian?) to explain why the term *behemah* is sometimes taken as a collective and *includes* the class of wild animals (*ḥayyah*), while at others it is the reverse. Who this Yaakov Mina'a was is difficult to say at this point, but it is clear that Rava was the target of such questions, not only from within the Jewish community, as in the case of *hahu merabbanan*—a certain *talmid*, who asked about the operation of a *midrash halakhah* on the doubled verb of *hashev teshivem* ("you shall certainly return them") in Deut 22:1 (BM 31a)—or the household of Dr. Benjamin, but also from outside. Indications are that Rava had already concerned himself with such questions even before he became *Mara de-Aṭra* of Maḥoza; he was approached with such questions because he had gained a reputation for answering them. In ten places in the Bavli the question of the consistent application of the *middoṯ* is raised, and in eight of them it is Rava who answers the question (Qid 9a, BQ 77b, Mak 8a, Tem 6b, Yom 63b, Ar 30b, Ned 80b, 88a). Moreover, some of his understanding of the *middoṯ* he

---

15 See Mary Boyce, "Middle Persian Literature," in B. Spuler, *Handbuch der Orientalistik* 4.2.1 (Iranistik), Literatur, Lieferung 1, Leiden/Koln: E.J. Brill, 1968, pp. 31-66; see pp. 34, 45, n. 1.

16 See *Otzar ha-Geonoim*, Yevamot, no. 107, and the discussion in my "Orality and the Redaction" n. 12 above) pp. 72-76.

learned from R. Ḥisda. Thus, the analysis of *gezerah shavah*s in terms of *don mineih u-mineih* or *don mineih ve-uqe' be-aṯra* is applied by R. Ḥisda and R. Hamnuna (Men 62a), Rava, R. Papa, Rava's *talmid muvhaq* (Nid 43b) R. Papa and Ravina (Men 2a), and R. Papa's *talmidim* (Shev 31a, Zev 91b, and Neb 107a). Another line of research pioneered by Rava and his *talmidim* (especially R. Papa) is whether combinations of *limmudim* are possible: for example, can a *qal va-homer* be applied to a *din* that had already been derived by a *heqesh*? (Zev 41a, 49b) Or by another *heqesh*? (Zev 41a), and so on through many combinations of that sort.

Perhaps Rava's most important contribution to the study of *midrash halakhah* was his insistence that every letter or word must be interpreted. This principle was implicit long before Rava, of course, but he went one step further: he pointed out cases in which there were "missing *derashoṯ*" (see BQ 54a, BM 27a, Men 10a). We will look at the second case:

> אמר רבא: למה לי דכתב רחמנא שור חמור שה ושמלה? צריכי, דאי כתב רחמנא שמלה, הוה אמינא: הני מילי - בעדים דגופה וסימנין דגופה, אבל חמור בעדים דאוכף וסימנין דאוכף - אימא לא מהדרינן ליה, כתב רחמנא חמור, דאפילו חמור בסימני האוכף. שור ושה דכתב רחמנא למה לי? שור - דאפילו לגיזת זנבו, ושה - לגיזותיו. ולכתוב רחמנא שור, דאפילו לגיזת זנבו, וכל שכן שה לגיזותיו! אלא אמר רבא: חמור דבור לרבי יהודה, ושה דאבידה לדברי הכל קשיא.

> Said Rava: Why does the All-Merciful mention "an ox, a donkey, a sheep and a garment" [in Deut 22:1, 3: "You shall not see your brother's ox or his sheep go astray and hide yourself from them; you shall surely return them to your brother....So shall you do with his donkey, and so shall you do with his garments"]?

After deriving various *dinim* from each of these terms, Rava notes that the word "donkey" in Exod 21:33 is problematical, as is the word "sheep" in Deut 22:1, 3, since there is a missing *derashah* for each.

> But, says Rava, [the word] "donkey" that is [mentioned] in connection with a pit ["And if a man should open a pit...and an ox or a donkey should fall in....."][is difficult] on R. Yehudah's view, and [the word] "sheep" that is [mentioned] in connection with a lost article [in Deut 22:1. 3] on all views is difficult [since we do not have R. Yehudah's *derashah* for donkey in Exod 21:33, nor any *derashah* for "sheep" in Deut 22:1.3].

R. Yehudah rejects the Sages' *mi'ut* of *ḥamor ve-lo' kelim*, that the word "donkey" comes to exclude vessels that are broken, but we have no substitute *derashah* in his name, so the word still poses a problem to his view. Similarly, we have no *derashah* for "sheep" in the Deut passage. In other words, Rava is telling us that, ideally, we should have a *derashah* for every seemingly "excess" word in the Torah. Now, with the passing of the *tequfah* of the Tannaim it was no longer possible to *darshan* a *vav ha-ḥibbur*, as R. Akiva and other Tannaim had done, and so that ideal could no longer be achieved. But we should be aware of that ideal.

Indeed, it is clear from Yev 72b that R. Yoḥanan in the second generation of Amoraim already realized this. Thus, in an exchange with R. Eleazar b. Pedaṯ, his *talmid ḥaver*, he criticized the latter because he thought (wrongly) that R. Eleazar had expounded a *vav-heh*; Resh Lakish however pointed out that the *derashah* was actually already in Sifra, the Midrash on Leviticus.

> כי הא דיתיב רבי יוחנן וקדריש: נותר בזמנו - אינו נשרף אלא ביום, שלא בזמנו - נשרף בין ביום בין בלילה, ואיתיביה רבי אלעזר לרבי יוחנן: אין לי אלא נימול לשמיני שאין נימול אלא ביום, מנין לרבות לתשעה, לעשרה, לאחד עשר, לשנים עשר (מנין)? תלמוד לומר: וביום, ואפילו למאן דלא דריש וא"ו, וא"ו וה"י דריש; אישתיק. בתר דנפק, א"ל רבי יוחנן לר"ל: ראיתי לבן פדת שיושב ודורש כמשה מפי הגבורה, א"ל ר"ל: דידיה היא? מתניתא היא. היכא תנא ליה? בתורת כהנים. נפק תנייה בתלתא יומי, וסברה בתלתא ירחי

> R. Yohanan was sitting and expounding: *Noṯar* at its proper time [on the third day, as per Lev 7:17] must be burned in the daytime [since the word "day" was used]; if not at its proper time [after the third day], it may be burned either by night or by day.
> R. Eleazar [b. Pedaṯ] raised an objection: I know only that the child who must be circumcised on the eighth day must be circumcised during the day, how do I know it for the ninth, tenth, eleventh or twelfth [day after its birth]? Because it was stated: "And in the day" (*uva-yom*—Lev 12:3), and even [R. Eleazar b. R. Shimon], who does not expound a *vav* [alone] will expound a *vav-heh*!
> [R. Yohanan] remained silent.
> After [R. Eleazar b. Pedaṯ] went out, R. Yoḥanan said to Resh Lakish "Did you see Ben Pedaṯ sitting and expounding like Moshe [Rabbenu] from the mouth of the Most High (*mi-pi Ha-Gevurah*)!" [Rashi: In the language of the Tannaim, {even though} R. Eleazar b. Pedaṯ was not a Tanna; he was an Amora, the *talmid* of R. Yoḥanan.]

Resh Lakish replied: "Was it his? It is really a *baraiṯa*.
"Where was it taught?"
"In Torat Kohanim."
R. Yoḥanan went out and memorized it in three days and *darshend* it for three months.

Clearly, R. Yoḥanan felt that only a Tanna could expound a *derashah* on a *vav*, and criticized R. Eleazar for doing so, unaware that he was quoting a *baraiṯa*. The *derashah* is in fact in the text of our Sifra [Tazri'a, *perek* 1, *parashah* 1]. Moreover, we do not find an Amora in all of the Bavli expounding a *vav* after the time of Rav and Shmuel, who as members of the transition generation between the tannaitic era and that of the Amoraim were in a special category (*Rav Tanna hu' u-palig*, Ket 8a, Git 38b, BB 42a, Sanh 83b).[17] The system of *midrash halakhah* was already closing down, though we find that Rava could still expound *mi'utim* and make use of some other *middoṯ*. Apparently, in the two cases he mentions in BM 27a he did not have a tradition to account for the missing *derashoṯ*.

V

As *Mara de-Aṯra* of Maḥoza and spokesman for its community, Rava had to address another issue that had much broader resonance among Jews and non-Jews alike, the problem of theodicy, *tzaddik ve-ra lo*. Once again, I will choose only three examples out of many that provide us with a view of Rava's thoughts on this complex, difficult and fraught question. The three will be Ḥul 7b, Sot 21a, and MQ 28a.

The first of these passages is made up of three *memroṯ* on *yissurim* and *kapparah*, two from Eretz Yisrael, and the final one by Rava.

ואמר ר' חנינא: אין אדם נוקף אצבעו מלמטה אלא א"כ מכריזין עליו מלמעלה, שנאמר: (תהלים ל"ז) מה' מצעדי גבר כוננו, (משלי כ') ואדם מה יבין דרכו. א"ר אלעזר: דם ניקוף מרצה כדם עולה. אמר רבא: בגודל ימין ובניקוף שני, והוא דקאזיל לדבר מצוה.

---

17 It is true that Tosafoṯ note in their comments in Pes 92a, s.v. *ve-amar R. Yoḥanan*, that R. Yoḥanan has the same status, but he himself apparently did not think that the Torah could be expounded in this way any longer.

1. Again, R. Ḥanina said: No one bruises his finger (or: leg) below unless it was so decreed against him from Above [There follow pesukim from Ps 37:23 and Prov 20:24].
2. R. Eleazar [b. Pedaṯ] said: The blood of a bruise atones as [does] the blood of a burnt-offering.
3. Rava added: Only the blood of a second bruising of the right thumb, and only if it happened to one who was about to perform a mitzvah.

Rava here seems to limit providential, atoning suffering to those who are injured while engaged in performing a mitzvah, and in only strictly limited circumstances. If Rava's comment relates only to no. 2, other bruising must be attributed to causes other than the need for atonement, perhaps "sufferings of love," *yissurim shel ahavah*; if it relates to no. 1 as well, he denies even providential status to most bruises. In short, he detaches suffering and atonement. What purpose then do these sufferings serve if they do not atone?

The next passage is another case in which Rava reacts to earlier opinions, limiting them also in the same way he did in Ḥul 7b. The question in Sot 21a is to what extent the study of Torah and the performance of mitzvoṯ protect the one engaged in them from temptation, sin or punishment.

The *sugya* begins with the view of R. Menaḥem b. R. Yose that performance of mitzvoṯ protects one only temporarily, while the study of Torah protects one permanently. It continues with the view of R. Yosef that a mitzvah protects the one engaged in it only while he is actively involved with it, while the study of Torah does so at all times. In part this is a slightly more concrete formulation of the previous statement, but R. Yosef introduces another distinction. Torah study not only protects the scholar from suffering, but also "rescues" him from the evil inclination. Thus, the essential premise of this *sugya* implicitly rejects R. Yaakov's statement in Qid 39b, which is introduced by Rava, that "there is no reward for mitzvoṯ in this world."

Modifying R. Yosef's formulation, Rava points to the cases of Doeg and Aḥitophel, the classic instances of scholars who came to a bad end; he proposes that:

אלא אמר רבא: תורה, בעידנא דעסיק בה - מגנא ומצלא, בעידנא דלא עסיק בה - אגוני מגנא, אצולי לא מצלא; מצוה, בין בעידנא דעסיק בה, בין בעידנא דלא עסיק בה - אגוני מגנא, אצולי לא מצלא.

> Torah protects [one from misfortune] and rescues [one from the evil inclination] when one is occupied in its study; when one is not occupied with it, it protects but does not rescue. Mitzvoṯ protect one [from misfortune] whether he is actively occupied with them or not, but they certainly do not rescue him [from the evil inclination].

Rava argues from historical experience: two great scholars came to bad ends: Aḥitophel committed suicide, and Doeg died at age 37, having lost his *heleq la-olam ha-ba'*. In Qid 39a, R. Yaakov's statement about there not being any reward for mitzvoṯ in this world is also an argument from experience, based on the incident of the son who climbed a ladder to perform the two mitzvoṯ that bring the doer long life—*kibbud av* and *shilu'aḥ ha-qen*—and fell to his death.

Our final source finds Rava also arguing from experience, the lives of two of the *gedolei ha-dor* of the generation before his: Rabbah and R. Ḥisda, the latter his own (second) father-in-law. Rava attributes to the workings of fate—*mazzal*—the three elements that we may see as components of individual contentment: "[length of] life, [surviving] children, and sustenance (MQ 28a)." Rava asserts that these three aspects of human life are astrologically determined and are not dependent on religious merit; he proves this by contrasting the lives of two great—"righteous"--authorities of the previous generation, Rabbah, the head of the Pumbediṯa school, and his own father-in-law, R. Ḥisda.

Rava presents in graphic terms the presence or absence of each of these components in the lives of these sages. Rabbah lived to the age of only forty; R. Ḥisda lived to the ripe old age of 92. Rabbah experienced "sixty" [i.e., a large number of] bereavements; R. Ḥisda celebrated sixty happy occasions. And finally, R. Ḥisda was so wealthy that he could afford to feed wheat bread even to the dogs of his household, while even the human members of Rabbah's household had to be content with the inferior barley bread—and did not have enough of that.

> אמר רבא: חיי, בני ומזוני, לא בזכותא תליא מילתא, אלא במזלא תליא מילתא. דהא רבה ורב חסדא תרוייהו רבנן צדיקי הוו, מר מצלי ואתי מיטרא, ומר מצלי ואתי מיטרא. רב חסדא חיה תשעין ותרתין שנין - רבה חיה ארבעין, בי רב חסדא - שיתין הלולי, בי רבה - שיתין תיכלי. בי רב חסדא - סמידא לכלבי ולא מתבעי, בי רבה - נהמא דשערי לאינשי, ולא משתכח.

ואמר רבא: הני תלת מילי בעאי קמי שמיא, תרתי יהבו לי, חדא לא יהבו לי; חוכמתיה דרב הונא ועותריה דרב חסדא - ויהבו לי, ענותנותיה דרבה בר רב הונא - לא יהבו לי.

Rava said: [Length of] life, children, and sustenance depend not on merit but [rather on] *mazzal.*
For take Rabbah and R. Ḥisda. Both were absolutely righteous rabbis; [the proof of this righteousness is that] each master prayed for rain and it came.
[Despite this,] R. Ḥisda lived to the age of 92; Rabbah lived only to the age of 40. In R. Ḥisda's house--60 marriage feasts, in Rabbah's—60 bereavements. At R. Ḥisda's house there was purest wheat bread for dogs, and it went to waste;[18] at Rabbah's house there was barley bread for humans--and that could not be found.
This too Rava said: I requested these three things of Heaven; two were given me, but the third was not: the scholarship of R. Huna and the wealth of R. Ḥisda were given me, but the modesty of Rabbah b. R. Huna was not given me.[19]

By attributing these three essential elements of human existence to *mazzal* and not merit, Rava articulates a vision of human life that is unflinching, unsparing—and perhaps terrifying—but honest. There is no comfort or security in his doctrine, except that it reflects the reality that many people either experience or observe. Piety, prayer, learning, good deeds—all these staples of the moral life—will not provide the doer with the elements of a classical "good life," what Ashkenazic Jews call *nachas*. An absolutely righteous rabbi (a *tzaddiq gamur*)—Rabbah in this case—could live a life that

18 Whether R. Ḥisda himself countenanced this is doubtful; see Shab 140b: Said R. Ḥisda: Whoever can to eat barley bread and eats wheat bread [instead] violates the prohibition of "You shall not destroy." Again, R. Ḥisda himself attributed his wealth to more pragmatic causes—his decision to become a beer brewer; see Pes 113a. What his view of astrology was is not clear, though he was greatly concerned with the interpretation of dreams, and several of his observations on that matter are preserved; see Ber 55a, and, in a legal context, Shab 11a=Taan 12b.

19 R. Huna, Rav's *talmid muvhaq*, was the undisputed Gedol ha-Dor, while his son Rabbah, though inheriting his father's position in Sura, was not considered on a par with R. Naḥman in Maḥoza or Rabbah in Pumbedita, and yet he remained totally without resentment.

was short, difficult—and tragic. After twenty or twenty-five adult years of penury, of repeated tragedies and bereavements, but great scholarly and religious achievement, Rabbah dies at age 40—and this despite reaching the heights of rabbinic scholarship. According to another Gemara, his end was of a piece with his life: he died in flight from the Persian authorities, one of the inhabitants of Pumbediṭa having slandered him (BM 86a). Indeed, his unpopularity with the townspeople was well known to his disciples and he himself was well aware of it (see Shab 153a). We should note that the Bavli in Taan 25a R. Eleazar b. Pedaṭ, on complaining to Hashem regarding his abject poverty was told: Eleazar, my son, should I turn the whole world to its beginnings, and *perhaps* then you will be born in an hour of sustenance? Upon hearing this, R. Eleazar gave up his objections!

This is not Rava's sole contribution to the matter, however, as we have already seen. Rava reshapes R. Yosef's statement in Sot 21a as to the limited utility of Torah study and the performance of mitzvoṭ; he asserts (in Ber 5a) that in some cases one's merit may bring upon him yet more suffering, albeit "sufferings of love." As if all this were not enough, he reflects on the perilous nature of Israel's life in exile as played out in his own life (Ḥag 5a-b). All of these (the limited protection from the exigencies of human existence afforded by Torah study and the performance of mitzvoṭ, humanity's own frail nature, and the "sufferings of love") contribute to the tragic dimensions of the human condition.

In the end, however, Rava's view of the astrological influences on the basics of human happiness was not universally accepted by the Bavli, which elsewhere rejected astrological influence as affecting Jews (see Shab 156a-b). The only exception is R. Hanina, who lived about a century before Rava, in Eretz Yisrael. But Rava's view is likewise a minority one. It is worth noting that he bases it on experience, which we may call a *sevara*, and—as the Gemara often tells us by equating *qera* and *sevara*, or even declaring a *pasuk* as unnecessary when we have a *sevara*[20]— a *sevara* is equivalent to a *de-oraiṭa*, a

---

20 See Pes 21b, Yev 35b, Ket 22a, BQ 46b, Sanh 30a {twice}, Shev 22a, AZ 34b, Zev 2a, 7a, Men 2a, 13b, 73b, Ḥul 114b, Nid 25a.

Torah teaching. Thus we see what stands behind Rava's views in Qid 39b, Ḥul 7b, and Sot 21a.

We may wonder how effective such a view of the limitations of Divine Providence was in addressing this issue of *tzaddiq ve-ra lo*, and what Rava's intentions were in presenting such a picture. The proverb that Rava quotes regarding "length of life, children, and sustenance," which appears often in Middle Persian and Arabic literature, indicates that this was a common view—as uncomfortable an observation of the human condition as it was. It seems that Rava understood his community: they preferred a realistic assessment of life in order to cope with its hardships and difficulties rather than a simplistic, rose-colored one. However, the Rishonim and Aḥaronim recognized that such a view, which either puts limits on Hashem's Providence or His justice, could not be interpreted in its plain sense.[21]

But as we have seen, the Bavli does not speak with one voice. Along with the rule that *ein somekhin al ha-nes*—"we do not rely on miracles" (see Pes 50b for the Aramaic version) we also have Naḥum Ish Gamzu's view that *gam zo le-tovah*—"all is for the best" (Taan 21a). Kelal Yisrael's experience has perhaps inclined it to the latter rather than the former.

In the foregoing we have emphasized the unity of Rava's halakhic and theological thought; it is more difficult to point to such a melding here, in Aggadah, the realm of the Providential ordering of the world, But Rava's profound and nuanced view of the world may be discerned in the following passage from BM 36b.

אתמר, פשע בה ויצאת לאגם, ומתה כדרכה. אביי משמיה דרבה אמר: חייב, רבא משמיה דרבה אמר: פטור. אביי משמיה דרבה אמר: חייב, כל דיינא דלא דאין כי האי דינא לאו דיינא הוא.

לא מבעיא למאן דאמר תחילתו בפשיעה וסופו באונס חייב - דחייב. אלא אפילו למאן דאמר פטור - הכא חייב. מאי טעמא - דאמרינן: הבלא דאגמא קטלה. רבא משמיה דרבה אמר: פטור, כל דיינא דלא דאין כי האי דינא לאו דיינא הוא.

לא מיבעיא למאן דאמר: תחילתו בפשיעה וסופו באונס פטור - דפטור. אלא אפילו למאן דאמר חייב - הכא פטור. מאי טעמא - דאמרינן: מלאך המות, מה לי הכא ומה

21 See my "The Contribution of Rabbinic Thought Towards a Theology of Suffering," in S. Carmy, ed., *Jewish Perspectives on the Experience of Suffering*, Jason Aaronson, Inc., 1999, pp. 155-212.

לי התם? ומודי אביי דאי הדרא לבי מרה ומתה דפטור. מאי טעמא - דהא הדרא לה, וליכא למימר הבלא דאגמא קטלה. ומודי רבא כל היכא דאיגנבה גנב באגם ומתה כדרכה בי גנב דחייב. מאי טעמא, דאי שבקה מלאך המות - בביתיה דגנבא הוה קיימא. ...

It has been stated: If he [the *shomer*] was negligent about it, and it went out into a meadow and died naturally, Abaye in Rabbah's name ruled that he is liable, [while] Rava in Rabbah's name ruled that he is not liable.

Abaye in Rabbah's name ruled that he is liable, [and] any judge who does not give such a verdict is not a judge: not only is he liable on the view that, if the beginning is through negligence, and the end through an accident, one is liable; but even on the view that one is not liable, in this case he is. Why? Because we say: The air of the meadow land killed it.

Rava in Rabbah's name ruled that he is not liable, [and] any judge who does not give such a verdict is not a judge: not only is he not liable on the view that, if the beginning is through negligence, and the end through an accident, one is not liable; but even on the view that he is liable, in this case he is not. Why? *Because we say: What difference does one place or another make to the Angel of Death?*

Now, Abaye admits that if it returned to its owner [that is, the bailee] and then died, he is free. Why? [It is] because it had returned, and it could not be said that the air of the meadow killed it, while Rava admits that if it was stolen from the meadow and died naturally in the thief's house, he [=the *shomer*] is responsible. Why? [Even] had the Angel of Death left it alone, it still would have been in the thief's house...

While the discussion continues, we already see from the opening declarations that Rava holds that since many animals pasture in the meadow and do not die, even the negligence of the *shomer* in allowing the animal to go out to the meadow is not sufficient to make him liable, since the animal might have died even in the *shomer*'s house (or barn). In this case, it was the owner's *mazzal* that caused the animal to die, and not the *shomer*'s negligence, in accordance with Rava's dictum in MQ 28a regarding *mazzal* and sustenance (*mezonei*). As we know from BQ 2b, animals themselves have no *mazzal*, and so it must have been the owner's *mazzal* and not the animal's. Thus, once again, Rava's view is consistent in his aggadic and halakhic positions—as we might well expect.

Rava was at once *Mara de-Aṯra*, Rosh Yeshiva and Dayyan, and the Gemara gives ample evidence of his fulfilling all three roles; we have examined only his activities as *Mara de-Aṯra*. This summary is based on studies published over a period of more than 20 years, and much, much more can be said. For the time being, this must suffice. ☙

Reconciling Divergent Estimates in Property Assessment Cases

By: SHELDON EPSTEIN, BERNARD DICKMAN and YONAH WILAMOWSKY

Introduction

This paper reviews a *Baraisa*,[1] *Bava Basra* (B"B) 107a, which offers three *tannaic* opinions with respect to the determination of the value of a property when three designated court-appointed experts cannot agree on a single fair price. The *Gemara* explains each of the *Baraisa's* Tannaim and offers an opinion as to which one to follow halachically. The *Gemara* concludes with Rav Ashi saying he does not understand the *Gemara's* recommended approach. He does not offer an opinion as to which alternative he considers best. The *rishonim* interpret the *Baraisa* in ways that raise many logical problems they have difficulty resolving. We will discuss the *Gemara* and the traditional explanations of the three *tannaic* positions, and then offer a different interpretation of the *Baraisa* that leads to results that are consistent with how a modern quantitative analyst might address the issue.

The Two Cases of the *Baraisa* and Basic Statistical Terminology

The *Baraisa* begins with the unchallenged ruling that when two of the three valuations are identical, the "one being in the minority is overruled." We will henceforth refer to this as the "majority" rule. In statistical studies when we want to find a single value to

1 The *Gemara* as well as an English translation is provided in the *Appendix*. When the meaning of the Aramaic word is ambiguous we transliterate it.

Sheldon Epstein, Bernard Dickman and Yonah Wilamowsky are professional educators. Their joint works on Biblical and Talmudic topics appear in *Tradition*, *Higayon*, and *Location Sciences*.

represent a set of numbers, the most commonly used measures are the:

- Mean: Sum the list and divide by the number of numbers there are in the list,
- Median: The value with as many numbers in the set less than it as more than it,
- Mode: The most frequently occurring value

The *Baraisa's* decision to follow the "majority" rule, in a situation where two out of three values in a set of numbers are identical, is consistent with both the Median and Mode values.

The *Baraisa* follows with three suggested methodologies for dealing with cases where the three evaluations are different and the "majority" rule is ostensibly not applicable. It illustrates this situation for assessments of: 80, 100 and 120:

- *Tanna Kamma* (T"K): 100
- R. Eliezer b.R. Zadok (REbRZ): 90
- *Acherim*: *Osin shuma bainaihen umeshalshin.*

Explaining *Tanna Kamma*—מציעתא

The *Gemara*[2] proceeds to explain the reasoning for each of these positions. It attributes T"K's choice of 100 to מציעתא (*Metsiasa*=middle). In statistical studies the search for a designated representative for a distribution of numbers is referred to as looking for a "Measure of Central Tendency." The Mean and Median always result in numbers that are in some way "central" to the distribution they represent. This may or may not be true for the Mode.[3]

---

2 The explanations do not appear to be part of the *Baraisa* but rather the *Gemara's* analysis of each position.

3 In our case there is no unique Mode (i.e., all values appear once). Even in cases with a unique Modal value, it is possible that the Mode appears at the lower or upper end of the list of numbers and a more representative value from the center may be preferred.

The Mean and Median as "middle" representative values, date back to the Greeks. The words Mean and Median come from the Indo-European root *medhyo*, and Pythagoras and the mathematicians of his school used the word *mesotetes* for Mean. Other words drawn from the same root as Median include: mediate (in the middle of the opposing parties), medium, mitten (put your hands in the middle), meridian, and Mediterranean (the middle of the world). The *Gemara's* מציעתא, from a historical, logical as well as linguistic standpoint, could thus conceivably be referring to either the Mean or the Median. In the 80, 100, 120 case T"K's choice of 100 as the מציעתא is consistent with both the Mean and the Median. In most cases the Mean and Median will not be the same. For example if the assessments were 90, 100 and 130, the Median would be 100 while the Mean would be 106⅔.

In reviewing the commentators on B"B 107a we found none who suggest T"K is referring to the Mean.[4] In fact we know of no example of any *Gemara* ever clearly employing a Mean for any purpose.[5] Although we do not know of any commentator

---

4 The reason, in our case, not to select the Mean as the final assessment value is understandable since a single extreme assessment could have an unduly high impact on the final value.

5 Rambam, *Hilchos Kiddush HaChodsesh* does use the word *Emtszai* to refer to the Mean:

ו:ג משיתקבץ הירח והחמה לפי חשבון זה, עד שיתקבצו פעם שנייה במהלכם האמצעי-- תשעה ועשרים יום ושתים עשרה שעות מיום שלושים מתחילת לילו, ושבע מאות שלושה ותשעים חלקים משעת שלוש עשרה; וזה הוא הזמן שבין כל מולד ומולד, וזה הוא חודשה של לבנה.

The way the ancient world determined the average length of a lunar cycle was based on the fact that a Solar eclipse can only occur at the time of a lunar conjunction. Thus they noted how many days there were between two consecutive Solar eclipses and divided it by the number of lunar months that occurred during that period. The resulting value is thus the Mean lunation. However, when the *Gemara* discussed this figure it referred to this length of a lunar cycle as a minimum, not *Emtszai*, i.e.,

ר"ה כה. אמר להם ר"ג כך מקובלני מבית אבי אבא אין חדושה של לבנה פחותה מעשרים ותשעה יום ומחצה ושני שלישי שעה וע"ג חלקים.

We should also note that there is some discussion as to whether this reference in the *Gemara* was a later insertion. See, e.g., Epstein et. al. "A 5765 Anomaly," *Tradition*, Vol. 38, No. 3, pp. 40-59, Fall 2004.

who directly associates the *Gemara's* מציעתא with the Median, יד רמה (Yad Ramah) adopts the "majority" rule given in the opening case of the *Baraisa* to eliminate both the lower and the upper assessments,[6] i.e.,

- Those who assess 80 and 100 agree that the value is ≤ 100. Hence its value cannot exceed 100,
- Those who assess 100 and 120 agree that the value is ≥ 100. Hence its value must be at least 100.

Thus, by applying the "majority" rule twice, the resulting evaluation must be 100. Although this is not the rationale behind the general selection of the Median (i.e. that it is literally the value in the middle of the list), this reasoning always results in the selection of the Median assessment value regardless if it is exactly midway between the two extreme values or not.[7]

Other than in B"B 107a, מציעתא appears many times in Talmudic works as being the middle between two extremes. For example, with respect to Mishnayos[8] that present three cases, מציעתא is the middle case between the רישא and סיפא. Other usages of מציעתא from Targum, *Gemara* and Midrash include

***Shemos* 26:28**

וְהַבְּרִיחַ הַתִּיכֹן, בְּתוֹךְ הַקְּרָשִׁים, מַבְרִחַ, מִן-הַקָּצֶה אֶל-הַקָּצֶה.	and the middle bar in the midst of the boards, which shall pass through from end to end.

תרגום ועברא[9] מציעאה בגו דפיא מעבר מן סיפי לסיפי

6 ועוד דהאי דאמר עשרים דאינון שמונים זוז ואידך דקאמר מנה תרוייהו מודו לא שויא טפי ממנה ואידך דקאמר שלשים סלע דאינון ק"ך זוז הוה ליה חד ואין דבריו של אחד במקום שנים והא דקאמר מנה ודקאמר שלשים תרוייהו מודו דלא שויא פחות ממנה והאי דקאמר שמונים הוה ליה חד ואין דבריו של אחד במקום שנים

7 Also mentioned in שלטי גיבורים as an explanation of Rashbam on B"B 107a.

8 One interesting example is יבמות פד. where the Mishna says there are 4 cases and proceeds to explain the first, second and fourth. When the *Gemara* then refers to the Mishna it calls the second case מצעיתא.

9 Targum for תיכון is מציעאה. In Hebrew the Mediterranean is ים התיכון.

Yerushalmi Sanhedrin 1:1

What is the signature of the Holy One blessed be he? Rebbe Bibi in the name of R' Reuven "Emes." What is "Emes"? Resh Lakish says *aleph* is at the start of the *aleph-bais*, *mem b'emtsiasa* {middle}, *tav* at the end, to say I Hashem am first, that I did not get it from another, and other than Me there is no deity, because I have no partner, and I am the last because in the future I will not hand it over to another.

Pnei Moshe *d"h* Resh Lakish: The reason is that aleph at the beginning of the a*leph-bais*, *mem* in the middle, *tav* at the end, indicate past, present, future. [10]

Devarim Rabba 1:10

R' Reuven said, What is the signature of the Holy One blessed be he? "Emes." Why "Emes"? Emes has three letters. *Aleph* is the first letter, *mem emtsais*, *tav* the end, to say I am first, I am last and there is no deity other than Me.

Chidushai H'Rashah *d"h mem emtsais*:
That is with the doubled letters.[11]

The *Yerushalmi* and *Devarim Rabba* citations both express the idea that the word אמת is a composite of letters from the beginning, אמצעיתא (middle) and end of the Hebrew alphabet. However, since there are 22 letters in the Hebrew alphabet, the 11th or 12th letters in the Jewish alphabet should be the middle letter, and *mem* is the

---

10 **ירושלמי סנהדרין א:א** מהו חותמו של הקדוש ברוך הוא? רבי ביבי בשם ר' ראובן אמת. מהו אמת? ...אמר ריש לקיש אל"ף רישיה דאלפא ביתא מ"ם באמצעיתה תי"ו בסופה לומר אני ה' ראשון שלא קיבלתי מאחר ומבלעדי אין אלהים שאין לי שותף ואת אחרונים אני הוא שאיני עתיד למוסרה לאחר.
פני משה ד״ה ר״ל אמר היינו טעמא דאלף רישיה דאלפא ביתא מ״ם באמצעיתא תי״ו בסופה ורמז היה הוה ויהיה.

11 **דברים רבה א:י** א״ר ראובן מהו חותמו של הקדוש ברוך הוא? אמת... ולמה אמת? אמת יש בו שלש אותיות אל"ף ראשון של אותיות מ"ם אמצעית תי"ו סופן לומר אני ראשון ואני אחרון ומבלעדי אין ה'.
חידושי הרש״ש ד״ה מ״ם אמצעיא היינו עם אותיות הכפולות.

13th.[12] *Chidushai HaRashash* therefore explains that in addition to the 22 regular letters, there are 5 letters that are written differently when they are at the end of a word. The middle item in an ordered set of 27 items is the 14th item. Assuming that when ordering letters, the regular letter precedes the end form letter, the 14th letter is the regular מ.

All of the above examples deal with sequencing of words or cases and not with numbers, and refer to something that lies exactly in the center of two other things. Thus, it is possible that מציעתא refers to a central item exactly midway between two extreme values (we will call it the mid-range) and not the Median which may not be in the exact middle. Indeed, Rambam explains מציעתא in B"B 107a in such a way:

> Three who went to make an assessment—if one says 100 and two say 200, or if one says 200 and two say 100, the individual is nullified because he is in the minority. One says manna {100}, one says 80 and one says 120 the judgment is 100. One says 100, one says 90 and one says 130, the judgment is 110. And this is the manner in which judgments are always made.[13]

---

12 This assumes מציעתא means the precise middle. However, the word the *Gemara* uses for the precise middle is חציו, e.g.,
קידושין ל. לפיכך נקראו ראשונים סופרים שהיו סופרים כל האותיות שבתורה שהיו אומרים וא"ו דגחון חציין של אותיות של ס"ת דרש דרש חציין של תיבות והתגלח של פסוקים יכרסמנה חזיר מיער עי"ן דיער חציין של תהלים והוא רחום יכפר עון חציו דפסוקים בעי רב יוסף וא"ו דגחון מהאי גיסא או מהאי גיסא ... בעי רב יוסף והתגלח מהאי גיסא או מהאי גיסא
Perhaps then מציעתא means something close to the middle but not necessarily the exact middle. Thus, although the exact middle of 22 letters are the 11th and 12th, i.e., כ and ל, the triplet of letters have to spell an existing word. אמת is such a word and since it is "a" (even though it is not "the") central letter, it was used.

13 **מלוה ולוה כב:יד** שלושה שירדו לשום--אחד אומר במנה ושניים אומרים במאתיים, או אחד אומר במאתיים ושניים אומרים במנה--בטל יחיד במיעוטו. אחד אומר במנה ואחד אומר בשמונים ואחד אומר במאה ועשרים, נידון במאה; אחד אומר במאה ואחד אומר בתשעים ואחד אומר במאה ושלושים, נידון במאה ועשרה. ועל דרך זו שמין ביניהן לעולם
Rambam clearly implies mid-range although he does not say how he derives 110. *Shulchan Aruch Choshen Mishpat* 103:3 spells it out in detail. Meiri also explains the T"K as Rambam does but offers as an example 80, 120 and 140 (with the midrange still 110 as in Rambam's example). Rashbam

The Median for 90, 100 and 130 is 100, but Rambam's מצעיתא is 110. His interpretation, however, leads to an apparently illogical mathematical conclusion[14] in that it assigns a higher valuation for 90, 100, 130 (i.e., 110) than for 100, 100, 130 (i.e. 100, based on "majority" rule) even though all the numbers in the latter triplet are greater than or equal to those of the former. One possible solution is that the 90, 100, 130 ruling is based on *peshara* (compromise) whereas the 100, 100, 130 ruling is based on the halachic principle of "a*charei rabim*" (majority rules) and the two cases need not be mathematically consistent. Rambam's position also leaves open the question as to why the *Gemara* illustrates the dispute with 80, 100 and 120 rather than the more revealing 90, 100 and 130?

Explaining Reb Elazar ben Rav Tzadok—Ignoring the Highest Assessment

The *Gemara* next explains that REbRZ's 90 valuation is based on

- dropping the highest assessment (i.e., 120),
- assuming that 90 is the correct value, and
- attributing an equal error of 10 to both the 80 and the 100 assessors, i.e., one erred on the high side and the other on the low side.

The *Gemara* asks, why not drop the lowest value of 80 and apply the same type of reasoning to the upper two assessments which results in an assessed value of 110? The *Gemara* responds:

נקוט מיהת תרי קמאי בידך דמתורת מנה לא מפקי ליה.

Use, in any event, the first two, for they do not take {the land} out of the category of *maneh*.

mentions another case according to T"K where one of the evaluations was 28 (i.e., 112). He is, however, unclear as to:

- Whether he means the middle estimate was 112 (rather than 100) or the highest estimate was 112 (rather than 120).
- Whether the final estimation stays the same as in the 80, 100, 120 case

14 See, e.g., אולם המשפט חו"מ סימן קג.

Rashbam's explanation (Tosafos concur) that it is a result of תפשת מרובה לא תפשת (do not take an overly large sum) is unclear. Whatever assessment is made will benefit one party at the expense of the other, i.e. a low value (which the *Gemara* is suggesting) benefits the creditor and a high value benefits the debtor. On the one hand the borrower is in possession of the field, מוחזק, and this should give him the stronger position.[15] On the other hand, it is also true that he is in possession of the creditor's money. In a case where the value of the property is uncertain, it seems unclear as to who should get the advantage.

Although the *Gemara* here does not mention anything about how the arrived-at valuation is implemented, *Shulchan Aruch* (*Choshen Mishpat* 103:1) says that this number is simply an initial value that is placed on the field, which is then put up for sale at this price.[16] Potential buyers are then encouraged to bid up the value of the property. If the field is ultimately sold at a value greater than its opening assessment, the new actual sales price is used to pay off the creditor. If on the other hand no one is willing to pay the initial offering price, the initial price is used to determine the creditor's payment. Thus, the estimated value the *Baraisa* is discussing is meant as a minimum value protecting the borrower's interest.[17] From this perspective Rashbam's תפשת

15 Ramban indeed argues that the borrower has the upper hand for precisely this reason. He then struggles to answer why we accept the lower estimates to the borrower's detriment.

16 Although the *Gemara* discusses the estimation process here in *Bava Basra*, and the public auctioning of the property in several places (e.g., *Arachin* 21a, *Bava Metzia* 35b) the exact sequencing of the procedure and the consequences of not getting a bid equal to the property valuation amount is not definitively stated in any *Gemara* (see Gra *C"M* 103, *S"K* 3). Rambam מלוה ולוה 22:6-8 gives the general outline of the procedure but does not specifically say what happens if the initial assessment is not met. *Maggid Mishna* explains that Rambam is consistent with the position of *Shulchan Aruch*.

17 The New York Times Thursday October 28, 2010 page 26A writes:
"It's not impossible that the sale of the conservatee's house to the conservator might be in the conservatee's best interest," Ms. Scott said, "but to avoid the appearance of self-dealing, a careful conservator would get three

מרובה לא תפשת is very reasonable. Although we want to protect the borrower from getting too low a price for his property, it is unreasonable to place this lower-limit safety net at what appears to be an inflated value.[18]

Explaining Acherim—משלשין

The *Gemara* continues with an explanation of the "*Meshalshin*" position of Acherim. It says this means:

- Divide the range (in this case 40: 120-80) by three[19] (i.e., 40/3 = 13⅓),
- Ignore the upper most value (like REbRZ), and
- Assume that both lower assessments meant 93⅓ (i.e. 80+13½) but erred on either side of it.

Rashbam explains that Acherim agree with REbRZ that the two lower values both were deviating from the same number, but disagrees that the deviation is 10. Since the numbers here are greater than 80, Acherim feel the amount of deviation is greater. Rashbam offers neither a rationale for 80 being the critical number, nor a me-

---

appraisals by commercial realtors unrelated to him and then buy the house for the highest estimate."'

18 The fact that Ramban struggles with the positions presented in this *Gemara* and does not mention that this number is only an initial minimum bid, would seem to indicate that he would disagree with *Shulchan Aruch's* description of the procedure.

19 משלשין appears several times in Shas and generally means to divide into 3 parts. In the following case:

מכות משנה א:ג מעידים אנו את איש פלוני, שהוא חייב מלקות ארבעים--נמצאו זוממין, לוקין שמונים: משום "לא תענה ברעך עד שקר" (שמות כ,יב), ומשום "ועשיתם לו, כאשר זמם לעשות לאחיו" (דברים יט,יט), דברי רבי מאיר. וחכמים אומרין, אין לוקין אלא ארבעים. משלשין בממון, ואין משלשין במכות. כיצד: העידוהו שהוא חייב לחברו מאתיים זוז--נמצאו זוממין, משלשין ביניהן; העידוהו שהוא חייב מלקות ארבעים--נמצאו זוממין, כל אחד ואחד לוקה ארבעים.

Rashi *Makkos* 3a offers an alternate explanation:

משלשין בממון אם שלשה עדים הן או ארבעה משלשין ביניהם בית דין נעשין שליש ביניהן להשוותם בפרעון איש לפי חלקו אי נמי האי משלשין לישנא בעלמא הוא מחלקין הפרעון בין שלשתן והוא הדין נמי אם ארבעה הן מרבעין.

thodology for determining the error amount.[20] Moreover, the Gemara's presentation seems to relate the error amount to the difference between the highest and lowest assessments (i.e., 40) and not the size of the assessments themselves. Thus for evaluations of 20, 40 and 60 it would appear that Acherim would decide on a compromise value of 33⅓.

The *Gemara* explains that according to Acherim both the 80 and the 100 assessments err by 13⅓ from 93⅓, and that the one who valued the property at 100 really wanted to say 106⅔ but thought to himself "It is enough that I have exceeded my colleague's by so much."[21] This presentation raises two issues. The first issue is that in effect the 100 assessment is being completely ignored and not contributing towards the final evaluation. The 106⅔ that we are assigning to the middle assessor is derived by dividing the two extreme assessments (i.e., 80 and 120) by 3 (hence 40/3 = 13⅓). This 106⅔, when averaged with the lowest assessment of 80, yields the final 93⅓. Presumably anything that the middle assessor would have said between 93⅓ and 106⅔ would have still been assigned the value of 106⅔.

The second issue is how the 100 assessor knew what his colleague was going to say. Tosafos explain that "this is the order of things that the two lower assessors speak first." We are not sure how this is operationally done. How does anyone know which assessors are going to come in with the lower assessments?[22] Moreover, as explained above, having the lowest assessor go first is not sufficient since the number the *Gemara* says the middle assessor really wanted to say is 106⅔. This number however can only be calculated after we know both the lowest and the highest assessments. Rashbam addresses the question more broadly than Tosafos:

---

20 It is also not clear from Rashbam whether REbRZ holds that 10 is a fixed amount of error or whether he too considers it the midrange between the two lower valuations.

21 I.e., he does not wish to exceed the lower estimate by too much.

22 Tosafos seem to take the word קמאי in the following expression literally.
נקוט מיהת תרי קמאי בידך דמתורת מנה לא מפקי ליה.

...even though we do not know the words of the first one, nevertheless, they have been discussing the matter and everyone knows what is in the heart of his friend.

Rashbam's view seems to be adopted by ביאורים משה"א *Shulchan Aruch Choshen Mishpat* 103:3 *seif katan* א, who says that the three assessors should deliberate together and discuss the matter so as to get the best possible estimate.

Just as it did with REbRZ, the *Gemara* questions Acherim's primary reliance on the 80 and 100 assessments rather than on the 100 and 120. In applying Acherim's reasoning to the 100 and 120 assessments, the *Gemara* suggests that the correct number should be 113⅓ and that the lower assessor deviated from the correct number by the full 13⅓ and again, the person who estimated 120 did not want to exceed the 100 by too much. Tosafos ask (and do not answer) that it is illogical that three assessments 80, 100 and 120 result in a valuation of 113⅓ since in a case where there are only two assessors with assessments of 100 and 120 the value of the property would be placed at 110 (i.e., each deviated by 10 from the correct value). How could a third assessment of only 80 raise the final value from 110 to 113⅓? Ramban answers that in the case of two assessors, the result would not be the average of the two. Rather, the rule of "*hamotzi mechavero*" would apply.[23]

The *Gemara* concludes with two different assertions that the halacha is according to Acherim. Each assertion concludes with Rav

---

[23] See footnote 16. Ramban also suggest that there is no such thing as having only two assessors. This, however, does not really answer the question since Tosafos' question can be formulated in a case of three assessors who came in with values of 100, 100 and 120. In this case there is no question that the value of the property would be placed at 100 (the first case of the *Baraisa*). How then could the lower triplet of assessments of 80, 100 and 120 result in the *Gemara's* suggested value of 113⅓ (i.e., 13⅓ more)? This variation of Tosafos' question is exactly the same as the one we previously mentioned with respect to Rambam. The fact that Ramban feels that he has an answer to Tosafos' question, and the fact that Tosafos did not ask the question from the case of three assessors, support the position previously given that we have to differentiate between cases decided by majority rule and cases decided by *peshara.*

Ashi saying he does not understand Acherim's reasoning.[24] Where does this leave the halacha? As we have seen, Rambam indeed does not follow the opinion of Acherim but rather that of T"K.

In the next section we offer a different interpretation of the *Baraisa* and explain how it addresses the difficulties we have raised with the way the Rishonim understood the *Gemara's* explanation of Acherim.

A Mathematical Analysis of the *Gemara*

From a practical perspective, the classical commentators' explanations of the *Gemara* that we have until here presented are, at best, incomplete. The *Baraisa* begins with the assertion that when two of the three assessors agree on a value, this is the value to be assigned. Does the word "agree" mean identical? Suppose the assessments offered were 80, 81 and 120:

- Are 80 and 81 treated as being the same (since they are so close) and based on the "majority" rule, the final assessment is placed somewhere between 80 and 81?
- Are 80 and 81 treated as different and according to Rambam's previously mentioned position the assessment is placed at 100?

If the *Baraisa* meant that to apply the "majority" rule, the two numbers would have to be literally identical, the practical application of the halacha is very limited and gives us no guidance of what to do in the overwhelming majority of cases that are not identical. On the other hand, if the *Gemara* held that when two values are

---

24 The exact words of Rav Ashi are

אמר רב אשי טעמא דאחרים לא ידעינן הלכתא עבדינן כוותייהו.

> We do not know the reason of Acherim; shall we administer the law in accordance with their view?

All of the commentators take this as a rhetorical question, i.e., I cannot follow this ruling since it is illogical. It is, however, possible to read this in an affirmative way, i.e., we will follow this decision even though we do not understand it. The argument in favor of this reading is that if Rav Ashi meant to disagree then why did he not say what he suggests be done?

"close" they can be considered as "identical," how do we define close? For example, if rather than 80, 100 and 120 the Gemara had offered an example of 80, 100 and 480, would we say that the 480 assessment is so out of line with the other two that it may be dropped? More extreme examples can be devised until we reach the point of saying that "identical" means "close" and that "close" is relative. This means that the *Baraisa,* in the final analysis, has really not conveyed a usable methodology for dealing with the problem.

We suggest that in fact this *Baraisa* is addressing two separate issues and that the three Tannaim cited may not necessarily be in total disagreement, i.e.,

- How to handle situations where several of the estimates are identical or close.
- How to handle situations where all of the estimates are far apart.

The *Baraisa* begins with the universally accepted "majority rule" that when two estimates are identical they alone determine the value of the property. The *Baraisa* next turns to an opposite-extreme case where no two assessments are identical and the middle assessment is equidistant from the lowest and highest assessments, and offers the position of T"K. As noted previously, although Rambam understood *metsiasa* to mean mid-range, יד רמה says it is the middle assessment. Using the middle assessment in the case of:

- 90, 100 and 130 (Rambam's case) - yields 100,
- 80, 81 and 120 - yields 81,
- 100, 750 and 800 - yields 750.

Thus according to *Yad Ramah* T"K's methodology will never allow a valuation that is totally out of conformity with the other two (whether on the high side or the low side) to overly influence the final result. T"K does not have to deal with the issue of closeness since the choice of the middle assessment (Median) guarantees that the estimates that are closer to each other will carry the most weight

The opening rule of the *Baraisa* also drives REbRZ's approach. However, whereas T"K meant to apply his approach in all cases, we suggest that REbRZ is limiting his suggestion to a case where none of the estimates can be considered close, e.g., they are all equidistant from each other. Rather than applying the opening majority rule twice (as T"K does), he prefers to view two of the three assessments as being the same (even though they are not). The two he chooses to use are the two lower ones and thus he adjusts the values of the property to the midpoint of these two numbers. The *Gemara* challenges this by saying that we can carry out this process equally well with the upper two assessments which would result in an assessment of 110. As we explained in a previous section, the *Gemara* responds:

נקוט מיהת תרי קמאי בידך דמתורת מנה לא מפקי ליה

I.e., if an assessment is to be discarded it is more reasonable that it be the highest one. What REbRZ's position would be in a situation where the 3 values are not equally spaced and where the middle value is closer to the upper value, is not addressed by him. We suggest that this asymmetrical case (i.e., where the middle assessment is not equidistant from the highest and lowest assessments) is what Acherim are primarily addressing in the final case of the *Baraisa*.

In dealing with the asymmetrical case, Acherim reject T"K's approach of always using the middle assessment, and instead offer a methodology to first measure "closeness" and then decide what to do. Their recommendation is to divide the range of the values by three and decompose the range of numbers into three intervals. In the 80, 100, 120 case, the intervals are thus 80–93⅓, 93⅓–106⅔, 106⅔–120. Trisecting the range in this way always results in the highest and lowest valuations falling into the two distinct end intervals. The "middle" assessment may however fall into any of the three intervals. For example, in Rambam's case of 90, 100 and 130, the three intervals are 90–103⅓, 103⅓–116⅔ and 116⅔-130, and the middle assessment falls in the same third as the lower assessment. In this case Acherim would consider the 2 lower assessments to be the same, and using the "majority" rule would eliminate the highest value from consideration. Thus, unlike Rambam's conclusion that the valuation is 110, Acherim put the final valuation between 90 and 100 and presumably would choose exactly 95 as REbRZ would. In a case of 80, 110 and 120, on the other hand, Acherim would part ways with both TK and REbRZ (since the two higher assessments are in the highest of the three intervals, 106⅔–120) and would give the final assessment as 115 (i.e., midpoint of 110, 120).

To support our position, that Acherim are dealing with something other than the 80, 100 and 120 case, note that they never mention 93⅓, nor offer any number, nor rejects outright either of the specific values offered by T"K and REbRZ. Acherim are merely trying to define when we consider two assessments to be the same and allow us to apply the "majority" rule in order to eliminate the third assessment.[25]

What will Acherim hold in a case where all assessments fall in different intervals, e.g., the symmetrical case of 80, 100 and 120? We offer the possibility that this is the case the *Gemara* is addressing when it places Acherim's evaluation at 93⅓, i.e., the upper end of the lowest of the three intervals. Thus,

- unlike Rashbam who attributes Acherim's disagreement with REbRZ to a desire to give more leeway for error when all the assessments exceed 80, and
- unlike the *Gamara's* explanation that the middle assessor modified his more extreme intentions because of knowledge of what the other assessors were going to say,

the choice of 93⅓ is chosen simply because it is the high point of the lowest *meshulashin* interval. This allows Acherim, like REbRZ, to give more credibility to the lower two assessments while not totally ignoring the 120 assessment[26] (as REbRZ does).

---

25 Is Acherim's choice of division by 3 arbitrary, or related to the fact that there are three assessors? Rambam seems to say that there are always 3 assessors:

מלוה ולוה כב:טו ואחר שכותבין הטירפא לטורף, מורידין שלושה בקיאין לאותה השדה, ושמין לו ממנה כשיעור חובו כפי מה שראוי לו מן הקרן, וחצי השבח כמו שביארנו.

However, Rashbam says three is not the designated number of assessors but the minimum:

ד"ה שלושה שירדו לשום... .ואין שימת ב"ד פחות משלשה

If so, had *Bais Din* appointed 4 assessors would Acherim suggest division by 4 or still stick with 3? As we will explain at the end of this section, division by 3 parallels the "3 sigma rule" used in modern statistics.

26 I.e., the range of the lowest interval is directly related to the 120 assessment.

From a modern statistical perspective, Acherim's choice of 93⅓ in the symmetrical case is appealing for another reason. In studying distributions of numbers, the "3 Sigma" rule (*meshulashin*?) says that almost all data from a Normal Distribution (bell-shaped curve) lies within 3 Standard Deviations (i.e. 3σ) of the Mean.[27] Thus σ is roughly estimated for a distribution by dividing its range by 6. As a result, for the *Baraisa's* case of 80, 100 and 120 the "3 Sigma" rule yields a σ estimate of 6⅔ ((120-80)/6) and the choice of 93⅓ is tantamount to choosing as the assessment a value that is exactly one standard deviation below the mean value[28] of 100.

Our explanation of what Acherim hold in the symmetrical case preserves the *Gemara's* basic contention that Acherim place the assessment at 93⅓, albeit not for the reason the *Gemara* gives. In this way the *Gemara* may have had a Mesorah on the amount Acherim said, but not on the reason. Thus, when Rav Ashi says he cannot understand Acherim's reason, he in effect is saying that he cannot halachically follow the Mesorah without understanding the reason. By us explaining the rationale of Acherim in a more intuitively (statistically) appealing manner it justifies Acherim's position and allows it to be halachically applied.

---

27 This rule is generally extended to include non-Normal symmetrical unimodal-distributions. For a Normal distribution about 99.7% of the population lies within three standard deviations of the Mean. For "all" distributions there is the more general Chebyshev Rule which says that at least 89% of the data lie within 3 standard deviations of the Mean.

28 While the "middle" concept of Mean and Median dates back to the Greeks and presumably might have been known to the Chachamim, the reasoning they used to arrive at their conclusions seems to be driven by a different set of logic (majority rule). The standard deviation is of much more recent vintage and was certainly not formally known to the Chachmei HaTalmud. Chebyshev Rule (see previous footnote), tying the percent of the numbers in the list to the number of standard deviations they are from the center, was not formulated until 1867. Nevertheless, we have shown that by using an alternate analysis the Chachmei HaTalmud could have come up with a solution that parallels some elements of this later mathematical discovery.

A Final Thought

In this final section of the paper we would like to discuss a broader implication of the way we have explained the *Gemara* in *Bava Basra*. Our explanation has the Tanna Acherim promulgating a position far more complex than the one the *Gemara* attributes to them. While there is much leeway in explaining a *pasuk* in Chumash differently from the way the *Gemara* does,[29] as well as explaining a Mishna far differently from the way the *Gemara* does,[30] the caveat is always that the difference in explanation may not change a halacha. In this case our explanation of Acherim, particularly in the asymmetrical case, results in a different numerical valuation of a property from the one the *Gemara* offers. Indeed, had the *Gemara* not concluded with its statement that Rav Ashi "did not understand Acherim," we would not have offered our explanation no matter how many questions the *Gemara's* explanation of the *Baraisa* raised. However, in this case Rav Ashi's concluding remark rejects the *pesak* previously given by the *Gemara*. Moreover, neither Rav Ashi nor the *Gemara* offers an alternate opinion as to what to do and in fact Rambam does not conclude according to Acherim. In such a situation we feel there is no problem with our offering a different explanation.[31] Since the *Gemara* does not end with a halachic decision, our explanation does not contradict the *Gemara's* conclusion. ൽ

---

29 See, e.g., *Ohr HaChaim Devarim* 32:1.

30 See, e.g., Rambam *Perush HaMishnah, Nazir* 5:5.

31 In many ways what we are doing is analogous to an explanation of the Mishna *Kesubos* 93a given by Nobel Prize winner Prof. Yisrael Aumann "Game Theoretic Analysis of a Bankruptcy Problem From the Talmud," *Journal of Economic Theory*, Vol. 36, Issue 2, August 1985, pp. 195-213. The Mishna there describes 3 scenarios of how much money to pay 3 debtors of different amounts, from an estate that cannot meet the full debt. The *Gemara* challenges the Mishna's recommendations and concludes with Rebbe ostensibly rejecting the Mishna's conclusions. The Rishonim discuss many difficulties with the *Gemara's* presentation and are unable to offer a satisfactory explanation of the Mishna's recommendations. Prof. Aumann showed that using modern Game Theory the Mishna's recommendations are perfectly consistent.

Appendix

Bava Basra 107a

תנו רבנן שלשה שירדו לשום אחד אומר במנה ושנים אומרים במאתים אחד אומר במאתים ושנים אומרים במנה בטל יחיד במיעוטו אחד אומר במנה ואחד אומר בעשרים ואחד אומר בשלשים נדון במנה רבי אליעזר ברבי צדוק אומר נדון בתשעים אחרים אומרים עושין שומא ביניהן ומשלשין מאן דאמר נדון במנה מילתא מציעתא רבי אליעזר בר' צדוק אומר נדון בתשעים קא סבר הא ארעא תשעין שוה והאי דקאמר עשרים דקא טעי עשרה לאחוריה והאי דקא אמר מנה קא טעי עשרה לקמיה אדרבה האי ארעא מאה ועשרה שויא והאי דקאמר מנה קא טעי עשרה לאחוריה והאי דקאמר שלשים קא טעי עשרה לקמיה נקוט מיהת תרי קמאי בידך דמתורת מנה לא מפקי ליה אחרים אומרים עושין שומא ביניהן ומשלשין קא סברי האי ארעא תשעין ותלתא ותילתא שויא האי דקא אמר עשרים קא טעי תליסר ותילתא לאחוריה והאי דקאמר מנה קא טעי תליסר ותילתא לקמיה ובדין הוא דלימא טפי והאי דלא קאמר סבר מיסתאי דקא מטפינא כולי האי אחבראי אדרבה הא ארעא מאה ותליסר ותלתא שויא האי דקאמר מנה קא טעי תליסר ותלתא לאחוריה והאי דקאמר שלשים טעי תליסר ותלתא לקמיה ובדין הוא דקאמר טפי סבר מיסתאי דקא מטפינא כולי האי אחבראי נקוט מיהת תרי קמאי בידך דמתורת מאה לא מפקי ליה אמר רב הונא הלכה כאחרים אמר רב אשי טעמא דאחרים לא ידעינן הלכתא עבדינן כוותייהו תנו דייני גולה עושין שומא ביניהן ומשלשין אמר רב הונא הלכתא כדייני גולה אמר רב אשי טעמא דדייני גולה לא ידעינן הלכתא עבדינן כוותייהו:

English Translation

Our Rabbis taught: three went down to assess, one says it is a *maneh* {100 zuz} and two say 200 {*zuz}*, one says 200 and two say a *maneh*, the one being in the minority is overruled. One says a *maneh*, one says twenty {80 zuz}, and one says thirty {120 zuz}, it is adjudged at a *maneh*. R. Eliezer b.R. Zadok, said: It is adjudged at 90. Acherim said: we make an estimate between them and are *meshalshin* {divide into three parts}. He who said, 'It is adjudged at a *maneh*,' adopts the middle course. R. Eliezer b. R. Zadok, who said, 'It is adjudged at ninety,' opines that the land is worth 90, and he who said twenty made a mistake by 10, and he who said *maneh* made a mistake by 10. On the contrary! Assume it is worth 110 and he who said a *maneh* underestimated it by 10 and he who said thirty overestimated it by 10? Adopt the first two lower values, since neither exceeds the sum of one *maneh*. Acherim said to make an estimate and be *meshalshim* holds the land is worth 93⅓; he who valued it at twenty underestimated it by 13⅓; he who valued it at a *maneh* overestimated it by 13⅓. Logically the latter should have given a higher estimate but did not do it because he thought, 'It is enough that I have exceeded my colleague's by so much.' On the contrary! Assume the land is worth 113⅓; he who valued it at a *maneh* underestimated it by 13⅓, and he who valued it at thirty overestimated it by 13⅓; logically he should have submitted a higher estimate. He thinks, 'It is enough that I have exceeded my colleague's by so much.' At all events one should adopt the first two, since both do not exceed a *maneh*. R. Huna said: The *halachah* is like Acherim. R. Ashi said: We do not know the reason of Acherim; shall we administer the law in accordance with their view? The judges of the Exile taught: The difference between them is calculated and divided by three. R. Huna said: The law is in accordance with the Judges of the Exile. R. Ashi said: We do not know the reason for the opinion of the judges of the Exile, shall we administer the law in accordance with their view?

Completing Creation

By: ASHER BENZION BUCHMAN

עשרה דברים נבראו בין השמשות--פי הארץ, פי הבאר, פי האתון, והקשת, והמן, והמטה, והשמיר, והכתב, והמכתב, והלוחות. ויש אומרין אף המזיקין, וקבורתו של משה, ואילו של אברהם. ויש אומרין אף צבת בצבת עשויה. (אבות ה:ו)

Ten things were created at dusk. The mouth of the earth; and the mouth of the well; and the mouth of the ass; and the rainbow and the manna; and the rod; and the shamir-worm and the writing; and that which was written, and the tablets. And some say, the spirits; and the sepulcher of Moses and the ram of Avaham our father. And some say, [the first] tongs to make tongs. (*Avos* 5:6)

The Creation of Miracles

In his commentary on the above Mishnah, Rambam reiterates what he had explained in the eighth chapter of his introduction to *Avos*, that miracles do not defy the laws of nature and thus all were put into nature at creation:

> They do not believe that G-d's will is renewed time after time, but at the very creation it was put into the nature of things to do all that that they will do, whether it be a constant performance which is nature, or only rare occurrences which is a miracle, and so they say it was put into the earth in the sixth day that it would split beneath Korach and his congregation. (*Perush HaMishnah Avos* 5:6)

The ten items listed in the Mishnah differ from all other wonders, only in that their creation was at dusk of the sixth day. All other miracles are a function of the matter from which they were

---

Asher Benzion Buchman is the author of *Encountering the Creator: Divine Providence and Prayer in the Works of Rambam* (Targum, 2004), and *Rambam and Redemption* (Targum, 2005).

created and were placed into that matter on the day they were created.

> For example, on the second when the waters were divided, it was put into their nature that the *Yam Suf* would split for Moshe, and the *yarden* for Yehoshua... and so too all the other miracles, besides for these ten which were put into nature at dusk. (ibid.)

Elsewhere, Rambam supports this fundamental principle, that miracles were programmed into nature at Creation, with a midrash regarding the splitting of the *Yam Suf*:

> R. Yochanan said, G-d made an agreement (תנאי) with the sea that it should divide before the Israelites: thus it is said, "And the sea returned to its strength (איתנו)[1] when the morning appeared" (*Shemos* xiv. 27). R. Yirmiyahu, son of Elazar, said: Not only with the sea, but with all that has been created in the six days of the beginning [was the agreement made]: this is referred to in the words, "I, even my hands have stretched out the heavens, and all their host have I commanded" (Isa. xlv. 12); i.e., I have commanded the sea to divide before Israel... the sun and moon to stand still before Yehoshua. (MN 2:29 from *Bereshis Rabbah* 5:5 and *Pirkei D'R Eliezer*).

Even Rabbenu Bachye, a commentator associated more with the mystical school of thought of Ramban, believed this Midrash was clear testimony to Rambam's position and states it emphatically:

> This midrash proves that all miracles and wonders that G-d did in all the generations through the prophets, were placed into the nature of the things created during the six days of creation... and thus when there is [an apparent] change of nature in the eyes of the observers, there is no change in the will of G-d as if to will something He had not willed earlier, for this had been His primeval will that nature should change at the appointed time in the eyes of the observers via the righteous of the generations. (*Shemos* 14:27)

---

1 The midrash relates the word איתנו to תנאי.

Rabbenu Bachye notes that the ten things created at dusk that Chazal speak of also conform to this idea, and raises Rambam's question as to why they are singled out, without giving an answer. "And it must be asked why these ten things were singled out [to be created at] at dusk." (ibid.) Although Rambam offers a technical distinction, he does not provide a conceptual reason for this uniqueness, and thus Rabbenu Bachye is troubled.

Chazal also see a reference to this concept in the second chapter of *Bereishis. Targum Yonasan* on the verse אשר ברא אלקים לעשות "That G-d created to do" translates דברא ה' ועתיד למעבד "That G-d created and will in the future create." He also translates ויכל אלקים ביום השביעי מלאכתו אשר עשה "And G-d finished on the seventh day the work He had done" as ושלים ה' ביומא שביעתא עבידתיה דעבד ועשרת עיסקין דברא ביני שמשתא "And He finished on the seventh day the work He had done and the ten things He created at dusk" making reference to these ten things as something additional implied by the text. Rav Menachem Recanti (ibid.) interprets the Targum in line with the understanding that is explicit in a later midrash (*Pesikta Zutrasi)* which comments on the word לעשות "These are the ten things that were created on Shabbos eve at dusk, for G-d created all these things to performs miracles and wonders... to fulfill the scripture 'there is nothing new under the heavnes.'"[2] This version of the *derash* differs from Rambam, in that it would seem that only those things created at dusk had these properties. But according to both versions, there is something unique about that which was created at dusk.

The Creation of Bilaam's Dream

The Rema in his *Toras HaOla* takes it as a matter of course, based on the *Midrash Rabbah* which he notes is cited in the *Moreh,*[3] that all

---

2 אלה עשרה דברים שנבראו בערב שבת ביה"ש כי כל אלה ברא אלקים לעשות ניסים וגבורות, ברוך שם כבוד מלכותו לקיים מה שנאמר אין כל חדש תחת השמש. The still later *Midrash HaGadol* that generally follows the opinions of Rambam elaborates in this vein as well. It is also possible that this is the meaning of the midrash rabba which on לעשות says כל מה שהיה הקב"ה עתיד לבראות בשביעי הקדים וברא בשישי.

3 And also the *Sefer HaAkeda.*

miracles were put into nature at creation as G-d's will (רצון) is unchanging, and thus raises Rambam's and R. Bachye's question of why *Chazal* singled out the ten creations of dusk. He couples this query with a question that he notes had puzzled many before him. Rambam in the *Moreh* (2:43) writes:

> We have already shown that the appearance or speech of an angel mentioned in Scripture took place in a vision or dream; it makes no difference whether this is expressly stated or not... That which happened to Bilaam on the way, and the speaking of the donkey, took place in a prophetic vision, since further on, in the same account, an angel of G-d is introduced as speaking to Bilaam.

How, asks Rema, could Rambam say that the donkey (אתון) was a dream character and yet justify its being listed among the ten items? He notes that while Ralbag follows Rambam in this opinion, many had felt that the Mishnah was ample reason to disprove this radical approach. He himself has the answer, which also answers the previous question concerning the uniqueness of these ten things:

> These ten things are natural things like all things created, and had the "mouth of the donkey" been meant literally it would be something miraculous and not natural, and thus it is said to have been created at *bain hashmoshos,* which is in doubt *(safek)* as to whether it is part of the day or of the night of the seventh. For it is known that all which was created on the six days of creation was new and not part of nature, and from the seventh day and on the world proceeded in a natural course... and while these things seem miraculous they have a natural quality... thus the "mouth of the donkey" qualifies as natural since it was part of a vision, and so too the tablets and the writing and the written as he explains well. (*Moreh* 1:76) (*Toras HaOlah 2:18)*

According to Rema, these ten miraculous things are singled out to explain that in fact they were miraculous although they appear to be natural. He goes on to explain how the other items, such as the rainbow and the earthquake that swallowed the congregation of Korach, are natural phenomena or at least phenomena that seem natural. The crucial element of his revolutionary answer, which he states with little fanfare, is that *Chazal* were referring to the phenomenon of Bilaam's dream when they spoke of the creation of the "mouth of the donkey" (פי האתון). Whereas Ralbag sees the Mishna as contradicting Rambam's stance, that the donkey appeared in a vision and consequently opts to differ with the Mishnah, Rema realizes that the Mishna must be consistent with Rambam's interpretation. In Rambam's commentary on the Mishnah he explains that "mouth of the donkey" refers to the donkey's speaking and expresses no difficulty with it, while taking great pains to describe the concept that the Mishnah puts forth. One could argue that in his later years when he wrote the *Moreh Nevuchim*, Rambam changed his attitude, but in fact Rambam apparently contradicts himself in the *Moreh* itself. In *Moreh* 2:6 he proves that even animals are affected by angels (מלאכים) from the story of Bilaam's donkey, and in 3:17 he proves that there is a Biblical prohibition against causing pain to animals (צער בעלי חיים דאורייתא) from the verse "Why have you smitten your donkey." Biblical allegory must be read at two levels, and both levels teach us laws and concepts. Of course it was a vision, but *Chazal* have identified what the donkey represents, and what it represents was created at dusk on the sixth day.

Interpreters of Midrashim

Rambam divides the interpreters of midrashim into three categories.

> The first group constitutes the majority of those whom I have met and whose works I have seen and heard about; they understand them literally and do not understand them at all, and all things that are impossible are considered by them to be necessary, and this is because of their lack of knowledge of the wisdoms and sciences... this group destroys the beauty of the Torah and darkens its light. The second group is also large who also take the words [of the Midrash] literally believing there is no other meaning intended and thus they mock and degrade them and consider strange that which is not strange, and make fun of the words of the *chachamim* considering themselves smarter than they... and they are dumber than the first group and greater fools... had they prepared themselves with the [study of] the wisdoms until they understood how one writes about G-dly matters and other abstract issues in a way that it

> can be read both by the masses and the scholars[4] and had they understood anything of practical philosophy, they would understand if the *chachamim* were indeed wise, and could understand the meaning of their words. The third group is... very small, and they are those who have recognized how great the *chachamim* are and... realized that in their words there is the simple meaning and the secret meaning (סוד) and in all statements of impossibilities the intent is allegorical and metaphorical." (*Perush HaMishnah,* Introduction to tenth chapter of *Sanhedrin*)

There is no question that Rema is in this third category. He struggles to find meaning to midrashim with the knowledge that their thought must be reconciled with the philosophical principles of Rambam. He saw *kabbala* as a language for expressing philosophical ideas, and his *Toras HaOla* integrates the philosophy of Rambam with the philosophical ideas expressed in the Zohar in a different, and even more abstract manner.

Rambam explains in his introduction to the *Moreh*, that he decided against writing a book explaining midrashim. "For I observed that by expounding these passages by means of allegorical and mystical terms, we do not explain anything, but merely substitute one thing for another of the same nature, whilst in explaining them fully our efforts would displease most people; and my sole object in planning to write those books was to make the contents of midrashim and the exoteric lessons of the prophecies intelligible to everybody." To some degree Maharal set out to write this book that Rambam had intended to write,[5] and of course Maharal's work is important and valuable. Being faced with the difficulty Rambam articulated, however, he too was forced to "substitute one thing for another of the same nature," and the meanings often remain hidden. In works like *Toras Haolah*, *Tzror HaMor*, *Meiri*, *Rabbenu Bachye*, and sometimes in *Abarbanel* and *Akedas Yitzchok,* as well as in later works of a mystical nature such as *Kedushas Levi,* a clearer picture of *Chazal's* intent is often presented.

---

4 To each on their own level.

5 See Rav Chaim Eisen's essay "Maharal's Be'er Ha-Golah and His Revolution in Aggaidc Scholarship," *Ḥakirah* 4 pp. 137–195.

The Creation of Creativity

In the *Tzror Hamor* (צרור המור), Rav Avraham Saba elaborates further on the idea of future miracles lying within creation:

> By saying which G-d had created 'to do' there is a hint of including all that exists in the world until the end of time, that appears new but really is not new... as if to say that G-d created on the sixth day all the things that will be done in the future and put into them the power to create, and this is what is referred to in the Mishnah in *Avos* as the ten things that were created at dusk... for these things are like fathers (אבות מלאכות) [of categories] of work that include all the other types of work that came into existence afterwards which are the extensions (תולדות)[6] of these things. Thus when the earth opened up it was nothing new, for it is a function of 'the mouth of the earth'... and when one sees a work of a smith made up of [so] many fine figures that it would appear that a human could not have made it, this is a function of the 'first tongs'... and so too 'the writing and the written' refers to when an author or *chochom*... composes new books, for in fact 'there is nothing new under the sun' for on the Sabbath eve this power was put into writing that it could emerge. (*Tzror Hamor, Breishis* Ch. 2)

The *Tzror HaMor* adds a dimension. First he broadens the concept of "mouth of the earth" to encompass all physical changes in nature, but then even more significantly he explains that the forces of human creativity were themselves part of this final creation. One of the objects that is in the supplementary list was the key in pointing to this interpretation—"the first tongs." Any new artistic and physical work was implied by the first tongs, and similarly any great literary work was implied by "writing." Rav Hai Gaon was a precursor to this line of thought in commenting on "writing and the written" (כתב ומכתב).

> The 'writing and the written' refer to speech and writing, as in them mankind is distinguished from other living beings. In them G-d placed in the beginning the ability to express letters

6 Lit., "children." R. Avraham uses the language of אבות ותולדות as it is used to categorize the types of work on Shabbos.

> and words to speak with so that all things can be understood; and so too He placed another power in him enabling writing of all these things with a pen so that later generations could understand these words, for without this the wisdom of the wise men would be lost upon their demise.[7]

The things created at dusk are not merely the ability for natural objects to depart from nature, but the ability for humans to change and to create change. Following this explanation we gain added insight into the explanation of the Rema with regard to the donkey. When we say Bilaam's dream was created, we are in fact saying that some element within the human psyche was created at dusk, that would enable change—or perhaps we should say progress—later on.

Completing Creation

The Meiri, well-known as a rationalist, echoes the words of R. Bachye with regard to the medrash on the word איתנו indicating that G-d's will (רצון) did not change after Creation, and he emphasizes also that the subsequent miracles give evidence to the world's having been created (חדוש העולם) and refutes the claim that the world always existed (קדמות העולם). He then refers to Rambam's[8] distinction between these ten miraculous creations and the other miracles, which leads him to ask the question that R. Bachye had asked. What reason is there for these things to be singled out as coming last? He answers that they are of particular interest to man who was created last. These miracles will serve to convince man of reward and punishment and hence continue to change man.[9]

Yet, upon further analysis, and being the rationalist he is, he finds reason to question our fundamental premise. Some of the members of the list are not miraculous. Why are the rainbow and

---

7 See the commentary on *Avos* of R. Yitzchok (quoted in *Torah Shelema*).

8 Although surprisingly not quoting Rambam.

9 ואפשר שפי הבאר ופי הארץ עיקר מציאותם להעניים ולגמול בני אדם שנבראו בששי וכן שאר הדברים וכונת המאמר לקבוע בלבבות אמונת גמול ועונש אפילו ע"י שינוי הטבעים באין התחדשות רצון התחדשות הבריאה שכן הונח מתחילה בטבעיי הדברים לשנות את תפקידם ברצון האומר והגוזר ומ"מ אף באחרים ראוי לומר כן:

the *shamir* included?[10] He feels compelled to explain the Mishnah's intention differently from what has been assumed until now.

> These things are the sustenance of the nation and the essence of success; some are beliefs and some are part of nature; and they are said to have been created at dusk, meaning that without them there would be no sustenance to our faith... which is the essence of perfection whose attainment is without doubt the purpose of Creation.[11]

According to this second explanation, these things make creation complete as their existence will enable the goal of Creation to be reached. Some represent beliefs that it is necessary for Israel to accept,[12] and others are functions within nature that make Israel's existence possible. There was no physical creation of these items; the midrash is merely teaching about their significance. In fact *bein hasmashos* refers not to the last moment of the creation process, but to the first moment of the world's existence. Israel, the purpose of creation, must have access to these things, to be able to prosper and accomplish its goals.

Completing Man's Creation

Both explanations of Meiri are compelling. Logic dictates that these things be last because they are the completion of Creation as the second answer states. On the other hand, man is created last. Should not these creations be related to man as proposed in the first answer? On the one hand, most of the elements are miraculous, and thus the first answer seems correct, that these are the miracles put into nature comparable to what the midrash clearly speaks of else-

---

10 He questions others on the extended list as well and does further acute analysis that is not fully recorded here.

11 הזכיר כאן הדברים שהם היו קיום האומה ותכלית ההצלחה קצתם מצד האמונה וקצתם מצד הטבע ומתוך כך ייחס בהם שהם נבראו בין השמשות כלומר שאומר דרך הפלגה שאלולא הדברים לא היה קיום לזאת האמונה שבה וכדומה לה תכלית השלימות שהוא בלי ספק תכלית כוונת זה המציאות ונמצאו אלו הדברים שהעמידו כוונת הבריאה על מכונה וענין בין השמשות הוא כלומר שתיכף לבריאה התחייבו מצד הקבלה להאמין כן והזכיר פתיחת פי הארץ להאמין בעונש הרעים ופי הבאר להאמין בגמול הטובים שהן פנות גדולות (בד"ת) [בדת].

12 Indeed these are the necessary beliefs that Rambam speaks of in *Moreh Nevuchim*.

where. On the other hand there are some exceptions, so perhaps it is not the miraculous nature that is important, but what these things represent that is important. There is overlap in these answers with the understanding of *tzror hamor* and R. Hai Gaon, in that they also stated that not all the elements are miraculous, but some are rather qualities that complete man and in several cases are related to man's creativity. Meiri adds to this list, man's "evil inclination" (יצר הרע) which he identifies with the "demons" (מזיקין) of the Mishnah.[13]

Meiri makes one final comment, which opens up a path of analysis for integrating his two explanations as well as those of *Tzror Hamor* and the Rema. He refers to a gemara in *Pesachim* that adds to our list "the cave that Moshe and Eliyahu stood in" and interprets it as referring to prophecy, since these two men "were the elite of the prophets... and there is no doubt that the sustenance of the religion and its continued success is contingent on prophecy." As we have noted previously, the Rema had explained that when Rambam teaches us that the donkey was created at dusk, he refers to a quality within man. Explanations for the "tongs" and the "writing" also refers to qualities within man—especially in *Tzror Hamor's* emphasis on human creativity. But while these commentators feel that certain of the ten things refer to man's abilities, what is unique about Rambam and his explanation of the "donkey" is the revelation that even those things that would appear to apply to creations in nature are in fact referring to creations within the human psyche. All ten items are aspects of human development.

Proper textual and midrashic analysis confirms the first explanation of Meiri that all ten things are related to the creation of man. Man was created last as he is the goal of earth's creation,[14] thus those things created *bein hashmoshos* must be elements within man that perfected him. Other midrashim detail how every hour of the sixth day marked a different level of man's development.

> In the first hour, his dust was collected into a mound, in the second his *tzurah* was created, in the third he was given a physical form, in the fourth his limbs were tied together, in the

[13] See the final footnote.

[14] See *hakdamah* to *Perush HaMishnah.*

> fifth the openings were made functional, in the sixth the soul was given, in the seventh he stood on his feet, in the eighth he was paired with *Chava*, in the ninth he entered *Gan Eden*, in the tenth he was commanded, in the eleventh he soured, in the twelfth he was driven out and left. (*Avos D'Rav Nosson*, ch. 1)

This midrash teaches that the Torah's depiction of man's creation and his fall are all part of an allegorical portrayal of the human psyche's natural development—ending with man's distancing from *Gan Eden*. The Mishnah of *bein hashmoshos*, however, explains that what was given to man by G-d would allow him to overcome his failings and return to Eden.

Meiri sensed, in his first answer, that the ten things had to be related to man, but was not willing to say that they were elements within man himself—but rather miracles put into nature that would influence man, so as to perfect him. But Rema has shown us that Rambam's profound grasp of Biblical metaphor and midrashic interpretation deciphered the totality of this midrash. Rambam's general philosophy, in fact, promotes the concept that "miracles" put into nature are in fact placed into the human psyche. Divine Providence[15] is on humans and commensurate to the level of perfection the individual has reached. As Meiri explains in his second interpretation, these ten things are necessary concepts rather than miracles. On the other hand, that which enables man to rise above his earthly essence and transcend to the heavenly sphere are the final miraculous creations of *bein hashmoshos.* As Rema explained, placing these elements at *bein hashmoshos* defines them as the supernatural elements of natural phenomena.

Creating the *Mikdash*

The concept of undoing man's exile from G-d that began with his banishment from Eden, is embodied in the building of the Mikdash—"Make for me a *mikdash* that I may dwell amongst them."

15 See *Moreh Nevuchim* 3:17-18.

The Messiah will build the mikdash and gather the exiles and enable us to do G-d's service as it had been intended.[16]

Our Mishnah is the last of a set of *mishnayos* that lists "tens." The first Mishnah of the chapter (Avos 5:1) speaks of the ten statements that constituted Creation, and thus our Mishnah's listing of the ten last elements in Creation is a fitting ending to the set. The Mishnah that directly precedes it lists the ten miracles that occurred in the *Bais HaMikdash*—thus a literary link and hint to the nature of our Mishnah exists. A cursory look at the ten objects reveals the link to *Mikdash* as well. The last 3 objects, according to the most standard explanation, which is Rambam's as well, refers to the *Luchos Habris* and the writing on them. This is the object placed at the heart of the Mikdash. The *manna* (מן) and the staff (מטה) were also placed there. The *shamir* (שמיר) was the creature necessary for building the Mikdash. Thus, without any in-depth analysis, we realize that six of the ten objects are central elements of the *mikdash*, with the very last being the most central. Thus it makes sense to assume that if we can ascertain the allegorical significance of all ten things, we will be able to discern in the Mishnah a pattern of ascending concepts that enable man's growth so that he can build the *Mikdash*.[17] We should note before we proceed further, that Rambam departed from the rationalists who quickly grasped upon the interpretations of "the writing and the written" as the ability to formulate abstract ideas, for he sees the Mishnah as an analysis of allegorical Torah messages. The Mishnah is commenting primarily not on the human psyche but on the teachings of the Torah texts.[18]

---

16 א המלך המשיח עתיד לעמוד, ולהחזיר מלכות בית דויד ליושנה הממשלה הראשונה, ובונה מקדש, ומקבץ נדחי ישראל. וחוזרין כל המשפטים בימיו, כשהיו מקודם: מקריבין קרבנות, ועושין שמיטין ויובלות ככל מצותן האמורה בתורה.(הל' מלכים יא:א)

17 Abarbanel explains כי יצר לב האדם רע מנעריו refers to the growth of the world just like that of the growth of an individual, and these steps perhaps reflect this chronological process.

18 Thus the writing on the tablets is what is being referred to. In the case of the שמיר, the Torah text never speaks of it explicitly, nevertheless its message is found in the Torah, as we will explain.

The Earth and its Mouths

The concepts of *chomer v'tzurah* (חומר וצורה), representing man's physical and spiritual aspects, are used by the early philosophers and *Chazal* when speaking of abstract ideas that merge philosophy and psychology.[19]

> Know that the *nefesh* of man is one, with many functions... and know that this singular *nefesh* of which we have described its forces or parts, is like *chomer*, and the intellect is its *tzurah*, and should it not acquire a *tzurah*, then its preparation for this *tzurah* would be for naught as if it were itself naught, and this is the meaning of 'For without knowledge the *nefesh* is not good' (*Mishlei* 19:2). (*Shemonah Perakim,* Ch. 1)

The *chomer* includes not only the physical body but also the emotions and even the imagination (כח המדמה), whereas the *tzurah* is the intellect.[20] In the *Moreh* (2:6), Rambam explains that this *chomer* is subject to the influence of "angels":

> **Even the movements of the brute creation without the power of speech, are sometimes due to the action of an angel, when such movements serve the purpose of the Creator, who endowed it with the power of performing that movement;** e.g., "G-d hath sent His angel, and hath shut the lions' mouths that they have not hurt me" (Dan. vi. 22). **Another instance may be seen in the movements of Bilaam's donkey, described as caused by an angel...** [the term angels] is also used for ideals, perceived by prophets in prophetic visions, and of man's animal powers, as will be explained in another place. When we assert that Scripture teaches that G-d rules this world through angels, we mean such angels as are identical with the Intelligences. (*Moreh* 2:6)

Thus, the "mouth of the donkey" is the ability of the *chomer* to interact with the angel of G-d (מלאך ה'). Within the *chomer* was placed the drive to elevate itself and seek sanctity, and this is the meaning of פי האתון. Normally a donkey is referred to in the Torah

---

19 See *Moreh Nevuchim* 1:17.

20 See first *perek* of *Shemona Perakim*.

as חמור, and this serves an allegorical purpose. Avraham "saddled his donkey" ויחבש את חמרו—when he began his mission of sacrificing Yitzchok. The donkey represents the *chomer* which he is subduing. Here the change of the word to אתון is to demonstrate another characteristic of the physical essence of man that was placed within it in *Bein HaShmoshos.* Onkelos translates בני אתנו in the poetic blessing of Yaakov to Yehuda (*Bereshis* 49:11) as יבני היכלי "will build the Mikdash." The term אתא means "to come" and denotes the drive within the physical to enter the sanctuary. It is this drive that diverted Bilaam from the road he was on, that caused him to bless rather than curse, to say "Let my *nefesh* die the death of the righteous and let my end be as them (Israel)"— תמת נפשי מות ישרים ותהי אחריתי כמהו.

The Mishnah's first three steps in establishing the Mikdash are all defined as פי "mouths" i.e. "openings" or "pathways," and each shows a facet of the *chomer* with which it interacts with the Divine. The "mouth of the earth," פי הארץ, is an obvious allusion to the *chomer* of man. As Meiri points out, the concept of punishment is implied by the mouth of the earth. The gemara associates it with a pathway to hell, גיהנם.

> 'If G-d will create a creation.' (*Bemidbar* 16) 'A creation' refers to hell, [meaning] if the creation of hell exists, then it is good, but if not then G-d should create it. Is this possible (that hell needed to be created)? We learned (in a *beraisa*) that seven things were created before the world was created... Torah, Repentance, *Gan Eden,* and hell... but this is the meaning, 'if the mouth of hell is not near, bring it close.' (*Nedarim* 39b)

Whereas the ultimate punishment for sin is גיהנם, which Rambam tells us means to not merit eternal life after earthly death, the pain and suffering that one brings to himself with his immersion in physicality is the concept of hell during life, חיים שאלה. It was the congregation of *Dasan* and *Aviram* who bemoaned the lack of the "milk and honey" and the lost bounty of Egypt who were swallowed up by the earth, ארץ. The immersion in the physical brings its own destruction naturally and costs man even this world. This is "the mouth of the earth," פי הארץ.[21]

> This class of evils originates in man's vices, such as excessive desire for eating, drinking, and love; indulgence in these things in undue measure, or in improper manner; or partaking of bad food. This course brings diseases and afflictions upon body and soul alike. The sufferings of the body in consequence of these evils are well known; those of the soul are twofold: First, such evils of the soul as are the necessary consequence of changes in the body, insofar as the soul is a force residing in the body, it has therefore been said that the properties of the soul depend on the condition of the body. Secondly, the soul, when accustomed to superfluous things, acquires a strong habit of desiring things which are necessary neither for the preservation of the individual nor for that of the species. This desire is without a limit, whilst things which are necessary are few in number and restricted within certain limits; but what is superfluous is without end. (*Moreh* 3:12)

Israel's recognition of this phenomenon steers them towards sanctity, קדושה, and away from the tent of *Dasan V'Aviram*. The Torah explains the impact on Israel when the earth swallowed up that congregation.

> And all of Israel that surrounded them fled at the sound for they said, perhaps the earth would swallow them up.

Rambam tells us that the "mouth of the well," פי הבאר, was unique in "that it brought forth water" (שהוציא המים). Meiri says that it refers to G-d's reward. Just as improper conduct by the *chomer* leads to man's destruction, proper conduct sustains it. This is the meaning of "the mouth of the well."

> If you worship G-d with joy, and follow His path—he will grant you these blessings and distance the curses, so that you

---

21 ואם עזבתם את ה' ושגיתם במאכל ומשקה וזנות ודומה להם--מביא עליכם כל הקללות האלו לב פנוי ולא גוף שלם .ומסיר כל הברכות, עד שייכלו ימיכם בבהלה ופחד, ולא יהיה לכם לעשות המצוות, כדי שתאבדו מחיי העולם הבא. ונמצא שאיבדתם שני עולמות: שבזמן שאדם טרוד בעולם הזה בחולי ובמלחמה ורעבון, אינו מתעסק לא בחכמה ולא במצוה שבהן זוכין לחיי העולם הבא (תשובה ט:א).

> will be free to grow wiser in Torah and immerse in it, so that you will merit the World to Come, and have the good of the world that is entirely good... and thus you will merit two worlds, life in this world which leads to life in the World to Come, for if you do not acquire wisdom and good deeds here, you will have nothing with which to merit. (*Hilchos Teshuva* 9:1)

This realization that physical rewards accrue from following the Torah's guidelines is the lesson of the well, and at its deepest level this is the understanding of the value of the mitzvos and how they bring G-d's providence, His *hashgacha* (השגחה).

> 'Speak to the rock'—When a child is young, his Rebbe hits and teaches him. Once he has grown, he is disciplined with speech. So too G-d told Moshe that when the rock was young you hit it as it says 'and hit the rock,' but now speak to it, teach a chapter upon it and the rock will bring forth water. (Midrash)

The *chomer* of Israel was to be molded during the forty years in the desert. First they recognized G-d's presence only by His might which they feared and this was represented by the earth's stone (סלע) that had to be hit. After forty years they were meant to recognize that serving G-d with joy will sustain them and the rock of their *chomer* was to be moved by speech and understanding. At that point they would attain to G-d's *hashgacha* which[22] would guide even their mundane decisions and sustain their existence. "Behold I stand before you on the rock." G-d Himself stands in front of Moshe on this rock.[23] This act was to determine "Is G-d in our midst or not," i.e., they were to learn that the *shechina*, שכינה,[24] was within the *chomer* of the world, within their own being.[25]

---

22 See *Moreh* (1:15-16), where Rambam explains that while the צור is a rock on the simple level, part of the earth, on a metaphoric level it refers to the presence of הקב"ה (הצור תמים פעלו)

23 שמשה לא היה יודע איזו צור הוא עד שאמר לו הקב"ה הסימן של אותו הצור שראה השכינה נראתה עליו, אז ידע כי הוא הצור (מדרש אגדה ת"ש 128 חקת).

24 Which Rambam equates with השגחה.

25 As Israel ends their journey they sing a song of this well.
טז וּמִשָּׁם, בְּאֵרָה: הִוא הַבְּאֵר, אֲשֶׁר אָמַר ה לְמֹשֶׁה, אֱסֹף אֶת-הָעָם, וְאֶתְּנָה לָהֶם מָיִם יז אָז יָשִׁיר יִשְׂרָאֵל, אֶת-הַשִּׁירָה הַזֹּאת: עֲלִי בְאֵר, עֱנוּ-לָהּ. יח בְּאֵר חֲפָרוּהָ שָׂרִים, כָּרוּהָ נְדִיבֵי הָעָם, בִּמְחֹקֵק, בְּמִשְׁעֲנֹתָם; וּמִמִּדְבָּר, מַתָּנָה.

The *chomer* of man is so made that wrongdoing itself destroys it (פי הארץ), good sustains it (פי הבאר) , and it yearns to elevate itself (פי האתון). As mankind realizes these truths about itself it begins its journey towards spirituality.

A Covenant with G-d

יג אֶת-קַשְׁתִּי, נָתַתִּי בֶּעָנָן; וְהָיְתָה לְאוֹת בְּרִית, בֵּינִי וּבֵין הָאָרֶץ. יד וְהָיָה,
בְּעַנְנִי עָנָן עַל-הָאָרֶץ, וְנִרְאֲתָה הַקֶּשֶׁת, בֶּעָנָן.טו וְזָכַרְתִּי אֶת-בְּרִיתִי, אֲשֶׁר
בֵּינִי וּבֵינֵיכֶם, וּבֵין כָּל-נֶפֶשׁ חַיָּה, בְּכָל-בָּשָׂר; וְלֹא-יִהְיֶה עוֹד הַמַּיִם לְמַבּוּל,
לְשַׁחֵת כָּל-בָּשָׂר. טז וְהָיְתָה הַקֶּשֶׁת, בֶּעָנָן; וּרְאִיתִיהָ, לִזְכֹּר בְּרִית עוֹלָם, בֵּין
אֱלֹהִים, וּבֵין כָּל-נֶפֶשׁ חַיָּה בְּכָל-בָּשָׂר אֲשֶׁר עַל-הָאָרֶץ.

I have set My bow in the cloud, and it shall be for a token of a covenant between Me and the earth. And it shall come to pass, when I bring clouds over the earth, and the bow is seen in the cloud, that I will remember My covenant, which is between Me and you and every living creature of all flesh; and the waters shall no more become a flood to destroy all flesh. And the bow shall be in the cloud; and I will look upon it, that I may remember the everlasting covenant between G-d and every living creature of all flesh that is upon the earth.

With regard to the rainbow, קשת, Ramban has already questioned the *mikra* itself for suggesting that it was created at the time of the flood, when the scientists explain that it is a fact of nature. It has a metaphorical meaning. It is the covenant (ברית) between the earth and G-d, between the earth within man, the *chomer*, and G-d. With the drive embodied in "the mouth of the donkey," man has elevated his *chomer*, and we now speak of man as a joint product of the physical and spiritual. Physical man reaches a point at which he cannot be destroyed for he has become inextricably bound with the *tzura*, that which the Torah characterizes as "the spirit of G-d" (רוח אלקים ממעל). Ramban calls the midrashic statement of this idea a secret, סוד.

The midrash tells us that these שרים are the *Avos*, and the well is the one first dug by Avraham. The accomplishment of Avraham, to connect man with the שכינה, is finally celebrated by his children.

'I have placed my *keshes* קשת'—קישותי [implies] that which has been compared[26] to me, is there any such thing? But rather the hard part of the fruit[27]... it was expounded otherwise, 'when the *keshes* is in the cloud, I will see it to remember the everlasting covenant between G-d and all living *nefesh'*; 'between G-d' is the attribute of justice above, and 'all living *nefesh*,' is the attribute of G-d below, the attribute of justice above is hard and that below is soft.

Man's recognition of G-d comes from recognizing Him in the patterns of nature

How does one come to love... of G-d, when he contemplates His great and wondrous actions and creations, and sees from them His wisdom which is beyond evaluation and limit—immediately he feels love and praises... and has a great desire to know the Great Name. (*Hilchos Yesodei HaTorah* 2:2)

When man recognizes G-d in nature, he develops a connection to the Divine, and this is what the *keshes* represents. Rambam quotes the blessing Chazal required because of this *parsha* together with the blessing instituted when seeing the new moon.

He who sees the rainbow in a cloud, blesses 'Blessed are you Hashem... who remembers the covenant, is trusted in His covenant, and is everlasting in His word.' One who sees the moon renewing blesses 'Blessed are you HaShem... who with His word created heavens, and by the breath of His mouth all their hosts, He gave them rules and times that they cannot change, they rejoice... to do the will of their possessor...'[28] And this blessing must be said standing, for all who bless the moon at its appointed time are as if they had greeted the face of the *shechina*. (*Hilchos Brachos* 11:16,17)

Seeing the rainbow reminds man that G-d gives rain to sustain life and yet limits it so that it will not destroy. This is a companion concept and an initial step in recognizing the wonder of all the hea-

---

26 The word קשת is similar to היקש—meaning something comparable or linked.

27 The word קשה means hard.

28 A new halacha begins here.

venly bodies that Rambam refers to in *Hilchos Yesodei HaTorah*. The moon was created earlier on the fourth day, and man would eventually turn to it and all the heavenly bodies for insight and inspiration—but the first step in this recognition and the more immediate link between the *chomer v'tzurah* was with the קשת.

He Who Takes Less will Not be Wanting

Rav Saadiah Gaon expresses a novel idea with regard to the *manna*, מן. He feels that since food affects not only the physical but the spiritual essence of man[29] therefore it was necessary for them to maintain a diet of this very fine food "so that they would be able to acquire wisdom."[30] This is apparently the intent of Chazal, in saying "The Torah could be given only to those eating the *man*."[31] In Rambam's elaboration on the quality of *histapkus*,[32] הסתפקות, he also relates it to the *manna*.

"He who lacks luxuries of life is missing nothing necessary, and he that gathered much had nothing over, and he that gathered little had no lack: they gathered every man according to his eating" (Exod. xvi. 18) (*Moreh* 3:12). The *manna* represents the mental state that fosters the quality of *histapkus*.

When the Torah speaks of *manna* it does not look at it from the perspective of what G-d has given Israel but rather calls it a trial, נסיון. "Remember the road which G-d led you upon for forty years

---

29 As we noted with regard to פי הארץ.

30 ואם יספיק לו המזון העב היבש, וינהיג עצמו בו ויעבה טבעו ויכער, תבטל זכות החכמה ודקותה, וכמ"ש (משלי כ"ה י"א) תפוחי זהב במשכיות כסף דבר דבור על אפניו. הלא תראה בני ישראל במדבר, זנם הבורא במזון דק רוצה לומר המן, כדי שילמדו החכמה, כמו שאמר (שמות ט"ז ד') ויצא העם ולקטו דבר יום ביומו למען אנסנו הילך בתורתי אם לא;(אמונות ודעות מאמר י').

31 Interestingly, Rambam equates the inability to understand midrashim to those who could not appreciate the מן.
כי לא יתאים לך ממנו מאומה, ולא עוד אלא שיזיק לך ותשנאהו, כי איך יתאימו מיני המזון קלי הכמות ממוצעי האיכות לאדם שכבר הורגל למיני המזון הרעים והכבדים, הלא רק יזיקוהו וישנאם, הנך רואה דבר אותם שהורגלו באכילת הבצלים והשומים והדגים על המן מה הוא ונפשנו קצה בלחם הקלקל. (פירוש המשנה לרמב"ם מסכת סנהדרין פרק י')

32 It is hard to translate this word. It is the quality of being content with the minimum that is really necessary of all worldly needs. Perhaps "abstemiousness" is the proper word.

in the desert, to cause you suffering and to test you, to know what is in your heart, whether you would keep his commands or not—He who fed you in the desert, in a way unknown to your fathers, to cause you suffering and to test you that it be to your benefit at the end." The prophet Yirmiyahu many years later calls it Israel's act of love. "I remember the kindness of your youth, your all-encompassing love—your following after me in the desert, in an unplanted land." Rambam explains as follows:

> Having shown that the term "to know" means "that all people may know," we apply this interpretation to the following words said in reference to the *manna*: "To humble thee, and to prove thee, to know what was in thine heart, whether thou wouldst keep his commandments, or not" (Deut. viii. 2). All nations shall know, it shall be published throughout the world, that those who devote themselves to the service of G-d are supported beyond their expectation. In the same sense it was said when the *manna* commenced to come down, "that I may test them whether they will walk in my law or not" (Exod. xvi. 4); i.e., let everyone who desires try and see whether it is useful and sufficient to devote himself to the service of G-d. It is, however, said a third time in reference to the manna: "Who fed thee in the wilderness with manna, which thy fathers knew not, that he might humble thee, and that he might test thee, to do thee good at thy latter end" (Deut. viii. 16). This might induce us to think that G-d sometimes afflicts man for the purpose of increasing his reward. But in truth this is not the case. We may rather assume one of the two following explanations: either this passage expresses the same idea as is expressed in the first and second passages, viz., **to show [to all people] whether faith in G-d is sufficient to secure man's maintenance and his relief from care and trouble,** or not. Or the Hebrew term *le-nassoteka* means "to accustom thee";... The meaning of the above passage would then be: "G-d has first trained you in the hardships of the wilderness, in order to increase your welfare when you enter the land of Canaan." **It is indeed a fact that the transition from trouble to ease gives more pleasure than continual ease. It is also known that the Israelites would not have been able to conquer the land and fight with its inhabitants, if they had not previously undergone the trouble and hardship of the wilderness.** Scripture says in

> reference to this: "For G-d said, Lest peradventure the people repent when they see war, and they return to Egypt. But G-d led the people about, through the way of the wilderness of the Red Sea; and the children of Israel went up harnessed out of the land of Egypt" (Exod. xiii. 17, 18). **Ease destroys bravery, whilst trouble and care for food create strength; and this was [also for the Israelites] the good that ultimately came out of their wanderings in the wilderness.** (*Moreh* 3:24)

> Perhaps this concept is best expressed in *Mishneh Torah*.

> Not only the tribe of Levi, but any man in the entire world whose spirit bequeaths itself and whose mind directs itself to separate and stand before G-d to serve Him and worship Him that he may know G-d, and go straight as G-d made him, and unburdens his neck from the yoke of many calculations that men seek out, becomes sanctified as the holy of holies (קדש קדשים), and G-d will be his portion and inheritance forever, and he will be granted in this world that which is necessary for him (דבר המספיק לו) just as He granted the priests and Levites. (*Hilchos Shemitta* 13:13)

Some interpret this passage as faith and indeed it is related to it, but it is in fact more complex, as it is joined with the quality that underlies *histapkus*.[33] מן represents the ability of the human spirit to endure hardship because of its faith—for the values of the spirit to rise above the needs of the flesh. Thus the מן was placed near the ארון as an exhortation to Israel, to strengthen themselves that they may enter the holy of holies, קדש קדשים.[34]

---

33 As Radvaz notes, דבר המספיק לו is the key.

34 לב וַיֹּאמֶר מֹשֶׁה, זֶה הַדָּבָר אֲשֶׁר צִוָּה יְהוָה--מְלֹא הָעֹמֶר מִמֶּנּוּ, לְמִשְׁמֶרֶת לְדֹרֹתֵיכֶם: לְמַעַן יִרְאוּ אֶת-הַלֶּחֶם, אֲשֶׁר הֶאֱכַלְתִּי אֶתְכֶם בַּמִּדְבָּר, בְּהוֹצִיאִי אֶתְכֶם, מֵאֶרֶץ מִצְרָיִם. לג וַיֹּאמֶר מֹשֶׁה אֶל-אַהֲרֹן, קַח צִנְצֶנֶת אַחַת, וְתֶן-שָׁמָּה מְלֹא-הָעֹמֶר, מָן; וְהַנַּח אֹתוֹ לִפְנֵי יְהוָה, לְמִשְׁמֶרֶת לְדֹרֹתֵיכֶם. לד כַּאֲשֶׁר צִוָּה יְהוָה, אֶל-מֹשֶׁה; וַיַּנִּיחֵהוּ אַהֲרֹן לִפְנֵי הָעֵדֻת, לְמִשְׁמָרֶת.

A Solitary Man and a Staff

The history of the *mateh* of Moshe is discussed in *Pirkei D'REliezer:*

> R. Levi says, the staff (מטה) which was created at dusk was handed to Adam HaRishon from Gan Eden and Adam handed it to Chanoch and Chanoch handed it to Noach and Noach to Shem and Shem handed it to Avraham and Avraham to Yitzchok, Yitzchok to Yaakov and Yaakov took it down to Mitzrayim and handed it to Yosef his son. When Yosef died and they looted his house it was given to the palace of Pharaoh. And Yisro, one of the magicians of Mitzrayim, saw the *mateh* and the signs (אותות) written on it and desired it in his heart and took it and planted it in the garden of his house and none could draw near to it again. When Moshe came to his house, he entered the garden and saw the *mateh* and read the signs which were on it. He pulled out his hand and took it. Yisro saw Moshe and said he will redeem Israel from Mitzrayim. He therefore gave him Tzipporah, his daughter, as a wife. (*Pirkei D'R Eliezer* (39))

Some midrashim say the symbols דצ"ך עד"ש באח"ב of the ten plagues were written on the *mateh,* while other midrashim say it was the name of G-d (שם הוי"ה). Rambam in the *Moreh* (2:38) explains what this *mateh* represents.

> Every man possesses a certain amount of courage, otherwise he would not stir to remove anything that might injure him. This psychical force seems to me analogous to the physical force of repulsion. Energy varies like all other forces, being great in one case and small in another. There are, therefore, people who attack a lion, whilst others run away at the sight of a mouse. One attacks a whole army and fights, another is frightened and terrified by the threat of a woman. This courage requires that there be in a man's constitution a certain disposition for it. If man, in accordance with a certain view, employs it more frequently, it develops and increases, but, on the other hand, if it is employed, in accordance with the opposite view, more rarely, it will diminish. From our own youth we remember that there are different degrees of energy among boys.
>
> The same is the case with the intuitive faculty; all possess it, but in different degrees. Man's intuitive power is especially

> strong in things which he has well comprehended, and in which his mind is much engaged. Thus you may yourself guess correctly that a certain person said or did a certain thing in a certain matter. Some persons are so strong and sound in their imagination and intuitive faculty that, when they assume a thing to be in existence, the reality either entirely or partly confirms their assumption. Although the causes of this assumption are numerous, and include many preceding, succeeding, and present circumstances, by means of the intuitive faculty the intellect can pass over all these causes, and draw inferences from them very quickly, almost instantaneously. This same faculty enables some persons to foretell important coming events. The prophets must have had these two forces, courage and intuition, highly developed, and these were still more strengthened when they were under the influence of the Active Intellect. Their courage was so great that **a solitary man with only a staff** in his hand, dared to address a great king in his desire to deliver a nation from his service. He was not frightened or terrified, because he had been told, "I will be with thee." (Exod. iii. 12) (*Moreh* 3:28)

The ability for man to transcend himself and do unfathomable acts of courage and accomplish miracles is symbolized by the *mateh* of Moshe.[35] The rod of Aharon (מקל של אהרן) was that very same staff according to some midrashim, while according to others the staff was sliced into 12 with one part being given to the heads of each tribe.[36] Only that which was given to Aharon of the tribe of Levi blossomed, and was placed near the ark (ארון) that Israel might learn what qualities were needed to enter the קדש קדשים.[37]

This enormous power is given only to G-d's chosen, those who possess "the spirit of G-d," רוח ה'[38], that comes from reaching the stage of "G-d is with you."

---

35 A staff is used for support, to strike with and extends the reach of he who hold it.

36 In the gemara *Pesachim* the מקל של אהרן is what is listed, not our term מטה.

37 וַיֹּאמֶר יְהוָה אֶל-מֹשֶׁה, הָשֵׁב אֶת-מַטֵּה אַהֲרֹן לִפְנֵי הָעֵדוּת, לְמִשְׁמֶרֶת לְאוֹת, לִבְנֵי-מֶרִי; וּתְכַל תְּלוּנֹּתָם מֵעָלַי, וְלֹא יָמֻתוּ. כו וַיַּעַשׂ, מֹשֶׁה: כַּאֲשֶׁר צִוָּה יְהוָה אֹתוֹ, כֵּן עָשָׂה.

38 Elsewhere in the *Moreh*, Rambam refers to this explicitly as רוח ה', the first level of prophecy.

If Your Sword Shall Wave upon it You Will Have Profaned It

כא וְאִם-מִזְבַּח אֲבָנִים תַּעֲשֶׂה-לִּי, לֹא-תִבְנֶה אֶתְהֶן גָּזִית: כִּי חַרְבְּךָ הֵנַפְתָּ עָלֶיהָ, וַתְּחַלְלֶהָ

> Should you build me an altar of stones, do not build it of cut stones, for if you wave your sword upon it, you will have profaned it.

Chazal explain that because the sword is a weapon of violence it could not be used in building the altar. While it was not practical to disallow cutting stone for the entire Bais HaMikdash, this principle was the source for requiring all iron cutting of stones to be outside the confines of the Mikdash. The building of the Mikdash had to be pure of the instinct for violence.[39]

The building of the Bais Hamikdash could not be by Dovid, because "your hands are full of blood," which Rambam interprets to refer to a quality of cruelty [40](אכזריות). The ability that is central to building the Bais Hamikdash was possessed by the king of peace, "Shlomo—the king to whom peace belongs,"[41] שלמה – המלך שהשלום שלו, and is embodied in the *shamir*, שמיר. Thus *Chazal* say that it vanished with the destruction of the *Bais HaMidkash.*[42]

The שמיר represents a power stronger than the forbidden iron sword—the power within man to substitute wisdom for force, to harness nature in order to build. Nature itself provides an animal

---

39 כשבונין ההיכל והעזרה, בונין באבנים גדולות; ואם לא מצאו אבנים, בונין בלבינים. ואין מפצלין את אבני הבניין בהר הבית--אלא מפצלין אותן ומסתתין אותן מבחוץ, ואחר כך מכניסין אותן לבניין: שנאמר "אבנים גדולות אבנים יקרות, לייסד הבית--אבני גזית" (מלכים א ה,לא), ואומר "ומקבות והגרזן כל כלי ברזל, לא נשמע בבית בהיבנותו" (מלכים א ו,ז).

40 *Shemonah Perakim.*

41 דרש על שיר השירים שלשלמה referring to Hashem, with Shlomo being the king who embodied this identity of G-d.

42 טו,א משחרב בית המקדש בטל שמיר ונופת צופים אמר ר' יהודה מה טיבו של שמיר זה [בריה היתה מששת ימי בראשית משנותנים אותו על גבי אבנים על גבי קורות מתפתחות לפניו כלוחי פנקס ולא עוד אלא כשנותנין אותו ע"ג ברזל הוא בוקע ויורד מלפניו ואין כל דבר יכול לעמוד בו כיצד עושין לו כורכין אותו במוכין של צמר ונותנים אותו לתוך מני של עופרת מלא סובין של שעורין ובו בנה שלמה את בית המקדש שנא' (מלכים א ו) ומקבות והגרזן כל כלי ברזל וגו' דברי ר' יהודה ר' נחמיה אומר מגוררת במגרה היה מבחוץ שנאמר (מלכים א ז) כל אלה אבנים יקרות כמדות גזית מגררות במגרה מבית ומחוץ מה ת"ל מבית ומחוץ בבית לא היו נשמעין אלא מתקנין אותו מבחוץ ומכניסין אותו לפנים] אמר ר' נראין דברי ר' יהודה באבני מקדש ודברי ר' נחמיה באבני ביתו (**תוספתא סוטה טו:א)**

that is stronger than iron. Shlomo asked G-d only for wisdom. Judaism sees existence not as a struggle, not of man against nature, nor man against man, but as mankind at peace with itself and in harmony with nature.

The Making of Moshe Rabbenu

Rambam did not interpret "the writing and the written" כתב ומכתב in the rationalistic way of R. Hai Gaon and Meiri—referring to the ability to form speech and writing—for these last elements are the culmination of the creation of man. As with all the other steps, they refer here to concepts described explicitly in the Biblical Narrative.[43] Just as the first three creations of *Bein HaShmashos* are a single group of ideas, the final three are a similar grouping. The first group are the creations that perfect the *chomer* while the final group perfect the *tzura*.

> The *kesav* is the Torah that is written before He the Exalted, and we do not know how (ולא נדע איך), as it says "and I gave you the *luchos* of stone, and the Torah and the commandment that I have written (אשר כתבתי) to teach them." And the *michtav* is the writing on the *luchos* as it says, "and the *michtav* is the *michtav* of G-d." (*Perush HaMishnah,* ibid.)

The ability of Moshe to perceive the word of G-d clearly "as it is written before Him" is the כתב and corresponds to the 7th *ikkar* of Rambam's 13 *ikkarim,* the unique prophecy of *Moshe Rabbenu.* The מכתב is the ability of Moshe to express it, and corresponds to the 8th *ikkar.*[44]

> That we believe that this entire Torah was given through Moshe Rabbenu, that it is completely from the Almighty, meaning that it reached him completely from G-d, in a manner that we refer to metaphorically as 'speech,' and we do not know how it reached him, but it was to Moshe that it reached, and he was like a scribe, to whom one reads and he writes all

---

43 Except for the שמיר which is nevertheless based on the *mikra* and described by *Chazal.*

44 Where we find the same phrase לא נדע איך that Rambam uses here for the כתב.

the events being recorded, the stories and the commandments, that is why he is called scribe, מחקק.

These qualities are within human potential but it was with Moshe that this potential was realized.[45] [46]

וַיִּפֶן וַיֵּרֶד מֹשֶׁה, מִן-הָהָר, וּשְׁנֵי לֻחֹת הָעֵדֻת, בְּיָדוֹ: לֻחֹת, **כְּתֻבִים** מִשְּׁנֵי עֶבְרֵיהֶם--מִזֶּה וּמִזֶּה, הֵם **כְּתֻבִים**. טז **וְהַלֻּחֹת**--מַעֲשֵׂה אֱלֹהִים, הֵמָּה; **וְהַמִּכְתָּב**, מִכְתַּב אֱלֹהִים הוּא--חָרוּת, עַל-הַלֻּחֹת.

And Moshe turned and went down from the mountain with the two tablets of the testimony in his hand, tablets written on both sides, on this side and that they are written. And the *luchos* are the action of G-d, and that which is written is that which is written by G-d—carved on the *luchos.*

The "tablets of testimony," לוחות העדות, are "the doing of G-d," מעשה אלקים, for they are a part of nature, created in the last moment of the six days of creation. On the meaning of the לוחות Rambam gives no explanation, as the literal meaning is self-evident. Their symbolic meaning should also be self-evident, as they lie at the heart of the *mikdash.* The midrash[47] connects the לוחות from G-d to those in the heart of man. "Why did He give them *luchos?* To indicate to them that they must write the words of the Torah on the *luach* of their heart. As it says 'Write them on the *luach* of your heart'" (*Midrash HaGadol*).

Midrash Tanchuma sees in them the call to emulate He who made them.

Every day a voice goes out from Mount Chorev and says, 'Woe to the creations because of the disgrace of the Torah,' for

---

45 Thus the surprising phrase near the end of the first chapter in *Hilchos Avodah Zara* become clear:
ומאהבת ה' אותנו, ומשומרו את השבועה לאברהם אבינו, **עשה משה רבנו** ורבן של כל הנביאים, ושלחו.

46 Rambam further clarifies the issue in the *Moreh* (1:66). He points us to the radical interpretation of Onkelos that G-d created what is called the אצבע of G-d's creation, from which to create the לוחות. Onkelos is saying that the quality that allowed the man called Moshe to write these *luchos* was a unique creation—referring to the כתב ומכתב rather than the *luchos* themselves, and it is this that Chazal tell us was created *Bain HaShmoshos.*

47 *Midrash HaGadol* is a late midrash based on the teachings of Rambam.

> anyone who is not perpetually [engaged] with the Torah is scorned before G-d for it says the 'luchos are the action of G-d,' in the manner of how a man[48] says to his friend, 'what is the work of that person?' [And the response is] 'pure silver.' So too the work of the King of kings is engaging in the Torah. (*Midrash Tanchuma (Warsa) Ki Sisa 16*)

The creation of mankind is complete when the human potential to emulate G-d is fulfilled. The creation of this potential to become מעשה אלקים—symbolized by the לוחות—was the final act of creation.

> The perfection, in which man can truly glory, is attained by him when he has acquired—as far as this is possible for man—the knowledge of G-d, the knowledge of His Providence, and of the manner in which it influences His creatures in their production and continued existence. Having acquired this knowledge he will then be determined always to seek loving-kindness, judgment, and righteousness, and thus to imitate the ways of G-d. (*Moreh* 3:54)[49] ☙

---

48 The person who is a silversmith is referred to by the product that he works with, 'pure silver.'

49 We have dealt with only one of the four that others contend were created בין השמשות—the צבת. We will leave it to the readers to contemplate what the others refer to, but one important note to be made is that the concept of מזיקין i.e. שדים, is, like all the others, not some magical force but a quality within man himself. The Meiri thinks it is the יצר הרע. Academics make much of the fact that Rambam does not believe in demons despite the Talmud's frequent reference to them. Of course Rambam does not mention them, because *Chazal* themselves did not believe in them. When they refer to them, they are referring to a function of the human psyche. Rambam (*Moreh* 1:7) refers to the midrash that says they were born to Adam during the first 130 years of his life when he was excommunicated by G-d—a form of evil created by man himself. According to one opinion in our Mishnah it is a destructive force G-d put into man. Like the donkey in Bilaam's dream, the demons are perceived by man as something external. Chazal understood, however, that the forces of destruction come from man himself.

The Mystical Spirituality of Rabbi Joseph B. Soloveitchik[*]

By: HESHEY ZELCER

> חוויות נמסרות בלחישה ואינן נלמדות בקול. אדם מוסר חוויה כדרך חולה שמוסר מחלה... אדם נדבק במחלה בהיותו במגע עם חולה. וכן נדבק אדם בחוויה מתוך מגעו עם הרב שחותמו־קדושה, שהוא חולה־אהבה. (הרב יוסף דב הלוי סולובייצ'יק, דברי הגות והערכה, דף רד)

Introduction

Rabbi Joseph B. Soloveitchik was imbued with a mystical spirituality that affected his life and thought. By recognizing his mystical spirituality we can better understand some of the Rav's disagreements with Rambam; his attitude toward ḥasidut; his relationship with his students; his attitude toward theodicy; and his dismissal of proofs of God as irrelevant.

What is spirituality?[1]

When we speak about the spiritual essence within ourselves, we often contrast it with the material, i.e., that the non-material spiritual spark within us is but a reflection of the ultimate spiritual existence that is God.

When we talk about our ability to act or feel spiritual, however, we usually do so in two different ways: as either an intellec-

---

[*] I lovingly dedicate this essay on spirituality to my father HaRav Yeraḥmiel ben Ẓvi Yehudah, *zẓ"l*, מחבר ספרי נר למאה, who passed away this 17th day of Kislev 5771 and who lived the ideal of והגית בו יומם ולילה.

[1] This section is not meant as a full discussion of Jewish spirituality. For a fuller treatment the reader is advised to consult The Orthodox Forum's *Jewish Spirituality and Divine Law*, ed. Adam Mintz and Lawrence Schiffman (Jersey City: Ktav, 2005).

Heshey Zelcer, a businessman, is the author of *Companion Mishnayot: Tractate Niddah* (1994) and *A Guide to the Jerusalem Talmud* (2002).

tual/philosophical endeavor, or as an emotional/mystical experience. Sometimes it is a combination of both.[2]

As an intellectual/philosophical endeavor, spirituality is our search for meaning in life. When religious people follow the dictates of their religion, they fill their lives with spirituality. In Judaism such spirituality is attained by accepting the beliefs of our religion and by performing the dictates of God, i.e., the mitzvoth. When the mitzvoth are performed, not by rote but with forethought and intent (*kavvanah*) as a means of obeying the will of God and connecting to Him, our lives become filled with spirituality. Certain commandments, such as prayer or the obligation to love and fear God, highlight our striving to connect with the Divine. According to Rambam, by contemplating the awesomeness of His wondrous creation, we recognize our own comparative insignificance and are filled with love and awe for the One Who created the endlessly complex and sophisticated universe (*Hilkhot Yesodei ha-Torah* 2:1-2, 4:12).

A person can also experience a connection with the Creator and/or the universe on an emotional/mystical level (*deveikut*). For some people the ability to experience or feel the Divine is natural and intense. For others it can be brought about, for example, through a religiously neutral action such as meditation.[3] Within the mystical strain of Judaism, i.e., kabbalah, we are told how to achieve this experience: we relax our body, still our mind and then visualize and focus on certain lights, *sefirot*, or names of God. The

---

2 For another definition of spirituality see R. Norman Lamm in *The Shema: Spirituality and Law in Judaism* (Philadelphia: JPS, 1998), quoted repeatedly in the Orthodox Forum's *Jewish Spirituality and Divine Law*. See, for example, p. 63, "By 'spirituality' I mean the intention we bring to our religious acts, the focusing of the mind and thoughts on the transcendent, the entire range of mindfulness—whether simple awareness of what we are doing, in contrast to rote performance, or elaborate mystical meditations—that spells a groping for the Source of all existence and the Giver of Torah."

3 Asceticism, which entails the denial of bodily pleasures, the removal from worldly affairs, and the focus on heavenly matters, is another example of a method used for achieving such spirituality.

ensuing meditation then enables us to achieve a mystical spiritual feeling of closeness to the Divine.

To summarize, in Judaism, the intellectual/philosophical type of spirituality is achieved through the observance of mitzvoth that require actions, forethought and contemplation, while the emotional/mystical type of spirituality is either inborn or achieved through meditative and other aspects of kabbalah. These two methods, however, are not mutually exclusive. The performance of mitzvoth, and concurrent meditative techniques, are often used in tandem to achieve spiritual experiences.

To contrast these two types of spirituality we should note that the intellectual/philosophical type of spirituality is bound to, and a natural outgrowth of, our performance of the mitzvoth with the proper forethought and intent. There is no halakhic obligation or halakhic ideal, however, to strive for or to achieve the emotional/mystical type of spirituality.[4]

The Rav's Spirituality

It needs no proof and it need not be said that from an intellectual/philosophical perspective the Rav was a very spiritual person.[5] His meticulous performance of the mitzvoth, his deep understanding of the halakhah and his all-encompassing view of reality through the prism of halakhah—all imbued his life, by definition, with meaning and spirituality.

What needs to be said, however, is that the Rav was also very spiritual on an emotional/mystical level. This spirituality was not

4 Even the "cleaving" to God mentioned, for example, in *Devarim* 4:4 and 30:20 is reinterpreted in *Ketubbot* 111b as an injunction to serve and benefit *talmidei ḥakhamim*.

5 Allan Nadler, "Soloveitchik's Halakhic Man: Not a Mithnagged" *Modern Judaism* 13: 119–147, 1993 argues against the view that "*Halakhic Man* is a mithnagged phenomenology of awesome proportions." Instead he writes p. 139 that "In rejecting completely the mithnagdim's adherence to Lurianic kabbalah's dualistic asceticism, and their sense of pessimism regarding the potentialities of man within the confines of this fragmented and alienated world, Soloveitchik has developed a highly original and uniquely optimistic alternative to hasidic spirituality."

something the Rav had to develop; it was simply there, a constant presence that was as real to him as the air he breathed—perhaps even biological and genetic.[6]

While the Rav may have inherited and imbibed his analytic nature from his paternal ancestors, he was also exposed, from his mother's side, to a more nurturing, warmer[7] and more mystical orientation:

> Most of all I learned [from my mother] that Judaism expresses itself not only in formal compliance with the law but also in a living experience. She taught me that there is a flavor, a scent and warmth to *mitzvot*. I learned from her the most important thing in life—to feel the presence of the Almighty and the gentle pressure of His hand resting upon my frail shoulders. Without her teachings, which quite often were transmitted to me in silence, I would have grown up a soulless being, dry and insensitive.[8]

A few paragraphs later (pp. 77-78) we find the following:

> [The Rebbetzen of Talne] was an outstanding teacher, even though she was a woman of few words. She taught, like my mother, how to feel the presence of God.

---

6 For discussions concerning the possibility of a biological/genetic basis for spirituality see, for example, Dean Hamer, *The God Gene: How Faith Is Hardwired into Our Genes* (New York: Anchor, 2004), and Andrew Newberg and Mark Robert Waldman, *Why We Believe What We Believe: Uncovering Our Biological Need for Meaning, Spirituality, and Truth* (New York: Free Press, 2006).

7 Shulamith Soloveitchik Meiselman, *The Soloveitchik Heritage: A Daughter's Memoir* (Hoboken: Ktav, 1995): "The Soloveitchiks are very unusual in that every act in their household is performed according to the letter of the Law... Your father is a saintly man, but he recognizes the importance of secular education, not only for his children but for all Israel, as long as it doesn't negate our tradition. At his table one feels free to discuss any subject—political, social, or literary. In addition, your home is permeated with warmth and tenderness," p. 11, as explained by her brother-in-law, Reb Menachem, to Pesha, the Rav's mother, prior to her engagement to R. Moshe Soloveitchik.

8 Joseph B. Soloveitchik, "A Tribute to the Rebbetzen of Talne," *Tradition* 17:2, Spring 1978, p. 77.

While yet a child, the Rav had already experienced this emotional/mystical spirituality:

> ... As a child I used to feel stimulated, aroused, and deeply inspired. I used to experience a strange peaceful stillness. As a child I used to surrender, using the language of the mystics, to a stream of inflowing joy and ecstasy. In a word, as a young child I felt the presence of kedushah [holiness] on these nights... Paradoxically, I must say that these emotions and experiences, however naive and childish, have always been the fountainhead of my religious life. My religious life has always been a colorful life. This achievement I derived from my childhood experience and not from my intellectual accomplishments.[9]

This mystical feeling stayed with the Rav throughout his life. Consider the effect that the sighting of the Baltic Sea had upon him:

> I remember that I was grown up when I went to Danzig [Gdansk, Poland]. I saw the [Baltic] sea for the first time, and it made a tremendous impression upon me. From afar, it looked like a blue forest. I was used to forests from Russia. When I drew closer and saw that it was the sea, I was overwhelmed. I made the benediction of "Blessed be He who wrought creation," which is recited when "one sees mountains, hills, seas, rivers and deserts" [Berakhot 9:2]. This blessing came from the depths of my heart. It was one of the greatest religious experiences I have ever had.[10]

---

9 Aaron Rakeffet-Rothkoff, *The Rav: The World of Rabbi Joseph B. Soloveitchik* (Jersey City: Ktav, 1999), volume 2 of 2, p. 172. We refer to these books hereafter as "Rakeffet Vol. 1" and "Rakeffet Vol. 2."

10 Rakeffet Vol. 2, p. 164. In another retelling of the same incident we find: "It was a religious reaction to viewing the majesty of God's creation. When I recited the blessing upon seeing the sea, I did so with emotion and deep feeling. I deeply experienced the words of the benediction: "Blessed be He who wrought creation" [Berakhot 9:1]. Not all the blessings that I recite are said with such concentration. It was more than simply a blessing, it was an encounter with the Creator. I felt the Shekhinah [Divine Presence] was hidden in the darkness and vastness of the sea. The experience was unique and unforgettable; the blessing welled out of me." (Ibid. 165:166)

The Rav also recounts how a traumatic event on Yom Kippur foreshadowed the death of his wife:

> ... It was Kol Nidrei, and I was holding a Sefer Torah for Kol Nidrei. Then the hazzan finished Kol Nidrei... I turned over the Sefer Torah to a talmid of mine and told him to put it into the aron ha-kodesh. He put it into the aron ha-kodesh. Apparently, he did not put it in properly. I don't know exactly what happened, but the Sefer Torah slipped and fell. It did not fall on the floor, but in the aron ha-kodesh. At that moment I knew that my wife would not survive. It was sealed. Don't ask me how I guessed it. Don't ask me why. I felt it was sealed. Nothing would help. Indeed it was so.[11]

God, the ultimate spiritual essence, was for R. Soloveitchik not merely something in which he believed but a presence which hovered above his shoulders.

> There are times at night when I feel as if someone [the Divine Presence] is standing behind me, bending himself to look over my shoulder to peer into the Talmudic text at the topic I am studying at that moment.[12]

Consider also how the Rav imagines Adam Two, the "man of faith":

> ... On the one hand, he beholds God in every nook and corner of creation, in the flowering of the plant, in the rushing of the tide, and in the movement of his own muscle, as if God were at hand close to and beside man, engaging him in a friendly dialogue. And yet the very moment man turns his face to God, he finds Him remote, unapproachable, enveloped in transcendence and mystery.[13]

The spiritual presence was also something he could turn to and find comfort in, in his darkest moments.

> ...However, I could not pray in the hospital; somehow I could not find God in the whitewashed, long corridors among the interns and the nurses. However, the need for prayer was great; I could

---

[11] Rakeffet Vol. 2, pp. 5-6.

[12] Rakeffet Vol. 2, p. 189.

[13] Joseph B. Soloveitchik, *The Lonely Man of Faith*, with a foreword by David Shatz (New York: Doubleday, 2006), p. 46.

> not live without gratifying this need. The moment I returned home I would rush to my room, fall on my knees and pray fervently. God, in those moments, appeared not as the exalted, majestic King, but rather as a humble, close friend, brother, father: in such moments of black despair, He was not far from me; He was right there in the dark room; I felt His warm hand, כביכול, on my shoulder, I hugged His knees, כביכול. He was with me in the narrow confines of a small room, taking up no space at all.[14]

To the Rav, the ability to experience God's presence is self-evident:

> She [the Jewish people] hears the rustle of footsteps on the hills, in the valleys, among the tender river-shoots, and in the garden paths where the almond and the pomegranate trees blossom. She bestirs herself and goes out to greet him [God]. Suddenly the echo melts away and disappears in the sun-drenched distance... their love cannot be realized, their yearning cannot be fulfilled...[15]

The above is not merely a poetic reading of *Shir ha-Shirim;* it is a manifestation of the Rav's deepest feelings:

> When God is apprehended *in* reality it is an experience; when God is comprehended *through* reality it is just an intellectual performance... The trouble with all rational demonstrations of the existence of God, with which the history of philosophy abounds, consists in their being exactly what they were meant to be by those who formulated them: abstract logical demonstrations divorced from the living primal experiences in which these demonstrations are rooted... Does the loving bride in the embrace of her beloved ask for proof that he is alive and real? Must the prayerful soul clinging in passionate love and ecstasy to her Beloved demonstrate that He exists? So asks Soren Kierkegaard sarcastically when told that Anselm of Canterbury, the father of the very abstract and complex ontological proof, spent many days in prayer and supplication that he be presented with rational evidence of the existence of God.[16]

---

14 Joseph B. Soloveitchik, "Majesty and Humility," *Tradition* 17:2, Spring 1978, pp. 25–37, on p. 33.

15 Rabbi Joseph B. Soloveitchik, *And From There You Shall Seek*, trans. from the Hebrew by Naomi Goldblum (Jersey City: Ktav, 2008) p. 2.

16 *The Lonely Man of Faith* p. 49, fn. 1. See also *And From There You Shall Seek*, p. 133.

> The religious sensibility does not offer decisive proofs, draw inferences, or make deductions. It "senses" and experiences God in its innermost ontological consciousness.[17]

Furthermore, this ontological consciousness far outweighs any and all of the proofs of God's existence:

> The proofs so prevalent in both general and Jewish philosophy attest to the human longing for God. These demonstrations can be divided into five categories. As mentioned in the text, we do not need these demonstrations as proofs, because the experience of God is the basis of certainty.[18]

The Rav's Difficulty in Passing on His Spirituality to His Students

Unfortunately for the Rav, his spirituality was not something he could easily pass on to his students:

> While I have succeeded, to a great or small degree, as a teacher and guide in the area of 'gadlut ha-mochin'... I have not seen much success in my efforts in the experiential area. I was not able to live together with them, to cleave to them and to transfer to them the warmth of my soul. My words, it seems, have not kindled the divine flame in sensitive hearts.[19]

When a mystical spiritual person discusses spirituality with a non-spiritual rationalist person, they often tend to talk **at** each other; they are not communicating **with** each other. They share different worlds and each has no idea what the other is saying. Consider this story within a story as related by the Rav to a student:

> ... With the aim of intensifying the emotional experience, the Rav announced that he was interested in teaching the *Likkutei Torah*,

[17] *And From There You Shall Seek*, p. 13.

[18] *And From There You Shall Seek,* p. 157, n. 3.

[19] "Al Ahavat Ha-Torah," p. 420; translation based on that of Rav Lichtenstein, "The Rav at Jubilee," p. 55. In another version: "I am not a bad teacher. However, I cannot transmit my recollections to them. If I want to transmit my experiences, I have to transmit myself, my own heart. How can I merge my soul and personality with my students? It is very difficult. Yet it is exactly what is lacking on the American scene... This is exactly our greatest need in the United States—to feel and experience God's Presence." Rakeffet Vol. 2, pp. 169, 170.

> authored by the founder of Habad Hasidism... Soon afterwards, the Rav learned that one of his closest students, who was a confirmed mitnaged [opponent of hasidim], was not exactly pleased with the choice of topic. Upon hearing of the student's objections, the Rav recounted the following tale... The *Bet ha-Levi* had a student who had become a devotee of the Hasidic movement... Time and again he invited the *Bet ha-Levi* to join him at a gathering of his hasidim. After many refusals, Rabbi Soloveitchik finally consented to accompany his student... Upon arriving, the two entered a room filled with song and spiritual delight. As the tunes of the hasidim grew louder and more intense, the sun suddenly peeked out of the clouds and shined forth over the *shtiebel*. Then the Rebbe began to speak... Suddenly the snow melted, the grass sprouted forth, the barren trees bloomed again, and the birds joined the hasidim in praising the Almighty.
>
> As the hour was late, the *Bet ha-Levi* glanced at his watch and suddenly told his student in a sharp tone: "Nu, nu, it is time for the Minhah [afternoon] prayers." The spiritual rapture of the gathering was broken, the weather outside once again turned bleak, the trees once again became bare, and the earth returned to a barren wilderness.
>
> After finishing the story, the Rav turned to the student who was not happy about studying a classic Hasidic text and exclaimed: "This story is about you!"[20]

As a postscript to the Rav's efforts mentioned above, to instill spirituality in his students, R. Aharon Lichtenstein quotes the Rav:

> "But," he confided to me subsequently, "it didn't really help."[21]

The Rav's Interpretation of Rambam's Imperative to Know that God Exists

Rambam, the ultimate rationalist, in the beginning of his *Mishneh Torah* rules that one has an obligation "to know that God exists." In paragraph 5 Rambam goes on to provide a proof for God's existence. For the Rav—whose spirituality allows him to experience the presence of God—any type of proof of God's existence is of second-

---

20 Rakeffet Vol. 2, pp. 180, 181.

21 *Memories of a Giant: Eulogies in Memory of Rabbi Dr. Joseph B. Soloveitchik zt"l*, ed. Michael A. Bierman (Jerusalem, New York: Urim, 2003) p. 68.

ary importance. He thus interprets Rambam's first paragraph as stating not that there is an obligation to know God but that knowing Him is self-evident. Only as secondary evidence does Rambam, according to the Rav, then provide a proof for His existence:

> Maimonides's term לידע (*Yesode ha-Torah* I:1) transcends the bounds of the abstract *logos* and passes over into the realm of the boundless intimate and impassioned experience where postulate and deduction, discursive knowledge and intuitive thinking, conception and perception, subject and object, are one. Only in paragraph five, after the aboriginal experience of God had been established by him as a firm reality (in paragraph one), does he introduce the Aristotelian cosmological proof of the unmoved mover.[22]

Analytic and Spiritual Explanations

While it is quite common for the Rav to give different explanations for a halakhah or a religious concept, we sometimes get the feeling that the two explanations he gives are meant to satisfy two aspects of his personality: the analytic and the spiritual. Consider the following two examples:

Reason for the Commandments—*Taamei ha-Mizvot:* In *Halakhic Mind*[23] the Rav explains why he disagrees with Rambam's attempt in *Moreh Nevukhim* to give a rational reason for the *ḥukim*—those commandments that we assume have no known rationale:

> For example, should we post [sic] the question: why did God forbid perjury? the intellectualistic philosopher would promptly reply, "because it is contrary to the norm of truth." Thus, he would explain a religious norm by an ethical precept, making religion the handmaid of ethics. Again, when the same philosopher attempts to sanction dietary laws on hygienic grounds, the specific religious content and meaning are supplanted by a principle of foreign extraction. If the Sabbath is to be seen only against the background of mundane social justice and similar ideals, the intrinsic quality of the Sabbath is transformed into something alien. It serves merely as a means to the realization of a "higher" end.

---

22 *The Lonely Man of Faith,* p. 50.

23 Rabbi Joseph B. Soloveitchik, *The Halakhic Mind: An Essay on Jewish Tradition and Modern Thought* (New York: Free Press, 1986) p. 93.

> Maimonides' efforts foreshadowed failure from the very outset of his "how" approach.

Going beyond why the Rav is unhappy with Rambam's approach to *taamei ha-mitzvot,* the Rav explains that the proper way to understand the *ḥukim* is not to ask "why were they commanded," but rather to construct reasons based on how the observations of the *ḥukim* make us feel; what these mitzvot mean to us subjectively. However, in *Majesty and Humility* the Rav gives a more esoteric/spiritual reason to explain the importance of *ḥukim.*

> Let me ask the following question: Is this Lurianic doctrine of צמצום just a Kabbalistic mystery, without any moral relevance for us; or is it the very foundation of our morality? If God withdrew, and creation is the result of His withdrawal, then guided by the principle of *imitation Dei*, we are called upon to do the same. Jewish ethics, then, requires man, in certain situations, to withdraw. Man must not always be victor. From time to time triumph should turn into defeat.[24]
>
> The Judaic concept of חק represents human surrender and human defeat. Man, an intelligent being, ignores the logos and burdens himself with laws whose rational motif he cannot grasp. He withdraws from the rationalistic position. In a word, withdrawal is required, in all areas of human experience and endeavor; whatever is most significant, whatever attracts man the most, must be given up.[25]

In other words, the purpose of *ḥukim* is to get man to admit that there are commandments of God that he cannot understand. By nevertheless accepting and observing these commandments, man admits defeat and surrenders himself to the will of God.

Theodicy and the Need for Mystery: In trying to explain why bad things happen to good people, the Rav similarly provides both an intellectual answer and a mystical answer. In one attempt to come to grips with "why bad things happen to good people," the Rav is emphatic that we should not try to provide a theodicy; we should not try to understand why God wants good people to suffer:

---

24 *Majesty and Humility*, pp. 35-36.

25 *Majesty and Humility*, p. 37.

> Man should not ask: Why evil? He should rather raise the question: What am I supposed to do if confronted with evil; how should I behave vis-à-vis evil? [26]

In other words, if we try to give a theodicy, a rational answer for why a person suffers, e.g., to cleanse him of sins so that he will reap a greater reward in the next world, we may then be tempted to say, "why should I help him; after all he deserves it, or it is for his own good." We might then be lax in helping such a person. The Rav thus advises us not to look for answers but to concentrate on helping the person who is suffering.

And yet elsewhere the Rav gives a totally different reason we should not offer a theodicy. The reason is similar to the mystical reason he provides for the *ḥukim*:

> The grandeur of religion lies in its *mysterium tremendum*, its magnitude, and its ultimate incomprehensibility... When a minister, rabbi, or priest attempts to solve the ancient question of Iyyov's suffering, through a sermon or lecture, he does not promote religious ends but, on the contrary, does them a disservice. The beauty of religion, with its grandiose vistas, reveals itself to man not in solutions but in problems, not in harmony but in constant conflict of diversified forces and trends.[27]

In both of the above cases (*Taamei ha-Mitzvot/ḥukim* and theodicy), the Rav sees the acceptance of the mysterious Will as the ideal. In *Taamei ha-Mitzvot* by observing the *ḥukim* we admit that we are not able to grasp everything that God commands. Similarly when it comes to the question of why bad things happen to good people, the Rav advises us that the ideal is to acknowledge that God's actions are sometimes unknowable and mysterious and yet to accept His edicts always.

---

26 As paraphrased by David Shatz in *Jewish Thought in Dialogue: Essays on Thinkers, Theologies, and Moral Theories* (Boston: Academic Studies Press, 2009), pp. 275-276.

27 "Sacred and Profane: *Kodesh* and *Chol* in World Perspectives," *The 1995 Book of Jewish Thought*, ed. Moshe Ch. Sosevsky (Orthodox Union and Yeshivat Ohr Yerushalayim, 1995) p. 57.

Attitude toward Ḥasidut, Lubavitch and the Rebbe

The Rav[28] describes how on one Rosh Ha-Shanah his father was about to begin to guide the blowing of the shofar when he noticed that a God-fearing Ḥabad ḥasid began to weep. Turning to the ḥasid, the Rav's father began chastising him: "Do you weep when you take the *lulav*? Why then do you weep when you sound the *shofar*? Are not both the commandments of God?"

The Rav then does something very strange. He spends two pages explaining why the ḥasid's weeping was justified. Toward the end of this explanation (p. 62) the Rav's writing takes an even stranger turn. He gives a biblical rationale for the actions of the Ḥabad ḥasid. He points out that "The Targum... translates the biblical name of Rosh Ha-Shanah... (*Yom Teruah*) (Num. 26:1) as 'a day of moaning' (*Yom Yevavah*). In contrast, the Torah enjoins special rejoicing on the festival of Sukkot: 'And ye shall rejoice before the Lord your God seven days' (Lev. 23:40)."

In short, the Rav makes an impassioned and detailed defense of the position of the Ḥabad ḥasid and portrays his father, the ultimate halakhic man, as being against an almost literal reading of Ḥumash. The Rav's sympathies seem to lie not with his father but with the Ḥabad ḥasid.

The Rav's warm feelings toward his first rebbe, a Ḥabad ḥasid who taught him Tanya; his visit to the Rebbe at the *farbrengen* celebrating his thirtieth anniversary as head of Ḥabad;[29] his sending two students to pick up a copy of every new sefer put out by the Rebbe; the Lubavitcher Rebbe's support for the Rav;[30] and the entire paean to ḥasidut described on pp. 145–163 in Rakeffet Vol. 1 all testify to the Rav's tendencies toward ḥasidut.

---

28 Rabbi Joseph B. Soloveitchik, *Halakhic Man*, translated by Lawrence Kaplan (Philadelphia: JPS, 1983), p. 60.

29 Rakeffet Vol. 2, p. 145.

30 Meiselman, regarding the effort to have the Rav succeed his father as *rosh yeshiva* at RIETS, writes: "The Lubavitcher Rebbe, Grand Rabbi Y. Y. Schneersohn (1880–1950), declared his support for Rabbi Soloveitchik," p. 256.

Conclusion

In *Halakhic Man* the Rav spends many pages denigrating *homo religiosus*—the mystical/spiritual ascetic—who removes himself from the material world to contemplate Heavenly matters.[31] We have shown, however, that on both an intellectual/philosophical level and an emotional/mystical level the Rav was a very spiritual person. We have shown further that the Rav's emotional/mystical spirituality was palpable, immediate and intense—a natural inborn part of his personality—and that his emotional/mystical spirituality affected his life and thought, his attitude toward proofs of God and the question of theodicy, and his relationship with his students.[32] ☙

---

31 See for example *Halakhic Man* pp. 92-94.

32 I would like to thank Rabbi Asher Benzion Buchman and Drs. Leib Litman, David Shatz and Meir Zelcer for reading and commenting on an earlier draft of this work.

Chimeras and the Limits of Casuistry in Jewish Bioethics

By: ALAN JOTKOWITZ

Chimeras,[1] organisms composed of two genetically distinct types of cells, have now been routinely created in the laboratory: Researchers are experimenting using sheep as a source of human liver transplant, and scientists have developed a line of pigs that have pig blood cells, human blood cells and a combination of both. Investigators have also created mice with a human immune system and are currently developing a strain of mice with human brains. Researchers have also claimed to have developed embryos containing a mixture of human and rabbit DNA,[2] and the British government announced in May 2008 that it will allow the use of embryos derived from human-animal hybrids in medical research.[3]

These rapid scientific developments have raised ethical questions which are slowly being addressed (e.g., disposal of embryos, status of chimeras). The most pressing issue, however, is whether the whole enterprise is morally objectionable due to its blurring of the distinction between man and animal, and the problem of the creation of new species. Although much has been written on this issue

---

1 In Greek mythology a chimera is a fire-spouting monster with a lion's head, a goat's body and a serpent's tail.

2 Mott, M. "Animal-human Hybrids Spark Controversy" *National Geographic News*, 2005 <http://news.nationalgeographic.com/news/2005/01/0125_050125_chimeras.html> (accessed June 1, 2008).

3 Donaldson, Kitty and Deen, Mark. "British Lawmakers Allow Hybrid Human-animal Embryos" *Bloomberg*, 2008 <http://www.bloomberg.com/apps/news?pid=20601102&sid=a6GcXDaQOX_E&refer=uk> (accessed June 1, 2008).

Alan Jotkowitz is a Senior Lecturer in Medicine and Director of the Jakobovits Center for Jewish Medical Ethics Faculty of Health Sciences, Ben-Gurion University of the Negev, Beer-Sheva, Israel.

from a liberal, Catholic and Protestant perspective, very little has been written from a Jewish perspective. This is probably due to two main reasons: one practical and the other theoretical:

1. Much of Jewish bioethics was developed from the rich tradition of responsa literature. Generally, Jewish decisors do not start by writing broad philosophical tracts but develop their positions in response to queries from petitioners. The questions thus tend to be practical in nature. For example, how to define death was first debated in the modern era when eminent decisors were asked whether transplantation is allowed from a Jewish perspective. Similarly, attempts to define the beginning of life came to the forefront with the debate over abortion. It is also important to note that Judaism is not monolithic in its responses to these questions. Equally valid differences of opinions on these crucial issues continue to this day. Thus, because of the more theoretical nature of the concerns with chimeras, less attention has been paid to the pressing moral dilemmas that it raises.
2. Methodology in Jewish medical ethics relies heavily on casuistry. There is a rich literature of Jewish ethics dating back two thousand years. This material was incorporated into the Talmud and serves as the source material for much of the modern discussion. Decisions are usually reached by a careful analysis of the relevant cases and an extrapolation to modern dilemmas. Newman has perceptively pointed out that this method works well when there are relevant cases comparable to modern dilemmas.[4] In the Talmudic and post Talmudic literature there are extensive discussions of the permissibility of abortion, and hence there is much material for contemporary decisors to build upon. But regarding, for example, euthanasia and withdrawal of care, there is only limited discussion and thus its relevance is questionable. The Rama rules:

   > It is forbidden to cause the dying to die quickly; such as one who is moribund for a prolonged time and cannot die, it is forbidden to remove the pillow from under him on the assumption that certain bird feathers prevent his death.

---

4 Newman, L. "Woodchoppers and Respirators: The Problem of Interpretation in Contemporary Jewish Ethics" *Modern Judaism*, 1990 10:2:17–42.

> So too one may not move him from his place. Similarly, one cannot place the keys of the synagogue beneath his head [because of the belief that their presence may hasten death] or move him that he may die. But if there is something that delays his death such as a nearby woodchopper making noise or there is salt on his tongue, and these prevent his imminent death, one can remove them, for this does not involve any action at all, but rather the removal of the hindrance to death.

This paragraph is the primary Jewish legal source relating to the care of a dying patient. But, as should be obvious to the reader, it is difficult to apply this ruling to modern palliative care for a number of reasons.

a. How does one define "dying" in an age of mechanical ventilation, left ventricular assist devices and dialysis? Due to the advance of modern medicine the dying can be kept alive for a prolonged period of time. Are such people therefore no longer considered dying?
b. The above medieval ruling deals with practices that, from a modern perspective, are difficult to understand. One is not allowed to move the pillow but one is permitted to remove the salt from his mouth. How do these "treatments" relate to modern medical care such as the use of antibiotics and insulin, not to mention mechanical ventilation or artificial nutrition? Do new therapies prevent the dying process, or are they akin to the feathers of the pillow which one is not allowed to remove? Or perhaps they belong to another category altogether? Brody has already commented on the difficulty in distinguishing, in the contemporary medical setting, between removing impediments to death and hastening it.[5]

Rabbi Joseph B. Soloveitchik, perhaps the most eminent Orthodox Jewish philosopher of the last fifty years, has argued forcefully that a genuine Jewish ethic is rooted in halakhic (legal) pers-

---

5 Brody, Baruch. "A Historical Introduction to Jewish Casuistry on Suicide and Euthanasia" ed. Baruch Brody. *Suicide and Euthanasia: Historical and Contemporary Themes* (Dordrecht: Kluwer Academic Publishers, 1989) pp. 39–75.

pective.[6] In other words, the attitudes and values that emerge from the details and minutiae of Jewish Law are what determine a Jewish ethic. Rabbi Immanuel Jakobovits, the founder of the modern discipline of Jewish medical ethics, expounds on this theme by commenting:

> Secular medical ethics is the effort to turn ethical guidelines or rules of conscience into law, i.e., into legislation. Attempts are made constantly to choose ethical insights and then to gradually distill these into legislative laws adopted by different legislatures; Jewish medical ethics does the reverse. We determine law or legislation, distill it, and then come to the conclusion that it contains certain ethical guidelines. Thus Jewish medical ethics derives from legislation. It does not lead to legislation. We look at legislation as rulings of law that have been given, i.e. halakhah which means law or legislation and then try and extrapolate ethical rules from the legislation. Therefore the Jewish concept of medical ethics is the very reverse of that commonly accepted in civilized countries of the world.[7]

Thus when faced with the issue of chimeras, where there is no relevant precedent literature, the methodology breaks down. In these instances, Bik has suggested that the rich Talmudic folklore literature can serve as a fertile source of insight into the Jewish view of modern moral dilemmas not dealt with directly by traditional legal texts.[8] For example, much has been written from a Jewish perspective on the ethical permissibility of human cloning, but all of these authors are keenly aware of the lack of traditional legal sources on which to base their respective arguments. There is, however, one ancient legend that many authorities feel is relevant to the discussion. The Talmud tells the story of Rava who created a man *ex nihilo* and sent him to his colleague Rav Zeira. Rav Zeira spoke

---

6 Soloveitchik, Joseph. "The Halakhic Mind" (New York: Simon and Schuster, 1986).

7 Jakobovits, I. "The Role of Jewish Medical Ethics in Shaping Legislation" ed. Fred Rosner, *Medicine and Jewish Law* (Northvale, NJ: Jason Aronson, 1990), pp. 1–18. For further discussion see Jotkowitz, A. "On the Methodology of Jewish Medical Ethics" *Tradition*, 2010, 43:38–55.

8 Bik, E. "Ovum Donations: A Rabbinic Conceptual Model of Maternity" *Tradition*, 1993, 28:28–45.

to the man but he did not answer [implying he was mute], thereupon Rav Zeira exclaimed "You are a creation of one of my colleagues; return to your dust."

Bleich, among others, infers from this legend that a human clone endowed with speech would have the full status of a human being and there is nothing inherently wrong with human beings using their scientific and technological know-how to create one.[9] Notwithstanding the fact that one does not normally learn halakha from aggadah, Rabbenu Tam, for example (*Sefer HaYashar* 619), maintains that if there is no halakhic source one may learn from midrash. But there are certainly limitations in applying the above legend to questions relating to modern human cloning. The Talmud relates this story in the context of the potential powers given to select righteous individuals, not ordinary scientists. In addition, there is nothing in the legend that is relevant to the discussion of making a genetic copy of another human being.

Due to the limitations of even folklore literature to help resolve ethical quandaries in Jewish bioethics, Mackler has suggested that Jewish ethical decision making is similar to Reflective Equilibrium (RE),[10] which is now touted as the methodology of choice in modern bioethics. RE is a method of moral reasoning that involves working back and forth between our moral intuitions about particular cases, the principles that we believe govern them and the theoretical considerations that impact on these deliberations. According to Rawls,[11] there is a constant back-and-forth between our intuitive or considered judgments and theoretical ethical principles until a morally accepted conclusion is reached. The role of the competent moral judge who is intelligent, impartial, well informed and empathetic is crucial to this process. Rabbi Soloveitchik maintains that the halakhic "competent moral judge" must have a mastery of all

---

9 Bleich, J.D. "Cloning: Homologous Reproduction and Jewish law" *Tradition*, 1998, 32:47–86.

10 Mackler, A. "Cases and Principles in Jewish Bioethics: Towards a Holistic Model" eds. Elliot N. Dorf and Louis E. Newman. *Contemporary Jewish ethics and morality: A reader.* (Oxford: Oxford University Press, 1995) pp. 177–193.

11 Rawls J. "A Theory of Justice" (Cambridge, Mass: Harvard University Press, 1971).

aspects of Jewish law, accept the sacredness and totality of the halakhah and interpret the halakhah in accordance with traditional methods.[12]

Regarding chimeras, Jewish tradition has reached the limits of casuistry as there are no relevant legal precedents or even folklore that can help us analyze the ethical dilemmas. Jewish ethicists must therefore rely on their intuitive judgments and ethical principles in rendering a decision.

Potential arguments against the production of chimeras include:

1. That it disregards the welfare of animals, particularly the higher primates. According to this view, animals have a right to exist without being tampered with for the benefit of human beings. While Judaism has specific laws forbidding the pointless suffering of animals, nevertheless, there is no prohibition against using animals for the benefit of humankind. Every effort must be made, however, to avoid or lessen the suffering of animals used in medical research.
2. Religions, particularly Catholicism, that give great credence to natural theology would understandably have difficulty with the creation of chimeras, similarly to their objections to artificial reproduction. According to natural law theorists, life is meant to be created through conjugal union of a female and male of the species, and mixing of the species is a violation of natural law. While there are some adherents to natural law among Jewish ethicists, this is not a dominant position and artificial reproduction is usually viewed favorably.
3. There is a tendency among selected bioethicists to attempt to restrict man's involvement in activities that tamper with the natural order. There are limitations to what man should do, notwithstanding his technological abilities or scientific prowess. Leon Kass has argued:

> The notion of man as a creature who is free to create himself... is problematic to say the least... Moreover, the freedom to change one's nature includes the freedom to de-

---

[12] Soloveitchik J. B. "Community, Covenant, and Commitment: Selected Letters and Communications of Rabbi Joseph B. Soloveitchik" ed. Netanel Helfgot (Jersey City: Ktav, 2005).

> stroy (by genetic manipulation or brain modification) one's nature, and thereby the capacity and desire for freedom itself. It is literally a freedom that can end all freedom.[13]

Among religious theorists this activity is viewed as tampering with God's creation. While echoes of this theme can be found in the Rabbinic literature, there are ample sources advocating an active role for man in the ongoing creation of the world. In the thought of Rabbi Soloveitchik there is a religious imperative for man to conquer and master the world. He is charged with being a partner of God in creation to fulfill the requirement of *imitatio Dei.* Man accomplishes this through scientific genius, technological creativity and communal activity. In the words of one authority:

> The Creator has granted man dominion over the world in which he lives and over the living species that are co-inhabitants of that world. Man has been given license to apply his intellect, ingenuity and physical prowess in developing the world in which he has been placed subject only to limitations imposed by the laws of the Torah, including the general admonition not to do harm to others, as well as by the constraints imposed by good sense and considerations of prudence.[9]

4. Notwithstanding the favorable attitude of traditional Judaism towards the creative activity of man, there is a biblical prohibition against interbreeding to create new species. While technically this law would not apply to the generation of chimeras, the rationale for the prohibition might be relevant. According to Ramban, the reason for the prohibition is that God in his wisdom created specific species and man does not have the right to change this Divine plan. This principle would certainly be relevant to the creation of chimeras, branding it an ethically problematic endeavor. Rashi, however, maintains that the reason for the prohibition is unknowable.

---

13 Kass, L. "Toward a More Natural Science" (New York: The Free Press, 1985).

5. It is plausible to suggest that there might be more of a hesitancy to create human chimeras than chimeras of two non-human species. The work of Rabbi Joseph B. Soloveitchik might be relevant to this question. Berger points out[14] that in the 1950s, R. Soloveitchik was preoccupied with the question of What is Man? In contrast to classic Greek philosophy and Christian thought, Judaism, according to R. Soloveitchik, views man as an organic being rooted in the natural world. Man is subject to the same biological processes such as birth, growth and death as are other living organisms. This is manifested in the clear vegetarian tendencies of the early chapters of Genesis and the grudging concession to allow meat eating after the story of the flood. The reason for this favorable attitude towards vegetarianism is due to the notion that all life is on a single continuum. God is the owner of all life and thus meat eating is an attempt by humans to control and consume that which belongs to God. Man is meant to live in harmony with nature. Sin, from this perspective, is regarded as a detachment from nature and leads to exile from and the loss of her blessings. Notwithstanding man's intimate connection to the natural, he nevertheless also exists very much apart from the rest of the world. R. Soloveitchik rejects the idea that man is simply another rung on the evolutionary ladder, and from a biological perspective simply a more complex organism than his competitors. He argues strongly for the distinctiveness of man which is biblically represented by the command to name the animals. This act, based on human cognition, forces man to identify himself as a unique personality. In this context God gave man stewardship over the earth and created a helpmate for Adam to combat his existential loneliness.

   At this point man also acquires the ability for ethical behavior based on the principle of human freedom as distinct from biological drives. Borrowing Buber's terms, R. Soloveitchik views mans' relationship with nature as an I - It relationship born from a common origin and fate, but man faces his fellow

14 Berger, M. "Introduction to Joseph B. Soloveitchik" *The Emergence of Ethical Man* (Jersey City, NJ: Ktav, 2005).

man as an I - Thou relationship based on a common future and destiny. In the words of R. Soloveitchik:

> Man as a natural being suddenly begins to discover in himself not only identity but also incommensurability with nature. Thus he enters into a new phase of viewing nature from a distance and meeting other human beings who act in a similar manner. Man can simultaneously be both unique and universal; the self is both isolated, shut off in its own paradoxical existence, but also flows into the non-self, merging with others. At this phase, the personality begins to assume shape and the ethical norm attains its full meaning. Man experiences the ethical must not as a natural necessity which he cannot flee but as a unique imperative which, if he decides so, he may disobey and ignore. By experiencing such a norm, he contrasts himself with nature and the consciousness of freedom begins to dawn upon him.[15]

This view of man, as part of nature but nonetheless distinct, has relevance to the creation of human-animal chimeras. God created man to be a unique creature trusted with the stewardship of the natural world and endowed with an ethical imperative. These new life forms might blur these divinely ordained distinctions. This theory of the uniqueness of man is also reflected in Jewish law. The principle of *kevod ha-beriyyot,* loosely translated as "respect for mankind," requires one to bury a corpse quickly and avoid displays of public nudity. Loike and Tendler[16] feel this insult to human dignity is a particular problem when dealing with the possibility of a human brain inside an animal body.

In conclusion, where there are no legal precedents to guide Jewish ethical decision making, as in the case of chimeras, decisors have to rely on moral principles derived from non-legal midrashic sources to help guide them. These component moral judges then

---

15 Soloveitchik, Joseph. "The Emergence of Ethical Man" (Jersey City NJ: Ktav, 2005).

16 Loike, John D. and Tendler, Moshe D. "Ethical Dilemmas in Stem Cell Research: Human Animal Chimeras" *Tradition*, 2008, 40:28–49.

weigh their intuitions against these principles in reaching a decision. What do our non-legal midrashic sources suggest? Ramban's rationale behind the biblical prohibition of interbreeding suggests a negative view of creating chimeras composed of DNA from two species. Similarly, the potential insult to the notion of human uniqueness suggests a negative view of human-animal chimeras. Both of these extra-halakhic indicators call for a thoughtful pause in the relentless scientific pursuit of new life forms. ☙

Clarifying Why the Muscovy Duck is Kosher: A Factually Accurate Response

By: ARI Z. ZIVOTOFSKY and ZOHAR AMAR

Introduction

Several years ago we summarized the halachik history of the kashrut of Muscovy duck, a story that had been static for nearly a century with the duck being accepted as kosher in Israel, France and South America and not accepted in the US.[1] Its lack of acceptance in the US and by some *badatzim* in Israel was due to its questionable mesorah [tradition] rather than a definitive statement that it is a non-kosher species. Within the last year a specific kashrut agency and its affiliated rabbinic group in the US issued strongly worded position statements declaring that Muscovy is unquestionably and definitively non-kosher because, they assert, it is a *dores* (predator) and therefore one would be required to kasher a pot in which Muscovy had been cooked. An investigation into the basis of

---

* This article is an expanded and updated version of the material that appeared in Hebrew as: Zohar Amar and Ari Z. Zivotofsky, "L'Taher et haTahor: Od b'Inyan Kashrut HaBerber," *HaMa'ayan*, *Tishrei* 5771 (51:1): 47-55.

1 A. Z. Zivotofsky and Z. Amar, "The Halachic Tale of Three American Birds: Turkey, Prairie Chicken and Muscovy Duck," *Journal of Halacha and Contemporary Society*, 46 (2003), pp. 81-103 and Z. Amar and A. Z. Zivotofsky, "Kashrut HaBerberi v'HaMulourd," *HaMa'ayan* 44:1 (5764): 35-42.

Ari Zivotofsky is a senior lecturer in the Brain Sciences program at Bar Ilan University and writes widely on themes related to Jewish traditions. Many of his articles can be found at <http://halachicadventures.com>.

Zohar Amar is a professor and former chairman of the department of Land of Israel Studies and Archaeology at Bar Ilan University. He is also director of the program in the History of Medicine.

these rulings reveals factual errors and flawed methodology. Because these statements have received wide circulation and attention within worldwide rabbinic circles they call out for a factually accurate response, which we provide herein.

First, however, we will give a brief background. With one exception, all domestic ducks are believed to be derived from the wild mallard (*Anas platyrhynchos*). The common mallard A. p. platyrhynchos is likely the sole progenitor of all domestic forms, with the most prominent breed (in the US and Israel) being the Pekin (*Anas platyrhynchos domestica* or *Anas peking*), introduced to the West from China in the late 19th century. The only exception is the Muscovy duck (*Cairina moschata*), also known as barbary duck. It is native to Mexico, Central America, and most of South America. The male weighs 2-4 kg and the female 1-1.5 kg. It is generally accepted that it was domesticated in pre-Columbian South America, where it was found in the very early 16th century by the Spaniards. There appears to have been an early and rapid diffusion into the Old World.

There is evidence that during this spread of the New World Muscovy to the Old World, Jews in parts of Russia treated it as kosher. Rabbi Aharon HaLevi Goldman wrote (*VaYalkut Yosef* 8(9):92) from Argentina in 1900 that he had refrained from *shechting* this New World bird until Jews from the Charshan and Besarabia areas of Russia emigrated and told him that it was eaten there without any hesitation. The early Jewish settlers in the southern U.S. also began eating Muscovy duck. The Muscovy has a peelable gizzard, an "extra toe," webbed feet, and a wide beak, all indicating that it is kosher. It does not have a standard crop, but has the same pseudo-crop found in other ducks and geese. Thus, these Jewish settlers treated it as kosher. It was its acceptance by the few Jews of New Orleans that led to the first known responsum about the Muscovy.

In 1861 Rabbi Yissachar Dov (Bernard) Illowy, PhD (1814-1871) arrived as the new rabbi in New Orleans and declared that the Muscovy duck could not possibly be treated as a kosher species because there was no valid mesorah for it. In a letter written in beautiful biblical, poetic Hebrew, Rabbi Illoway presented the question of the Muscovy duck to two European rabbis, Chief Rabbi Dr. Nathan Adler of London and Rabbi Shimshon Raphael Hirsch of Germany.[2]

Rabbi Illoway states in his letter that there could be no mesorah on this New World bird, and further that the eggs of the Muscovy have the signs of non-kosher eggs. Both Rabbi Hirsch and Rabbi Adler responded that Rabbi Illoway was correct in prohibiting the Muscovy.

That was not the end of the pre-21st century discussion regarding the Muscovy. Many other authorities dealt with the question and many permitted it, some using arguments similar to those used to permit a nearly universally accepted New World bird, the turkey. For example, the Netziv (*Meishiv Davar* 22), when asked about "geese that are larger and different from the common goose," permitted them and argued that once a bird is widely accepted the burden of proof falls upon those who would prohibit it to bring proof that it is a *dores* and thus prohibited. Barring such a proof the bird should remain permitted. This argument is equally valid for the turkey and the Muscovy duck.

Several decades after Rabbi Illoway, another European newly arrived on US shores seems to have addressed the same issue. Rabbi Leeber Cohen (born ca. 1874), upon taking a job as rabbi in Memphis, TN, discovered that he was receiving many queries about a new kind of "goose" about which he had previously answered several questions in Europe. In 1916 he published *Chiddushei Chaviva*, the first half of which is devoted to the question of the new "goose" which, according to his description, seems to have been the Muscovy duck. He concluded that based on the "egg signs" discussed in the Talmud, the bird under discussion was permitted.

Two South American rabbis also engaged in lengthy discussions about the Muscovy duck. The above-mentioned Rav Aharon Halevi Goldman permitted the Muscovy for several reasons, including a report that the Netziv and Rav Naftali (Hermann) Adler (1839-1911) had permitted it.[3] In response to the fact that some rabbis continued to challenge the kashrut of the Muscovy, Rav Yosef Aha-

2 See "The Controversial Letters and the Casuistic Decisions of the Late Rabbi Bernard Illowy," by his son Henry Illoway, Berlin, 1914, p. 162-165.

3 *Divrei Aharon*, Yerushalayim, 5741, 25-31 (pp. 72-81).

ron Taran, a *shochet* in Argentina, took up the gauntlet of rebuttal. He realized that the naysayers had not personally observed the bird and were under the misimpression that it was a *dores*.

In an effort to strengthen their position, those who sought to ban it sent a pair of birds to Yerushalayim to have Rav Shmuel Salant (1816-1909), the *av beit din*, rule on it. The male bird died en route, but the female successfully completed the lengthy journey. Rav Salant initially refrained from ruling on the matter due to his advanced age and requested that Rav Chaim Berlin, who was then visiting the city, rule on the matter. When Rav Berlin was fed all manner of fiction, such as that the bird breeds with snakes, he refused to rule and returned the question to Rav Salant. Rav Salant immediately ordered his *shochet* to slaughter the bird and on *erev Pesach* a letter was promptly dispatched to Argentina stating that the bird had been eaten following Rav Salant's ruling. Rav Shmuel Salant committed his opinion to writing in a responsum dated 25 Kislev 5668 (1908). Rav Taran publicized that letter, as well as several other permissive rulings from European rabbis, including one from Rav Naftali (Herman) Adler (1839-1911), chief rabbi of the British Empire and son of former Chief Rabbi Nathan Adler (1803-1890) who had prohibited it years earlier.[4]

Almost 50 years later, the chief rabbi of Yerushalayim, Rav Tzvi Pesach Frank (1873-1961) testified (*Har Tzvi YD* 75) that the Muscovy was eaten in his day in Yerushalayim based on the ruling that was issued to an Argentinean emissary who had brought a bird with him. Although he does not specify that it was his teacher Rav Salant who had permitted it, the significance of the fact that it was well known that it was accepted and that it had been permitted after observing a live bird cannot be overemphasized. Subsequently, the Muscovy was commercially raised in Israel for decades and accepted as kosher by the chief rabbinate and various local kashrut organizations. This was not merely theoretical; it was *shechted* by the tens of thousands for decades as "mehadrin" under the Jerusalem and Kiryat Shemona rabbinate. It was and continues to be accepted and slaughtered as kosher in France. In recent years in Israel the primary usage of Muscovy was to cross a male with a pekin female to

4 *Zichron Yosef*, Yerushalayim 5684, 1a-5b.

yield a mulard (also spelled moulard) for the production of *foie gras* (*foie gras de canard*; as opposed to goose liver *foie gras d'oie*). With the banning of gavage by the Knesset in 2006 the raising of Muscovy is Israel has been relegated to petting zoos.

The Reignited Muscovy Controversy

In *Tevet* 5770 the kashrut status of the Muscovy duck again entered the public arena. The debate started anew when a supplier of birds provided Muscovy ducks instead of the usual pekin to kosher slaughter houses in Pennsylvania and Kiryas Yoel, NY. In the former the *shochtim* noticed the difference and refrained from *shechting* while in the latter the birds were slaughtered before anyone noticed that it was a different species of bird.[5] The rabbinic authorities of the respective slaughter houses were consulted and an investigation that turned polemical was launched. In the course of researching the Muscovy, someone found a website[6] of one Muscovy breeder that supposedly describes the violent nature of the Muscovy. The site states:

> Muscovy do have a few characteristics that aren't very pleasant. One of the most distressing aspects of owning Muscovy that I have found is their omnivorous nature. They require more animal protein than mallard-derivative ducks and will eat mice, baby birds, chicks, sometimes even other Muscovy ducklings. The first time I witnessed this was when an adult Muscovy drake of mine snatched up a bantam chick from a broody & her clutch. Before I could rescue it he'd killed it and there was nothing I could do. Since that time, I've had to make sure that I do not allow chicks in the Muscovy pen, and pick up ducklings as soon as they're brought from the nest. In my ex-

---

5 It is interesting that they were slaughtering ducks in *Tevet*. The Rema (*YD* 11:4) cites a custom not to *shecht* geese, understood to include also duck, in the months of *Tevet* and *Shevat* unless the *shochet* eats from its heart. One would have expected the Kiryas Yoel slaughterhouse to observe this custom. There is no question that they *shechted* them, because KJ Poultry put an ad in the Jan 15, 2010 "Der Blatt" requesting the return of the ducks purchased while they investigated the matter.

6 <http://www.muscovyduckcentral.com/thefarm/whymuscovy.html>.

> perience juvenile drakes are the most likely to kill ducklings, although at times some adult drakes & ducks will do it, too. This need for animal protein is why I like to use a pork-based poultry premix in my feed, and I often recommend people feed cat kibble or hard boiled eggs as a treat. Another consideration is the Muscovy's incredible strength and their sharp, talon-like claws. Even ducks can be difficult to manage for a lot of people.

This quote, in a garbled Hebrew translation, formed the basis of the primary ruling prohibiting Muscovy.[7] In introducing it they stated that it was a consensus of "all the experts and farmers," when it is in fact the site and opinion of one breeder. It is based on this that they ruled that the Muscovy is a *dores* and hence definitively prohibited. It is clear from the various proclamations and pamphlets that the authors of these prohibitions never bothered to personally examine the bird or its behavior, or to compare its behavior with that of known kosher birds such as the chicken. It seems that that one Internet site was sufficient evidence upon which to base a halachik ruling. Subsequently a second similar site[8] was found and quoted in later pamphlets. This site reports that: "The Muscovy is the ultimate eater. They are known for eating anything that they can find, including bugs of all sorts, roots, stems, leaves, algae, seeds, small fishes, lizards, snakes, and vermin including mice, voles, and young rats... They love mosquito larva and will eat it from the water, but also enjoy eating flying ones, poisonous spiders, flies, and maggots. Because they are fierce eaters with a wide variety of food choices, they should be kept away from rabbit and guinea pig cages, especially if their [sic] are young there. They have no problems attacking the young for food." Strangely, these reports were enough to designate the Muscovy a *dores* and therefore non-kosher.

---

7 It formed the meat of "the proclamation" issued by *Mishmeret L'Mishmeret* of the *vaad hakashrut* and *beit din tzedek*, Brooklyn, dated 7 *Shvat* 5770.

8 <http://www.associatedcontent.com/article/804777/muscovy_ducks_an_unusual_bird_to_go_pg3.html?cat=58>.

What is a *dores* and who cares?

The Torah gives no identifying features to distinguish kosher from non-kosher birds and simply lists (Lev. 11:13-19 and Deut. 14:11-18) 24 categories of birds that are not kosher (*Chullin* 63b). By implication, all other birds are kosher. Over time the identity of those 24 non-kosher species has been lost and new methods of determining which birds are kosher developed. The Mishnah (*Chullin* 3:6 [59a]) states: "every bird that is 1) *dores* ("a predator") is not kosher. Every bird that has 2) an extra toe, 3) a *zefek* (crop, the biblical *more'eh*, e.g. Lev. 1:16), and 4) a *korkuvan* (gizzard, "pupik" in Yiddish) whose inner lining can be peeled, is kosher." While at first glance the rules in this Mishnah seem rather straightforward, they are anything but. How to understand each of the signs as well as how to use them is mired in controversy. However, what is generally agreed upon is that a bird that is a *dores* is not kosher.[9]

With that principle in hand, it becomes essential to define a "dores." This is no easy task as it is a debate amongst the early medieval commentators. Some of the opinions are:

1) Rashi (*Chullin* 59a) and Rav Ovadiah MiBartenura (*Chullin* 3:6, the first explanation) explain that it refers to a bird that seizes its food with its claws and lifts it off the ground to its mouth. Rashi (*Chullin* 62a, *Niddah* 50b) and Rambam (*Perush HaMishnah, Chullin* 3:6) explain that the bird holds down its prey with its claws and breaks off small pieces to eat. The Ra'avad elaborates and says that a bird is a *dores* if it holds down its food with its feet. The food can be a live or dead animal or even vegetables.
2) Tosafot (*Chullin* 61a, s.v. *hadores*; in the name of Rabbenu Tam) and Rav Ovadiah MiBartenura (*Chullin* 3:6, the second explanation) question Rashi's definition because it would seem to include chickens. Rather, they explain that a *dores* is a bird that ingests its prey while it is still alive.
3) Ramban (*Chullin* 59a; *Vayikra* 11:4) and *Sefer HaChinuch* define *dores* as birds that either claw their prey to death or inject them with venom.
4) Rambam (commentary to *Chullin* 3:6; *Maachalot Asurot* 1:20)

---

9 Rambam, *Maachalot Asurot* 1:16; *Shulchan Aruch, Yore De'a* 82:2.

echoes the Mishnah and provides two indicators that a bird is a *dores*. If, while standing on a rope, it spreads two toes to each side it is *dores* or alternatively if it snags its food in midair and eats in the air it is a *dores*.

Because of the debate, the halacha is that if a bird meets any of those criteria, it is treated as a *dores* and prohibited. Those who want to brand the Muscovy a *dores* do so because they claim it meets criterion 2, that of Rabbenu Tam. They fail to note the reason for Rabenu Tam's explanation; he was looking for a rule that does not apply to chickens. Hence, the Beit Yosef, Meiri, and Rashba all explain that the eating of live worms by chickens is not a problem because worms are not true "animals." This would apply to flies as well. The Rashba limits *dores* to birds that eat other birds alive. Furthermore, to be a *dores*, this must be the nature of the bird, not an aberration. After all, chickens also occasionally eat rats.

The Muscovy Facts

As might have been expected, the release of the 7 *Shevat* (January 22 2010) proclamation precipitated a debate and led to a flood of interest and assorted broadsides, pamphlets, notices, and articles.[10] In the proclamation it stated that the status of the Muscovy as a *dores* is attested to by the straightforward writings of experts and farmers. However, upon examination, it appears that the mountain is based on a molehill—the entire evidence is an anecdote found on one website and not facts investigated and confirmed by experts.

We decided to investigate Muscovy behavior with some experts. The Muscovy behavior as described on that website is not typical Muscovy behavior and is not substantiated by either Israeli or US experts whom we consulted. The sole commercial breeder of ducks in Israel, Naftali Levin of Kfar Baruch, has been raising ducks, in-

---

[10] For a list of these see the *haMa'ayan* article, note 15. A summary article appeared in *Kashrus Magazine,* 149(30:4), *Nissan* 5770/May 2010, pp. 86-91 called "The Great Duck Debate: Is the Muscovy Duck Kosher." Practically everything that was published in this recent controversy relied somewhat on our previous papers; we note that unlike most, *Kashrus Magazine* was honest enough to cite it by name.

cluding Muscovy for almost 30 years. He told us that Muscovy ducks can be quite aggressive but only when they are defending territory or engaged in mating behavior. He was emphatic that as regards eating they are not predatory and do not normally display the behavior described on that website.

Stan Searles, curator of birds and aquatics at the Cleveland (OH) Metroparks Zoo for two decades is an expert on Muscovy ducks and other birds and he stated:

> The question might be posed, 'Does the animal use these methods of hunting [*dores* descriptions] as its normal method to acquire the vast majority of its food? If that is the question, then ducks and chicken are not *dores*. Fowl (ducks, chickens, etc.) were not meant to be *dores*, but they can meet some of the criteria. The main difference is that raptors always act like [a *dores*]; the other birds rarely do so.

In analyzing the various definitions of *dores* he responded:

> 1) Chickens, pekin and Muscovy would only use their feet to catch an animal (although, more often would catch their prey with their mouth). 2) Chickens, pekin and Muscovy may hold their prey down with the foot, but I think the original description probably refers to the bird holding the prey in its talons like a bird of prey. 3) Chickens and ducks do not kill other creatures for food using their claws. Roosters may fight using their feet, but that is not for food acquisition. 4) Chickens, pekins and Muscovy do not catch prey airborne.

He concluded by observing that:

> Fowl (ducks, chickens, etc.) were not meant to be *dores*, but they can meet some of the criteria; the main difference is that raptors always act like that, the other birds rarely do so.

All of the above was in email exchanges. In a phone conversation he reiterated that his generalizations about duck apply to Muscovy and that there is no way that he would categorize Muscovy as a *dores*. Such testimony of people with long-term experience regarding thousands of Muscovy indeed carries halachik weight. Rabbi

Aryeh Lebush Bolchiver,[11] author of *Shem Aryeh*, when discussing turkey, reaches the startling conclusion that when the Rama requires a tradition, it is only where there is uncertainty regarding the bird's *dores* status. He posits that if a bird is no longer "new" but has been observed for a long period of time, i.e., 12 months, and observed to be non-*dores* it is appropriate to say with certainty that it is not a *dores*. These experts have observed many Muscovy for many years and attest to its non-*dores* status.

All of this begs the question—what about the author of the Internet site that is the source of information for the rabbis who prohibited the bird? She was contacted directly and responded[12] that "I have seen Muscovy kill young birds, ducklings, chicks, and wild birds but usually by the time they can eat them they are dead and have been basically pulled apart. I have not seen a Muscovy eat any of these whole." She does think that Muscovy are violent, but her description is not of a *dores*. Chickens also eat small dead vermin, but this does not qualify them as *dores*.

The proclamations also describe the Muscovy as eating the flesh of pig and having nails like a predator. These descriptions are inaccurate and irrelevant and are clearly designed to bias the reader into thinking that these are very non-kosher birds. Chickens will also eat meat of almost any animal and I have personally fed chicken to chickens. The claws of a Muscovy are indeed larger than those of other ducks but they are not talons and are not used for hunting prey and nowhere in halacha is it suggested that larger nails categorize a bird as a *dores*. But stooping to innuendos will not deter those who are intent on prohibiting this bird which had been eaten by hundreds of thousands of Israeli Jews for a century.

Rather than rely on inexact, nonscientific Internet descriptions we decided to investigate and observe Muscovy duck behavior with our own eyes. We arranged to observe range Muscovy and to see their behavior when offered one-day-old chicks. Their reaction was quite interesting. All of the Muscovy, en masse, rapidly approached the tiny chicks and appeared to be pecking at them. We were sure that they were attacking and killing them, and verbally stated that

---

11 *Arugot Habosem* (Russia, 1870) *kuntras ha'tshuvot* in the back, *siman* 16.

12 Personal email Feb 12 2010.

and expressed surprise at what we were seeing. In reality, first impressions can be misleading, and that is not at all what was taking place. The Muscovy were merely expressing curiosity and were, in an animated manner, checking out these newcomers. The chicks were not injured and within several minutes the Muscovy lost interest in the chicks and moved on to other activities.[13]

Within the US haredei community there was some dissent from the position expressed in the proclamation described above, and an anonymous cynical proclamation was issued strongly disagreeing with its position. They pointed out that there are Internet sites[14] that describe the chicken as a merciless eater that will devour live mice, and they therefore sarcastically called on all religious Jews to refrain from chicken and to realize that anyone who has ever eaten chicken has eaten non kosher-meat. This cynical broadside was the exception; for the most part the vast majority of major kashrut organizations in the US simply did not get involved. While they maintained their position of not certifying Muscovy, they did not form a chorus in declaring the Muscovy a *dores* and thereby an absolute non-kosher species. It may be that they treat it as non-kosher for lack of a mesorah, or that they actually deem it kosher but maintain the long-standing US custom and therefore do not certify it. But it appears that the OU and the other major agencies realized that an illegitimate halachik process was taking place, and stayed out of the fray.

It would seem much more significant that the information from the Internet sites is what our traditional sources reveal about the violent nature of chickens. Rav Yehuda ben Bava testified (*Eduyyot* 6:1) regarding a chicken that was stoned to death in Yerushalayim on account of it having killed a person. Despite this irrefutable evi-

---

13 The observations and experiment were conducted on 21 *Iyar* 5770 at Kfar Baruch. A short video of the experiment can be seen at: <http://www.youtube.com/watch?v=BjXtACakIi4>.

14 See for example: <http://en.wikipedia.org/wiki/Debeaking>; <http://www.cnr.uidaho.edu/range556/Appl_BEHAVE/projects/Chicken_Cannibalism.html>; <http://badapple.wordpress.com/2009/03/27/pecked-to-death-by-the-cannibal-chickens/>.

dence that a chicken is capable of much more than killing a rat—it can kill a human being—there is no commentary on that Mishnah that suggests that because of that behavior a chicken should therefore be treated as non-kosher. So too the (factually inaccurate) charges raised by those who seek to prohibit the Muscovy are based on its violent nature. Those accusations have no halachik bearing.

Interestingly, in the initial Muscovy controversy over a hundred years ago unsubstantiated facts that are incorrect were bandied about as well. Clearly, these who wrote the statements never saw the object upon which they were commenting and ruling. Rav Illoway wrote that the eggs of the Muscovy are round (as opposed to the shape of kosher eggs such as chicken eggs) and are greenish. There seems to be no question that Rav Illoway saw the Muscovy, but it is hard to reconcile his description of the eggs with a firsthand observation. The eggs of the Muscovy duck are shaped like every other kosher egg, rounder at one end and pointed at the other, and are uniformly white. While it can be assumed that Rav Illoway did not see the eggs, the same cannot be said of the anonymous author of the 2010 pamphlet *l'Taher Temaim,* where on page 96 a picture of the eggs is shown. Where that picture comes from is not clear, but it misrepresents the facts that we and our experts have seen of countless Muscovy eggs all looking like kosher eggs. And indeed if that picture is looked at carefully it too can be seen to be kosher. The documents from that debate talk about a bird that swallows chicks whole and mates with snakes. These are myths that anyone who saw the bird would know to reject.

Just like then, so too today, those who prohibit never bothered to verify the facts or even observe the bird. They simply based their position on a selection of quotes from those who prohibited last time and on a few Internet sites. They ignored all of Rav Taran's counterarguments that he presented to show it is not a *dores*. For example, there were those who argued that it grabs its food in the air and he thus did many experiments to show it is factually not true.[15] Rav Taran did experiments and verified facts; they, however, blustered and prohibited. In order to bolster their positions, when-

[15] Videos can be found on the Internet that show Muscovy catching in its beak small bits of food, but that is clearly not its natural behavior pattern.

ever one of those who permitted is mentioned it is to attack him. For example, they argue that Rav Naftali Adler, who permitted, was not as great as his father, Rav Natan Adler, who prohibited, so he must be ignored. The height of irony is when they argue that the Netziv and the Divrei Makiel, who permitted, were not familiar with the characteristics of the bird and therefore did not know that it is a *dores*. They ignore or question the ruling of Rav Shmuel Salant who permitted the Muscovy.

The proclamation states that in the original debate all rabbis prohibited it except for a few who were not informed that it is a *dores*. A more factually accurate statement would be that many of those who examined it and were given accurate facts permitted it, while those who were told that it breeds with snakes, eats live birds, and has round eggs prohibited it, as anyone who is told such facts would and should do. Since those "facts" have nothing to do with the Muscovy, a ruling based on those facts is inapplicable to the Muscovy. There were others who did prohibit it even recognizing that it was not a *dores*, for the simple fact that it lacked a valid mesorah. That was Rav Illoway's primary concern as well as the next occurrence of "Muscovy duck" in US literature in 1872, well before the major controversy.[16]

One of the stars of these anonymous pamphlets and proclamations is Rav Chaim Soloveitchik who prohibited the bird. What they fail to note is that he prohibited it after hearing that it is a classic *dores* who eats other birds and swallows them live and grabs and eats prey in the air before it ever reaches the ground. Given these facts, who would not prohibit? Such a bird of course may not be eaten. But that says nothing about the Muscovy, which does not have those characteristics. Yet Rav Chaim Soloveitchik's position is cited without providing the background. Furthermore, this position of Rav Chaim Soloveitchik is found quoted in a responsum attributed to Rav Chaim Berlin. It seems unusual that Rav Chaim Berlin would pen this in opposition to his father the Netziv and after he himself supposedly refused to rule on the issue while in Jerusalem. It is also strange that in Jerusalem this position was unknown and

16 See *Hatsofe B'erez Hachadasha* (Hebrew), NY, vol. 7, 2 *Tammuz* 5633 (June 27, 1873) p. 56.

Rav Tzvi Pesach Frank does not cite it. This has led some to question the authenticity of this responsum attributed to Rav Berlin.

Is Muscovy duck kosher?

We have previously discussed this in our earlier papers and it is not the main point of this article. But we cannot simply ignore that question. The Mishnah gives signs for how to determine which birds are kosher. For many centuries now we do not rely on those signs and eat only those birds for which a mesorah (tradition) exists. This is how both the *mechaber* (*YD* 82:2) and the Rema (*YD* 82:3) rule. The only exception is that the *mechaber* is lenient if the bird passes the "goose comparison," in that if it has a wide beak and webbed feet there is no need to be concerned that it is a *dores* and the signs of the Mishnah may be relied upon. The Rema says not to rely even on that and always require a mesorah. The Muscovy obviously passes the "goose comparison" and is thus clearly not a *dores*. The Rema still requires a mesorah to permit it, but it is absurd to label it a *dores* and a definitive *min tamei* (non-kosher species).

So is there a mesorah for the Muscovy? That depends on how widely one is willing to expand the mesorah of the similar pekin duck. They are clearly two different species and can readily be told apart. Yet the *shochtim* in Kiryas Yoel who slaughter ducks by the thousands did not notice the difference! They *shechted* the birds brought to them without any question. Clearly there is a great similarly between the birds or those *shochtim* are highly incompetent. We would rather believe the former option. Rav Eliyahu Klatzkin (1852-1932) from Lublin permitted a duck that he was asked about in 1911 (it may have been the Muscovy duck) because, he stated, it does not require its own mesorah due to its similarity to known kosher ducks (*Dvar Halacha*, 1921, #53, pp. 37a-b).

An additional reason the Muscovy duck is kosher is the "hybridization principle." The Talmud (*Bechorot* 7a) states that kosher species cannot mate with non-kosher species and therefore the fact that an unknown species can interbreed with a known kosher species confirms the kosher status of the unknown species. In the Talmud it is not explicitly stated if this principle applies only to animals or to birds as well. The Avnei Nezer (*Yoreh De`ah* 1:75:19-21) and many others explicitly apply this rule to birds as well as mammals. The pekin and Muscovy freely and happily crossbreed with each other without the need for human intervention. Most of the time, although not always, the cross is infertile and it has recently been suggested that this is a reason not to apply the principle in this case. Fertility of the offspring does not appear to be a requirement, merely the ability to produce live offspring. The free and frequent hybridization would seem to be icing on the cake that makes it an unquestionable proof of kashrut in this instance.

Finally, the logic of the Netziv regarding turkey should apply here as well. As Rav Amitai Ben David, author of *Sichat Chullin*, wrote (19 *Shvat* 5761) in letter to Rav Naftali Weinberger that is appended to R. Weinberger's book *Shaleach Tishalach* (5761, Jerusalem, p. 180), the Muscovy had been given a de facto okay by the Netziv and the Avnei Nezer because it was already being eaten by masses of Jews. In addition he states that he personally received a mesorah on the Muscovy from his teacher who taught him *shechita*, the well-known Rav Chochaima.

It is often difficult to know about which specific bird 19th century responsa are dealing. In the case of the Muscovy it may be immaterial. Based on the three points above: 1) similarity to the Muscovy as so poignantly demonstrated by the Kiryas Yoel *shochtim*, 2) the hybridization principle, and 3) the fact that Jews by the millions have been eating it, and of course the facts that it is not a *dorcs*, passes the goose comparison, and has kosher-type eggs, the Muscovy should certainly be treated as kosher.

Conclusion

Rav Tzvi Pesach Frank, a member of the court headed by Rav Shmuel Salant and later the long-time and well-respected chief rabbi of Jerusalem penned a response on the Muscovy years after the heated controversy. He sought to limit the eating of this New World bird, and he is thus sometimes quoted by those who seek to ban it. What they fail to note, and it is important to stress this, is that Rav Frank did not prohibit the bird, and attested to the fact that it was permitted and eaten in Jerusalem. That evidence alone should be sufficient to quell the voices that state that it was never really permitted. It is clear that for decades it was treated as a permitted bird in Jerusalem and Rav Frank did not contradict that fact or seek to reverse it. In a fair review of the history, Rav Shalom Landa[17] concludes that most of the significant rabbinic authorities indeed permitted the Muscovy and ruled that it may be eaten without question.

There is nothing new under the sun, and an analysis of the recent debate reveals that practically all of the arguments raised to prohibit it 100 years ago were raised again and that, "surprisingly" all of the century-old responses were ignored. Those seeking to prohibit the bird mobilized all tactics including utilized rumors, hearsay, suppression of facts, and simple lies.[18] There is no question that the discussion of the kashrut of the Muscovy was not carried out as a legitimate halchik discussion, the facts were not verified or examined in depth and thus the process and the conclusion are invalid from the start. This is a reckless ruling that should never have seen the light of day and through it the honorable names of Torah scholars of earlier generations and the masses who ate the bird relying on the earlier ruling were besmirched. It is legitimate and understandable if one personally wants to refrain from eating Muscovy due to a questionable mesorah, the issue of force-feeding ducks, or any of a host of other reasons. But one may not, in the name of "chumra" or "frumkeit," misrepresent the truth, distort the Torah, and make the pure impure. ☙

---

17 *Ohr Yisrael*, 59 (*Nissan* 5770) 19-30.

18 We are herein reporting facts and not attempting to assign motives. But one cannot avoid noticing that the events took place in a Satmar slaughterhouse and shortly thereafter an anonymous 5 part(!) series strongly prohibiting the Muscovy appeared in the weekly *Chomas Hadas* newsletter of the other Satmar faction.

Methodologies Used by Poskim to Determine the Orientation of the Synagogue

By: ARYEH SHORE

The *poskim* of the 16th to 19th centuries made use of the available scientific literature to determine the halachah. In the field of animal science this included performing experiments, using books of natural history and surveys.[1] The present paper discusses the methodology and sources used by the *poskim* for determining the direction of prayer towards Yerushalayim. Three methods are considered: camera obscura, the "great circle" and the compass.

The halachic discussion of why the synagogues in northern Europe faced east, in spite of the decisions of the *Lavush, Taz* and *Mishnah Berurah*[2] to pray to the southeast, have been summarized

1 Aryeh Shore. "The role of animal dissections in determining Jewish Law" BDD *(Bekal DarKekha Da'ehu*, Bar Ilan Univ. 1997 4:73-80; "Identification of the first-born calf" *Halichot Sadeh* 1997, 104: 51-55; "The use of scientific sources by rabbinical authorities to determine the nature of animal species" *Korot* (Heb. Univ.) 12 (1996-1997): 7-15; Laurence S. Shore. "Efforts by Jewish communities to prevent zoonoses" *Torah U'Maddah* 8 (1998-1999): 277–282. For example, in the 1700s there was a debate regarding the permissibility of a chicken with no visible heart. After R' Tzvi Ashkenazi, the *Chacham Tzvi*, appealed to experiments done by Galen to prove his point, R' Yonatan Eybeshutz consulted with the Halle Academy of Medicine (see *Chacham Tzvi* 74-78; *Kreiti Upleiti* 40:4).

2 *Lavush, Perek Techelet, Hilchot Tefillah OH* 94; *Mishneh Brurah OH* 94.

Aryeh (Laurence) Shore was born in Philadelphia, received his B.A. from Y.U. ('65) and his Ph.D. from Hahnemann Medical School ('72). Since making *aliyah* in 1977, he has been a Researcher at the Kimron Veterinary Institute, Bet Dagan, Israel. He has published over 90 scientific articles and recently co-edited a book entitled: *Hormones and Pharmaceuticals Generated by Concentrated Animal Feeding Operations: Transport in Water and Soil* (Springer).

by *Aruch HaShulchan.*[3] Briefly, the *Aruch HaShulchan* is apologetic as to why the European synagogues do not face southeast but states that the intent of Talmudic texts is that just the general direction of Eretz Yisrael is required.

The Jews of France and Germany had no problem in facing east as the general direction of Yerushalaim (*Tur* OH 94). As the Jews moved to more northern climes, the inconsistency of praying toward the east when Yerushalayim is in the southeast became more of a concern, especially since the Christian churches were oriented to the sunrise and deliberately orienting the synagogue to the east appeared to violate the injunction in the *Gemara* not to pray to the east as the idol worshippers do.

The first mention of the problem is by Rabbi Yeshayah ben Eliyah di Trani (d. *c.* 1280) brought in the *Shiltei Giborim* (*Hagaot Alfasi HaChadashim*).[4]

"This is what the ancients meant that one does not pray in the synagogues directly against the sunrise. In our synagogues, we pray toward the middle of the day." It would seem that the middle of the day would be south, as in all places north of Israel in Europe and Asia, the sun is in the south at noon. However, the *Mishnah Berurah* says that this isn't meant to be literal but just that one should face southeast. Alternatively, the middle of the day is referring to determining east by using the position of the sun at midday to determine true north and south and then turning to the east.[5]

Camera Obscura

A camera obscura or pinhole camera is a room or box where the sun shining through a small window or hole can be used to determine direction and the meridian. The most influential description of using a camera obscura is that of Mordechai Yaffe in *Lavush* OH 94 published in 1590 as his description was brought by the *Taz* and the *Divrei Chamadot*. However, the drawings from the early edi-

3 *Orach Chaim* 94; *Berakhot* 30a; *Bava Batra* 25b; Y. *Berachot* 8.

4 *Berachot* 23b (*Talmud Bavli*, Lemberg 1860).

5 Yom-Tov Lipmann ben Nathan ha-Levi Heller, *Divrei Chamadot* on the Rosh 19, *siman* 66; 1628.

tions of the *Lavush* (*Fig. 1* א, ב, ג), did not appear in later additions. The *Taz* does have a drawing (*Fig. 2*) in early editions, but in modern editions it is an incomprehensible composition of lines (*Fig. 3*).

While some thought the correction of the Lavush was an outstanding contribution to rational thought in the halachah ("Schon R. Mordechai Jafe hat dies ges suhlt und eine sudwestliche Richtung der Synagogen empsohlen."),[6] the drawings of the *Lavush* apparently were confusing to some, and according to a question asked of R. Eliyahu bar Shmuel from Lublin[7] this resulted in a synagogue with totally incorrect orientation, depicted in *Fig. 4*. R. Eliyahu states that the coordinates for Yerushalayim given in *Chukat HaShamayin*, p. 137, by R. Y. from Candia (Crete) (*Sefer Elim* by Joseph Solomon Delmedigo; 1629) calculated using spherical geometry[8] would be the best method to determine direction.

The question therefore arises as to why the *Lavush* adapted such a complicated system to determine the correct direction. It is possible that he was under the influence of a book of astronomy published a hundred years before in which Levi ben Gershon (1288–1344) described the meridian he made in a synagogue in Spain which he used to determine the position of the planets and the sun.[9] This work became the basis of the *meridiana* that were used in cathedrals in the 14th and 15th centuries. Levi ben Gershon describes a room in which the distance from the east to west walls is 40 *amot*. Observations are made using a window in the east wall so that the sun's ray shortly after sunrise can be used to determine the true east-west line. (Levi was well aware that a window was too large for a good camera obscura and made corrections for it in his treatise.) However, although the description would indicate that this was R. Jaffe's source, the Hebrew is not a direct quotation.

---

6 Zipser, Maier. "Die Rucksicht auf die Ostseite bei Synagogenbauten," *Ben Chananja*, 1860; 3:9-18.

7 Eliyahu bar Shmuel, *Yad Eliyahu*, Amsterdam, 1710, Responsa 1, p. 1–4.

8 The method of calculation of the actual distance to Yerushalayim, e.g., from Baltic Straits of "Zunti" between Riga and Norway, is given on p. 121.

9 Goldstein, Baruch R. "The Physical Astronomy of Levi ben Gerson," *Perspectives on Science*, 1997, 5: 1–30; "*The Astronomy of Levi ben Gerson (1288–1344)*." New York: Springer-Verlag, 1985. Chap. 14.

The Great Circle

In spherical geometry there are two potentially correct ways to calculate the distance between two points.[10] One can use a circle (the great circle) from the place of origin to the target. Alternatively, one can project the sphere surfacc onto a flat plane (Mercator map, rhumb line), which was more convenient for navigation by boat or carriage. The differences in length are insignificant for the distance between Europe and Israel. However, the direction and distances are quite different in North America since in distances over 1000 km, the curvature of the earth is apparent. In North America the shortest distance is counterintuitive. It is shorter to travel to the northeast, then through France and down to Israel.

The earliest reference to the problem of the great circle as opposed to the system of the *Lavush* was R. Y. Segal[11] in *Netzach Yisrael* (p. 52a on *Brachot* 30a, 1741). "The *Lavush* erred as did those who followed him" as it did not follow the rules of spherical geometry. "I wish to explain how even though a city can be North of Yerushalayim, a person living there should orientate himself slightly to the North, which is the opposite of the opinion of the Lavush." R. Yisrael Segal seems to be the first to illustrate the problem (*Fig. 5*). Although he based his calculations and method on the *Yesod HaOlam* (1320) by Isaac Israeli of Toledo and *Sefer Elim* by Joseph Solomon Delmedigo (1629) ("and at the end of the Elim you will find all the tables needed as well as in the books I have written"), the actual problem of prayer direction to Yerushalayim is not discussed in the *Sefer Elim*. The *Yesod HaOlam* and *Sefer Elim* based themselves on the works of Euclid and Ptolemy as well as in the

---

10 Levin, Daniel Z. "Which way is Jerusalem? Which way is Mecca? The direction-facing problem in religion and geography" *The Journal of Geography* 2002, 101:27-37.

11 Segal, Yisrael. *Netzach Yisrael, Kuntras Acharon*, 1741; Frankfort-am-Oder; Freudenthal, Gad. "Hebrew Medieval Science in Zamosc ca. 1730. The Early Years of Rabbi Israel ben Moses Halevy of Zamosc," in R. Fontaine, A. Schatz, I.E. Zwiep (eds.), *Sepharad in Ashkenaz*. Medieval Learning and Eighteenth-Century Enlightened Jewish Discourse (Amsterdam, Edita 2004), p. 25–68.

case of Joseph Solomon Delmedigo, actually studying under Galileo Galilei.[12]

The problem of the great circle was also addressed in the early part of the 19th century by R. Schneier Zalman from Liadi (1745–1812). Basing himself on the *Netzach Yisrael*, R. Zalman states that the further west and north one was to the meridian of Yerushalayim, the direction of prayer could move from slightly southeast to slightly northeast.[13] "It is easy to calculate this direction using spherical geometry (במשולש כדורי)."

The Compass

Using a compass to determine the direction of Yerushalayim can be problematical because of magnetic declination, which was mentioned by an early 20th century Rav, Y.H. Singer.[14] He pointed out that in Russia the magnetic north as shown by the compass is not the true north. (It would give an error of about 30 degrees to the west in Moscow in 1900.)[15] This is of interest, as in the last decade there have appeared advertisements for a kosher compass. This

---

12 Isaac Israeli ben Joseph (*fl.* 1310), *Yesod HaOlam*, Berlin, 1777; Delmedigo, Joseph S. (1591–1655) *Sefer Elim*, Amsterdam 1629.

13 *Shulchan Aruch* with commentary by Schneier Zalman (*Shulchan Aruch Harav*), *OH* 94, manuscript was completed by 1810. Although the NW orientation was never adopted by North American Jews, there is a recently built synagogue in Lakewood with a deliberately NW orientation. The Lakewood entry to Zmanim.com <http://www.myzmanim.com/day.aspx?vars=US08701> contains this chart:

Davening Direction In Lakewood

Following a *Rhumb Line* **[?]** Maintains a constant compass direction HaRav Yisroel Belsky and others	Bearing **95° ≈ East**
Following a *Great Circle* **[?]** A straight path of shortest distance HaRav Yechiel A. Zilber and others	Bearing **54°≈North-East**

(**Key:** Bearing 0° = True-North, 90° = East, 180° = South and 270° = West)

14 Singer, Yehoshua H., *Zichron B'Sefer*, Vilna, 1900 p. 24 on *Berachot* 30.

15 <http://www.ngdc.noaa.gov/geomagmodels/Declination.jsp>.

compass purports to show the direction of prayer to Yerushalayim anywhere in the world. It comes with directions for how to set the compass for each region. In the absence of seeing claimed pending patent, one can assume that it is a simple compass with a bezel that points 90 degrees from compass needle, similar to expensive compasses that correct for declination. However it is difficult to be sure of a device that claims to "appear to defy the laws of nature."[16] On the site itself, it is recommended by Rav Moshe Halberstam, Rav Moshe Sternbuch, Rav Yosef Lieberman and Rav Yaakov Perlow. Furthermore, in a web communication, "Moshe" (the inventor of the device)[17] states that anyone who claims that the great circle has halachic validity is going against all the great *gedolim* who endorsed his product. This seem disingenuous, as two *acharonim* specifically state that the great circle is the most correct method and explicitly state that the method of the Lavush or rhumb line will give you the wrong direction. In any event, no technical literature is brought in support of the device, so it is not known what sources the inventor used to verify its accuracy.

Summary

The literature used by *poskim* in the 15th to the 19th centuries to determine the halachah in astronomy differs from that used by the *poskim* determining zoological or anatomical decisions. In the case of astronomical determinations, the actual observations were done by the Rabbis trained in the discipline, and in the case of Levi ben Gershon, were important contributions to general scientific literature as well. On the other hand, the *poskim* determining the biological data were well educated but not trained in natural sciences.

---

16 <http://www.koshercompass.com/catalog/>, accessed Feb 2, 2010.

17 <http://observantastronomer.blogspot.com/2005/11/incredible-jerusalem-compass.html>, accessed Feb 2 2010; <http://parsha.blogspot.com/2005/12/further-info-on-jerusalem-compass.html>, accessed Feb 3 2010.

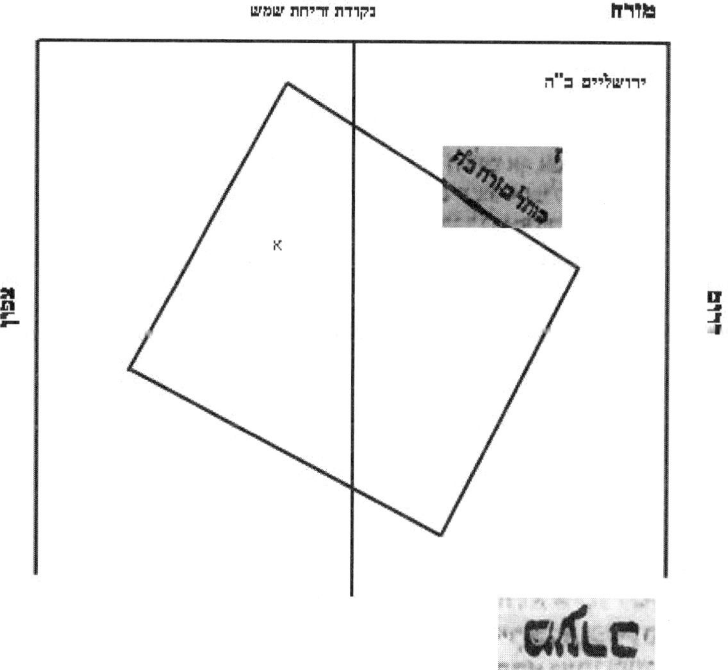

Fig. 1. א "According to the image of a sphere (תמונת צורת כדור), if we position ourselves on the first day of spring or first day of autumn, or close to it within six or seven days, as the sun shines in the morning through the window in the middle of the east wall of the synagogue, and the ray is directed to the western wall; if one moves the spot in the middle of the western wall, an hour or half hour after the sunrise (15 or 30 degrees) to the south (that is 15/360 degrees to the south of the middle of the wall), one reaches the position which is exactly opposite the window of the east, like this:" (All drawings are tracings made by the author.)

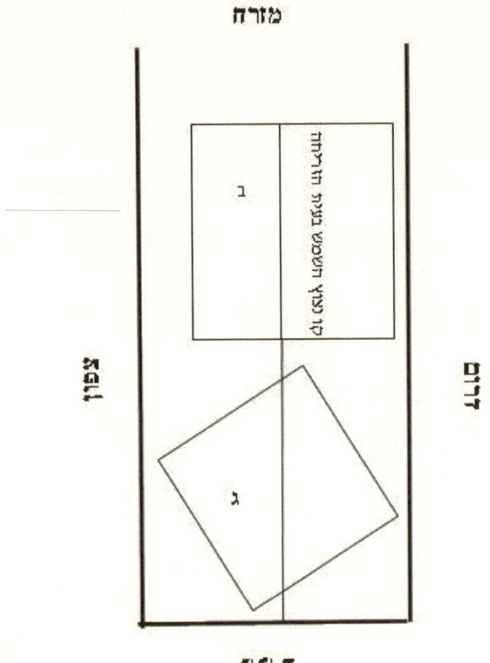

Fig. 1 ב. "If we position ourselves on the above mentioned days so that the ray of the rising sun through the eastern window directly strikes the western wall like this. Then it would strike the wall exactly due east and this indeed is the way of Magi... and not in the direction of Yerushalayim." (Magi is used for pagan sun worshippers. It is not clear if the author was aware that the Amogushi [Talmudic form of the word] or Zoroastrians placed a strong emphasis on sun worship.)

Fig. 1 ג. "If we position ourselves that the ray of the sunrise on the above-mentioned days and move it towards the north, this would not be in the way of the Magi... but would not be in the direction of Yerushalayim... and this is the picture ג that I have drawn."

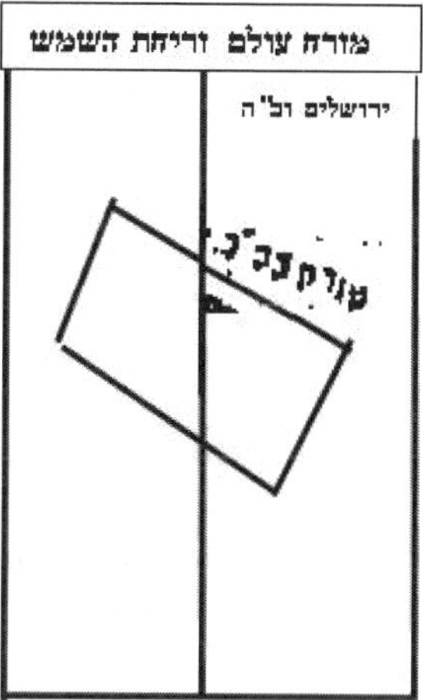

Fig. 2. The rendition of the *Lavush*'s drawings as it appears in an early edition of the *Shulchan Aruch* (*Magini Eretz,* Dyhernfurth, 1692).

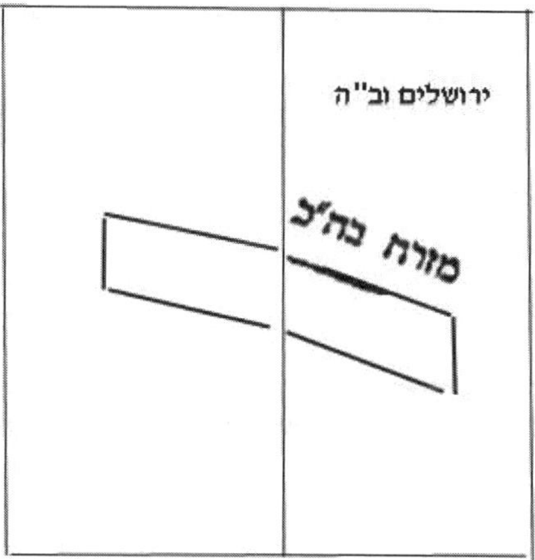

Fig. 3. The rendition of the *Lavush's* drawings as it appears in modern editions of the *Shulchan Aruch* (*El HaMekorot*, Yerushalayim, 1955).

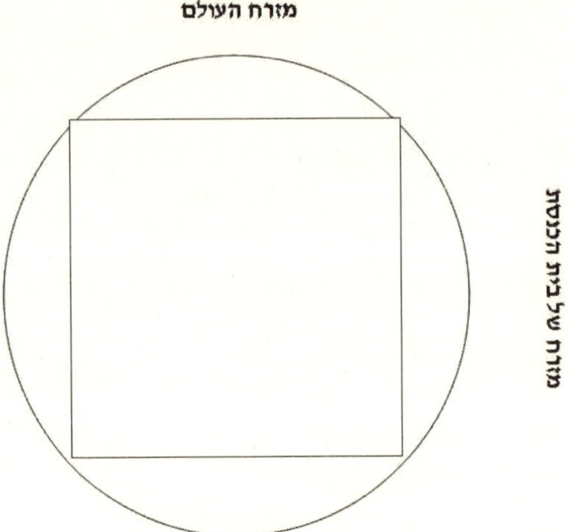

Fig. 4. Orientation of the synagogue that faced due South instead of Southeast discussed by R. Eliyah bar Shmuel. R. Eliyahu thought this could be the result of a misunderstanding of the Lavush.

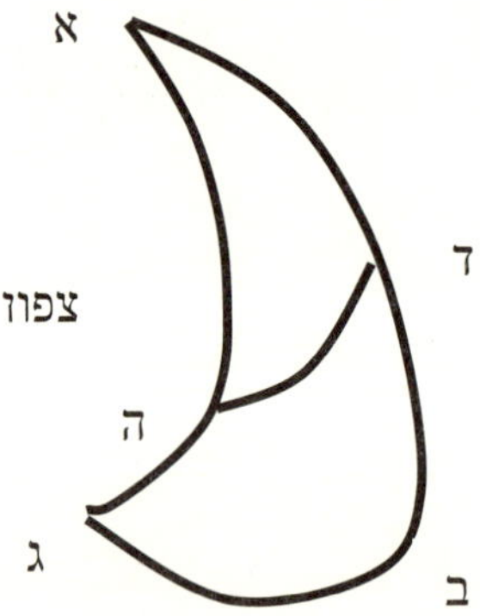

Fig. 5. "The second illustration is about the city of Bayonne, France whose distance in latitude from the equator is 42 degrees and the distance from prime meridian is 17 degrees west (French meridian), and I want to explain how in such a situation one has to face Northeast. This is the illustration: if we take ג as the city in France, and ב-ג is its latitude and א-ד-ב its (Yerushalayim) "quarter circle" from the equator and א-ה-ג is the quarter circle for the city of Bayonne and ד-ה is the arc from "half day" (due east) from Yerushalayim." *Netzach Yisrael, Kuntras Acharon,* p. 52b.

Glossary of Terms

Declination: The difference between the north geographic pole and the north magnetic pole is called *magnetic declination* or usually just declination. Depending on where you are on the earth, the angle of declination will be different—from some locations, the geographic and magnetic poles are aligned so declination is minimal, but from other spots, the angle between the two poles is fairly large. <http://www.compassdude.com/compass-declination.shtml>, accessed Nov. 3, 2010.

Degrees: A circle contains 360 degrees. Fifteen degrees would be about 4% of a circle and 30° would be about 8% of a circle.

Great Circle Route: By the great circle route, the shortest distance between New York and Mecca is 6,400 miles; the rhumb line, the line of constant direction, is 6,800 miles long.

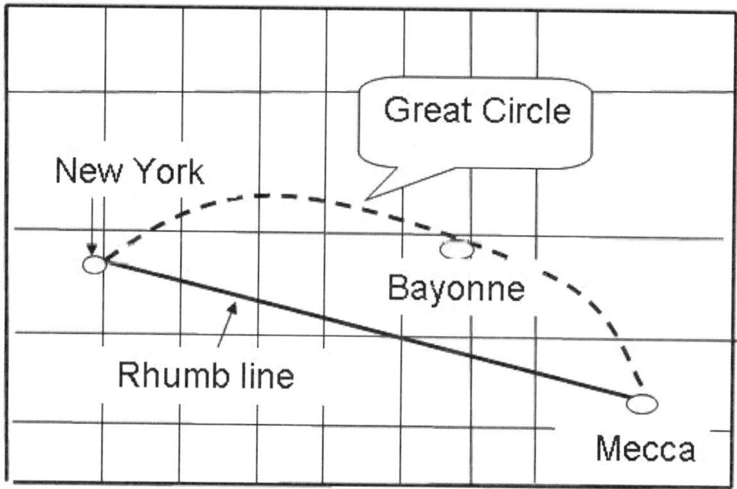

Meridian: A great circle that passes through the earth's poles and any other given point on the earth's surface. In ante meridian (A.M.) and post meridian (P.M), it is the line where the sun is at noon.

Meridiana: The Catholic Church provided the means and encouraged improvements for the measurement of the vernal equinox. Paolo del Pozzo Toscanelli, in 1475, designed the first *meridiana* in the Cathedral of Santa Maria del Fiore, Florence, Italy. He laid down a geographical North/South line (meridiana) and "pierced the lantern" (a hole in the ceiling) which acted as a gnomon. When the spot of sunlight crossed the meridiana it was noon, and when it reached a certain point along the line from north to south, the date of the equinox was determined. <http://www.analemma.org/presidentspen.html>; accessed Nov. 3, 2010.

Paris meridian: The present prime meridian (0 degrees) through Greenwich was adapted during the late 19th century. Prior to that time there were several prime meridians, including a meridian through Paris. en.wikipedia.org/wiki/Paris_Meridian

Rhumb line: A line on the surface of the earth that cuts all meridians at the same angle. It appears as a curved line on the surface of a sphere. Only one such line may be drawn through any two points. Although this is not the shortest distance, the direction is constant.

Spherical geometry: The use of trigonometric equations for determining the distance between two points on a sphere. The most extensive calculations were done by al-Khalili in 14th century Damascus, who calculated the distance from Mecca for all areas under Moslem control. <http://en.wikipedia.org/wiki/Al-Khalili>. ☙

Aleinu: Obligation to Fix the World or the Text?[1]

By: MITCHELL FIRST

The Jewish obligation of תקון עולם (=improving the world) is widely referred to and it is traditionally assumed that the *Aleinu* prayer is one of the texts upon which this obligation is based.

This article will show that a very strong case can be made that the original version of *Aleinu* read **לתכן** עולם (=to **establish** the world under God's sovereignty), and not **לתקן** עולם (=to **perfect/improve** the world under God's sovereignty.)[2] If so, the concept of תקון עולם has no connection to the *Aleinu* prayer.[3]

---

1 I would like to thank Yehiel Levy for showing me his Yemenite *siddur* which read לתכן, which inspired this research. I would also like to thank R. Moshe Yasgur for sharing his thoughts and for always being willing to listen to mine. I dedicate this article to my beloved wife Sharon, whose name has the *gematria* תקון, and who needs no improvement.

2 The above is how this phrase is usually translated. But *The Complete ArtScroll Siddur*, p. 161, translates: "to perfect the universe **through** the Almighty's sovereignty." Others adopt this translation as well. See e.g., J. David Bleich, "*Tikkun Olam*: Jewish Obligations to Non-Jewish Society," in *Tikkun Olam: Social Responsibility in Jewish Thought and Law*, eds. David Shatz, Chaim I. Waxman, and Nathan J. Diament (Northvale, NJ: Jason Aronson 1997), p. 61.

3 One scholar who has already suggested that the original reading was לתכן is Meir Bar-Ilan. See his "*Mekorah shel Tefillat 'Aleinu le-Shabeaḥ'*," *Daat*

Mitchell First resides in Teaneck and practices law in NYC. He has an M.A. in Jewish History from Bernard Revel Graduate School and is the author of "Jewish History in Conflict: A Study of the Major Discrepancy Between Rabbinic and Conventional Chronology" (Jason Aronson 1997); "The Origin of Taʻanit Esther" (*AJS Review* 34:2, November 2010); and other articles on liturgy at <seforim.traditiononline.org> and <seforim.blogspot.com>.

It is reasonable to assume that *Aleinu* was already included in the *Amidah* of *Rosh ha-Shanah* (=RH) by the time of Rav (early 3rd cent. C.E.).[4] But no text of *Aleinu* is included in the Talmud, nor is

---

vol. 43, Ramat Gan: 1999, p. 20, n. 72. Bar-Ilan did not cite any sources for his suggestion and seems to have merely intuited it. Also, an on-line article discusses the לתכן reading briefly and cites two of the sources that I will cite. See "תיקון עולם - תיקון טעות" at <www.yhn.co.il/articals/machshava/tikun-taut> (the site of the *hesder yeshivah* "*Ahavat Yisrael*" of Netivot). In 2005, Gilbert S. Rosenthal wrote a detailed article about the concept of *tikkun olam* throughout the ages, and merely assumed that the reading in *Aleinu* was לתקן. See his "*Tikkun ha-Olam*: The Metamorphosis of a Concept," *Journal of Religion* vol. 85:2, Chicago: 2005, pp. 214-40. The various articles in *Tikkun Olam: Social Responsibility in Jewish Thought and Law* also merely assume that the reading was לתקן (see pp. 26, 61 and 98).

4 The Jerusalem Talmud, at *Avodah Zarah* 1:2, includes the following passage:

א"ר יוסי בי רבי בון מאן סבר בראש השנה נברא העולם? רב, דתני בתקיעתא דבי רב זה היום תחילת מעשיך זכרון ליום ראשון וכו'.

A very similar passage is found at J. Talmud RH 1:3 (where the reading is בתקיעתא דרב). The sentence referred to from the liturgy (זה היום...) is from the introductory section to the ten verses of *zikhronot.* A reasonable inference from these Talmudic passages is that Rav composed (at least) the introductory sections to *zikhronot*, *malkhuyyot* and *shofarot. Aleinu* is part of the introductory section to *malkhuyyot.* Since the sentence quoted from the introduction to *zikhronot* corresponds to the present introduction to *zikhronot*, it is reasonable to assume that their introduction to *malkhuyyot* corresponded to the present introduction to *malkhuyyot*, i.e., that it included *Aleinu.* Admittedly, Rav could have made use of older material in the introductory section he composed. The fact that *Aleinu* has been found (in a modified version) in *heikhalot* literature is evidence for *Aleinu*'s existence in this early period, even though the prayer is not specifically mentioned in any Mishnaic or Talmudic source. (Regarding the dating of *heikhalot* literature, see below.) On the version of *Aleinu* in *heikhalot* literature, see Michael D. Swartz, "'*Alay Le-Shabbeaḥ*: A Liturgical Prayer in *Ma'aseh Merkabah*," *Jewish Quarterly Review* vol. 77, Philadelphia: 1986-1987, pp. 179-190. See also the article by Bar-Ilan cited above. For parallels in later sources to the two passages from the Jerusalem Talmud, see Swartz, p. 186, n. 20. See also RH 27a.

A statement that *Aleinu* was composed by Joshua appears in a collection of Geonic responsa known as *Shaarei Teshuvah* (responsum #44). But the statement was probably a later addition by the thirteenth century kabbala text of *Aleinu* included in any of the classical *midrashim*.[5] Therefore, we must look to later sources for texts of *Aleinu*.

When we do, we find that the reading לתכן is found in the text of the RH *Amidah* in the *Siddur* of R. Saadiah Gaon (d. 942),[6] and in the text of the RH *Amidah* in the *Mishneh Torah* of Rambam (d.

---

ist Moses de Leon. See Elliot R. Wolfson, "Hai Gaon's Letter and Commentary on *'Aleynu*: Further Evidence of Moses De León's Pseudepigraphic Activity," *Jewish Quarterly Review* vol. 81, Philadelphia: 1990-91, pp. 379-380. Statements that *Aleinu* was composed by Joshua are found in various Ashkenazic *Rishonim*. For the references, see Wolfson, pp. 380-381.

There is much evidence that *Aleinu* could not have been composed by Joshua. For example: 1) *Aleinu* cites verses from the prophet Isaiah (this will be discussed below); 2) *ha-kadosh barukh hu* was not an appellation for God in Biblical times; 3) *olam* was a time-related word, and not a word for "world" in Biblical times (see, e.g., *Daat Mikra*, comm. to Psalms 89:3, p. 138, n. 5); and 4) terms are found in *Aleinu* that are characteristic of *heikhalot* literature.

5 As noted, *Aleinu* has been found (in a modified form) in *heikhalot* literature. There are five manuscripts which include the relevant passage. But four of these manuscripts only include *Aleinu* in an abbreviated form and are not long enough to include the phrase לתכן/לתקן עולם. See Peter Schäfer, *Synopse zur Hekhalot-Literatur*, Tübingen: J.C.B. Mohr, 1981, sec. 551, pp. 206-207. The only manuscript that includes the phrase reads לתקן. But this manuscript, N8128, dates from around 1500. See Ra'anan S. Boustan, "The Study of *Heikhalot* Literature: Between Mystical Experience and Textual Artifact," *Currents in Biblical Research* vol. 6.1, Los Angeles: 2007, p. 137.

Regarding the dating of *heikhalot* literature, Bar-Ilan (*Mekorah*, p. 22, n. 85) estimates this literature as dating from the third through fifth centuries. Moshe Idel, in the second edition of the *Encyclopaedia Judaica* (11:592) summarizes the subject as follows:

> Even though it is quite possible that some of the texts were not edited until this period [=the geonic era], there is no doubt that large sections originated in talmudic times, and that the central ideas, as well as many details, go back as far as the first and second centuries.

6 *Siddur Rav Saadiah Gaon*, p. 221. Admittedly, what has been published here is not a manuscript composed by R. Saadiah himself. Neither R. Saadiah nor Rambam recited *Aleinu* in the daily service.

1204).[7] Moreover, it is also found in at least four texts from the Cairo Genizah which include all or part of *Aleinu*:[8] 1) a fragment of the RH *Amidah* first published by Jacob Mann in 1925;[9] 2) a fragment of the RH *Amidah* first published by Richard Gottheil and William H. Worrell in 1927;[10] 3) a fragment of the RH *Amidah* first published by Mordecai Margaliot in 1973;[11] and 4) a text of *Aleinu* first published by Mann in 1925.[12] In this last text, *Aleinu* is included in the *Pesukei de-Zimra* section of the Palestinian *shaḥarit* ritual.[13]

---

7 See the *Seder Tefillot Kol ha-Shanah* section at the end of *Sefer Ahavah*. I have looked at the *Or ve-Yeshuah* edition, the Frankel edition, the Mechon Mamre edition <www.mechon-mamre.org>, and the editions published by R. Yitḥak Sheilat and by R. Yosef Kafaḥ. All print לתכן. (The Frankel edition does note that a small number of manuscripts read לתקן.) In the standard printed *Mishneh Torah*, in the *al kein nekaveh* section of the RH *Amidah* (*Sefer Ahavah*, p. 154), only the first ten words were included (up to עוזך), followed by a וכו׳.

8 The Genizah includes more texts of *Aleinu* than I listed here. All the ones I have seen to date are noted above and all read לתכן. Most of the texts in the Genizah date from the tenth through the thirteenth centuries. See Robert Brody, *The Geonim of Babylonia and the Shaping of Medieval Jewish Culture*, New Haven: Yale Univ. Press, 1998, p. 32.

9 See his "Genizah Fragments of the Palestinian Order of Service," *Hebrew Union College Annual* vol. 2, Cincinnati: 1925, p. 329. (The fragment is known as Cambridge Add. 3160, no. 10.) When Mann published the fragment, he printed לתקן. But I had the fragment checked and it reads לתכן. I would like to thank Dr. Ben M. Outhwaite and Dr. Julia G. Krivoruchko of the Taylor-Schechter Genizah Research Unit at Cambridge University Library for checking the reading.

10 See their *Fragments from the Cairo Genizah in the Freer Collection,* New York: The MacMillan Company, 1927, plate XLIII (opposite p. 194). The volume includes a photograph of the fragment (plates XLIII and XLIV) but not a transcription. The authors remark (p. 195): "nor do the contents of this fragment appear, from any point of view, to justify transcription, translation and notes." Based on the word לתכן alone, a transcription would have been justified!

11 See his *Hilkhot Ereẓ Yisrael min ha-Genizah*. Jerusalem: Mossad Harav Kook, 1973, p. 148. The fragment is known as T-S 8 H. 23/1.

12 See above, pp. 324-325. See also, more recently, Ezra Fleischer, *Tefillah u-Minhagey Tefillah Ereẓ-Yisreliyyim bi-Tekufat ha-Genizah*. Jerusalem: Magnes Press, 1988, p. 238. The text is known as Cambridge Add. 3160, no. 5. Neither Mann nor Fleischer printed the full text of *Aleinu* in this

Furthermore, the reading לתכן survives in Yemenite *siddurim* to this day. It was also the reading in the original tradition of the Jews of Persia.[14]

Admittedly, the reading in Europe since the time of the *Rishonim* has been לתקן. See, for example, the following texts of *Aleinu*:

- *Maḥzor Vitry* of R. Simḥah of Vitry (daily *shaḥarit* and RH);[15]
- *Siddur Ḥasidei Ashkenaz* (daily *shaḥarit* and RH);[16]

---

fragment. I again would like to thank Dr. Ben M. Outhwaite and Dr. Julia G. Krivoruchko for checking the reading.

13 Since the second word of the *Aleinu* prayer is לשבח, it was probably seen as fitting to include this prayer in the *Pesukei de-Zimra* section. A main theme of both *Barukh she-Amar* and *Yishtabaḥ*, as well as of the entire *Pesukei de-Zimra*, is שבח.

A Palestinian practice of reciting *Aleinu* in *Pesukei de-Zimra* may also explain a statement found in several Rishonim (e.g., *Sefer ha-Maḥkim*, *Kol Bo*, and *Orḥot Ḥayyim*) in the name of *Pirkei de-Rabbi Eliezer* (a work composed in eighth century Palestine): שבח גדול יש בעלינו לשבח לכך צריך לאומרו מעומד. The statement is obviously not giving an instruction regarding the RH *Amidah* recited by individuals. Nor does the language of the statement (לאומרו) fit as an instruction to individuals listening to the repetition of the RH *Amidah*. The recital of *Aleinu* in a context outside of the *Amidah* seems to be referred to. (The statement is not found in the surviving texts of *Pirkei de-Rabbi Eliezer*.)

14 See Shelomoh Tal, *Nusaḥ ha-Tefillah shel Yehudei Paras*. Jerusalem: Makhon Ben Ẓvi, 1981, p. 154 (RH). The Persian-Jewish prayer ritual followed that of R. Saadiah in many respects. At the end of the eighteenth century the Persian Jews were influenced to adopt a Sefardic prayer ritual and their own ritual was forgotten.

15 Ed. Aryeh Goldschmidt. Jerusalem: Makhon Ozar ha-Poskim, 2004, pp. 131 (daily *shaḥarit*) and 717 (RH). The earliest surviving manuscript of *Maḥzor Vitry* seems to have been copied around the year 1145; a calendar for this year is found within it. See Israel Ta-Shema, "*Al Cammah Inyanei Maḥzor Vitry*," *Alei Sefer* vol. 11, Ramat Gan: 1984, p. 87.

16 Ed. Moshe Hirschler, Jerusalem, 1972, p. 125 (daily *shaḥarit*), and p. 214 (RH). (This work was published by Hirschler together with another work, *Siddur Rabbenu Shelomoh*; both are integrated into the same volume.) *Siddur Ḥasidei Ashkenaz* was compiled by the students of R. Judah he-Hasid (d. 1217) and presumably reflects his text of *Aleinu*. Hirschler's edition of this *siddur* is based on several manuscripts.

- *Peirush ha-Tefillot ve-ha-Berakhot* of R. Judah b. Yakar (RH);[17]
- *Peirushei Siddur ha-Tefillah* of R. Eleazar b. Judah of Worms (RH);[18] and
- *Sefer Arugat ha-Bosem* of R. Abraham b. Azriel (RH).[19]

The three main manuscripts of *Seder Rav Amram Gaon* also read לתקן.[20] But these manuscripts are not from the time of R. Amram (d. 875); they are European manuscripts from the time of the later Rishonim.[21]

Earlier than *Maḥzor Vitry*, we have circumstantial evidence for the reading לתקן in comments on *Aleinu* that were probably composed by R. Eliezer b. Nathan of Mainz (c. 1090-1170). Here, in

---

17 Ed. Samuel Yerushalmi. Jerusalem: Meorei Yisrael, 1979, sec. 2, pp. 91-92. R. Judah flourished in Spain and died in the early thirteenth century. Aside from the text of *Aleinu* in the manuscript published by Yerushalmi including the reading לתקן, it is also clear from the various explanatory comments by R. Judah that he was working with a text that read לתקן.

18 Ed. Moshe Hirschler. Jerusalem: Machon Harav Hirschler, 1992, p. 659. R. Eleazar died circa 1230. The text of *Aleinu* is found in his commentary to the *Aleinu* of RH. In his commentary on the daily *shaḥarit*, only the first two words of *Aleinu* and the last two (*timlokh be-khavod*) are recorded. In his *Sefer ha-Rokeaḥ*, his references to *Aleinu* in both the RH *Amidah* and the daily *shaḥarit* are similarly very brief.

19 Ed. Ephraim E. Urbach. Jerusalem: Mekiẓei Nirdamim, 1963, vol. 3, pp. 469-470. *Sefer Arugat ha-Bosem* was composed in 1234, in Bohemia. Aside from the text of *Aleinu* published here including the word לתקן, it is also clear from R. Abraham's explanatory comment (p. 469, lines 8-9) that he was working with a text that read לתקן.
Other early European texts of *Aleinu* include that of Ms. Cambridge Add. 667.1 (early thirteenth century) and the three texts of *Aleinu* in Ms. Oxford Corpus Christi College 133 (late twelfth century). I have not been able to check these readings. I have no reason to suspect that they do not read לתקן.

20 See *Seder Rav Amram Gaon*, ed. Daniel Goldschmidt. Jerusalem: Mossad Harav Kook, 1971, p. 142.

21 *Ibid.*, introduction, pp. 11-13. A few fragments of the *Seder Rav Amram Gaon* have been found in the Genizah, but these are very small and do not include our passage.

Hamburg MS 153,[22] the following explanatory comment about *Aleinu* is expressed (without a text of the line itself): ויהיו כל העולם מתקנים מלכותך וכולם יקראו בשמך...[23] Another manuscript, also largely composed of the comments of R. Eliezer b. Nathan, has essentially this same reading in two places.[24] Another manuscript, which is probably the *Siddur* of R. Eliezer b. Nathan, has a similar reading: ויהיו כל העולם מתקנים במלכותך. וכולם יקראו בשמך...[25]

Admittedly, I cannot prove that לתכן was the original reading. But this seems very likely, as לתכן is by far the better reading in the context. We see this by looking at all the other scenarios that are longed for in this section:

לראות מהרה בתפארת עוזך
להעביר גילולים מן הארץ
והאלילים כרות יכרתון
לתכן/לתקן עולם במלכות שד-י
וכל בני בשר יקראו בשמך
להפנות אליך כל רשעי ארץ
יכירו וידעו כל יושבי תבל כי לך תכרע כל ברך תשבע כל לשון
לפניך ה' אלקינו יכרעו ויפולו
ולכבוד שמך יקר יתנו

---

22 This manuscript is generally considered to be largely composed of the comments of R. Eliezer b. Nathan. See, e.g., Urbach, *Sefer Arugat ha-Bosem*, vol. 4, p. 24 and the facsimile edition of this manuscript published by Abraham Naftali Ẓvi Rot, Jerusalem: 1980, pp. 21-30. The manuscript itself is estimated to have been copied in the fourteenth century (Rot, p. 21).

23 See Rot, p. 20a (comm. to RH *Aleinu*).

24 See Alter Yehudah Hirschler, "*Peirush Siddur ha-Tefillah ve-ha-Maḥzor Meyuḥas le-Rabbi Eliezer ben Natan mi-Magenza (ha-Ravan),*" *Genuzot* vol. 3, Jerusalem:1991, pp. 1-128. In this *siddur* commentary (pp. 78 and 114), ויהיו כל העולם מתקני' מלכותך וכלם יקראו בשמך is found in the commentary to daily *Aleinu* in *shaḥarit*, and ויהיו כל העולם מתקנין מלכותך וכלם יקראו בשמך is found in the commentary to RH *Aleinu*. (One should not deduce from this manuscript that R. Eliezer b. Nathan recited *Aleinu* daily in *shaḥarit*.)

25 See *Siddur Rabbenu Shelomoh*, p. 212 (commentary on RH *Aleinu*). Hirschler published this work as the *siddur* of Shelomoh b. R. Shimson of Worms (1030-1096), but it is probably that of R. Eliezer b. Nathan. See, *e.g.*, Grossman, *Ḥakhmei Ashkenaz ha-Rishonim*. Jerusalem: Magnes Press, 2001, pp. 346-348.

ויקבלו כולם את עול מלכותך
ותמלוך עליהם מהרה לעולם ועד
כי המלכות שלך היא
ולעולמי עד תמלוך בכבוד

Beginning with the second line, להעביר, every clause expresses a hope for either the removal of other gods or the universal acceptance of our God. With regard to the first line, properly understood and its mystical and elevated language decoded,[26] it is almost certainly a request for the speedily rebuilding of the Temple.[27] Taken to-

---

26 Gershom Scholem recognized long ago that *Aleinu* includes several terms that are not only post-Biblical, but are characteristic of *heikhalot* literature. See his *Jewish Gnosticism, Merkabah Mysticism and Talmudic Tradition*, New York: Jewish Theological Seminary, 1965 (2d. ed.), pp. 27-28. He points to the terms *yoẓer bereshit*, *moshav yekaro*, and *shekhinat uzo*. Meir Bar-Ilan (*Mekorah*, p. 8) also points to the term *adon ha-kol*. (I suspect that *gavhei meromim*, another non-Biblical term, will eventually be found in this literature as well.) All of this suggests that *Aleinu* was composed by someone with some connection to *heikhalot* literature, or composed at a time after terms originating in *heikhalot* literature came to be in normative rabbinic use. This explains how *Aleinu* easily came to be borrowed into *heikhalot* literature. Due to the common terms, the authors of this literature probably saw *Aleinu* as a text "related to their own hymnology." Scholem, p. 28.
In *heikhalot* literature, *Aleinu* serves as a prayer of gratitude purportedly recited by R. Akiva (in the singular form עלי לשבח) on return from a safe journey to heaven. See the article by Swartz referred to above. Meir Bar-Ilan, *Mekorah*, pp. 12-24, argues that *Aleinu* originated here, and was then changed into the plural and borrowed into the RH service. This is very unlikely. There are too many themes in *Aleinu* that are out of context and extraneous under the assumption that *Aleinu* originated merely as a prayer of gratitude on return from a safe journey to heaven (e.g., the hope for God's future reign and that the nations shall acknowledge God's sovereignty). See Swartz, p. 188.

27 The idiom is based on verses such as Psalms 78:60-61 (ויתן לשבי עזו ותפארתו ביד צר) and 96:6 (עז ותפארת במקדשו), and Isaiah 60:7 (ובית תפארתי אפאר) and 64:10 (בית קדשנו ותפארתנו). This interpretation is probably implicit in the commentary of R. Judah b. Yakar. On לראות מהרה בתפארת עוזך, he writes: ע"ש [=על שם] כי תפארת עוזמו אתה, ונזכה לראות פני שכינה ולראות בתפארת בית המקדש דכתי' ובית תפארתך אפאר.

gether, this whole section is a prayer for the rebuilding of the Temple and the establishment God's kingdom on earth. This fits the reading לתכן perfectly.

That this section of *Aleinu* is fundamentally a prayer for the establishment of God's kingdom makes sense given that, most likely, this section was composed as an introduction to the *malkhuyyot* section of the RH *Amidah*.[28]

See the *Peirush ha-Tefillot ve-ha-Berakhot* of R. Judah b. Yakar, part II, p. 91. R. Judah's statements are adopted by R. David Abudraham in his commentary to the *Aleinu* of RH. See also R. Shemtob Gaugine, *Keter Shem Tov*, Kėdainiai, 1934, p. 104. Unfortunately, this interpretation of the phrase תפארת עוזך has generally been overlooked.

Scholem (p. 28, n. 18) notes the following passage found in other *heikhalot* texts: ברוך שמו במושב הדרו ומבורך בתפארת עזו. The parallel to מושב הדרו strongly suggests that תפארת עזו in this passage represents the physical Temple. For *heikhalot* texts with this passage see Mordecai Margaliot, *Sefer ha-Razim*, Jerusalem, 1966, pp. 107-09, and Martin Samuel Cohen, *The Shi'ur Qomah: Texts and Recensions*, Tübingen: J.C.B. Mohr, 1985, pp. 173 and 175.

28 Aside from the fact that the theme of the section fits as an introduction to verses of *malkhuyyot*, the section ends with four words from the root מלך: ויקבלו כולם את עול מלכותך ותמלוך עליהם מהרה לעולם ועד כי המלכות שלך היא ולעולמי עד תמלוך בכבוד.

I have little doubt that the first section of *Aleinu* (which includes the words מלך מלכי המלכים and מלכינו) was also composed at the same time. This is contrary to the view of many scholars who point to the two separate themes in the two sections as evidence of different authors. *Aleinu* is a short prayer, and in the earliest texts of *Aleinu* there is no division into sections. Therefore, our presumption should be one of unitary authorship. Close analysis of the verses cited shows that **both sections quote or paraphrase from the same chapter of Isaiah** (45:20: ומתפללים אל אל לא יושיע and 45:23: כי לי תכרע כל ברך תשבע כל לשון; there are quotes and paraphrases of other verses from chapter 45, and from 44:24 and 46:9 as well.) This strongly suggests that both sections were composed at the same time. (I have not seen anyone else make this point.) The terms characteristic of *heikhalot* literature are found in both sections as well.

While it cannot be proved that Rav (early third century, Babylonia and Palestine) was the author of *Aleinu*, it has been observed that "in some of Rav's homilies a tendency to a certain mystical thinking is discernible." See EJ 13:1578 and the citations there, as well as the statement of Rav at Ber. 55a: יודע היה בצלאל לצרף אותיות שנבראו בהן שמים וארץ... Also, several

Moreover, we can easily understand how an original reading of לתכן עולם might have evolved into לתקן עולם, a term related to the familiar term תקון העולם. The term תקון העולם (always with the definite article) is widespread in early rabbinic literature.[29] For example, it is found thirteen times in the Mishnah, and seventeen times in the Babylonian Talmud.[30] The alternative scenario, that the original reading was לתקן עולם and that this evolved in some texts into לתכן עולם is much less likely.

Finally, the ב of במלכות שד-י seems to fit better in לתכן עולם במלכות שד-י (=to establish the world under God's sovereignty) than in either of the two ways of understanding לתקן עולם במלכות שד-י.[31] Also, the lack of an את before the object עולם perhaps fits the reading לתכן better. I will leave a detailed analysis of these aspects to grammarians.

Talmudic passages record Rav's authorship or contribution to the text of other prayers. Most of these passages are collected at Ismar Elbogen, *Jewish Liturgy: A Comprehensive History*, tr. Raymond P. Scheindlin, New York: Jewish Publication Society and Jewish Theological Seminary, 1993, pp. 207-208. Most relevant is *Ber.* 12b where the המלך הקדוש and המלך המשפט changes for the Ten Days of Repentance are recorded in the name of Rav.

29 תקון העולם was the correct classical term, even though it has now been replaced in popular parlance by תקון עולם. Rosenthal, p. 214, n. 1.

30 Rosenthal, p. 214, n. 1. It is also found eight times in the Jerusalem Talmud and four times in the Tosefta. Most of the time, the term is used in the context of the laws of divorce, but it is found in other contexts as well (e.g., Hillel's enactment of *prozbol* at M. *Gittin* 4:3). Rosenthal suggests that the concept originated in the context of the laws of divorce, and was later expanded into the other contexts. See Rosenthal, pp. 217-219.

31 As mentioned earlier, in the reading לתקן עולם, there are two ways to translate במלכות: "under the sovereignty" or "through the sovereignty." If the translation is "under," **establishing** a world under the sovereignty of God is a simpler reading than **perfecting** a world under the sovereignty of God. If one wants to advocate for the translation "through," it requires investigation whether the prefix ב could have been used to mean "through" in the Talmudic period.

Conclusion

There is no question that social justice is an important value in Judaism.[32] Moreover, classical rabbinical literature includes many references to the concept of תקון העולם, both in the context of divorce legislation and in other contexts. The purpose of this article was only to show that it is almost certainly a mistake to read such a concept into the *Aleinu* prayer, a prayer most likely composed as an introduction to the *malkhuyyot* section of the *Amidah*, and focused primarily on the goal of **establishing** (תכון) God's kingdom on earth. Even if we do not fix the text of our *siddurim*, we should certainly have this alternate and almost certainly original reading in mind as we recite this prayer. ☙

32 See, e.g., *Tikkun Olam: Social Responsibility in Jewish Thought and Law* (cited earlier), and Jacob J. Schacter, "*Tikkun Olam*: Defining the Jewish Obligation," in *Rav Chesed: Essays in Honor of Rabbi Dr. Haskel Lookstein*, ed. Rafael Medoff (Jersey City: Ktav, 2009), vol. 2, pp. 183-204. For some citations to Biblical verses on justice, see Rosenthal, p. 215, n. 2.

A Proposal to Improve Rabbinic Decision-Making for Serious Medical Problems

By: BRENDA BREUER, FRED ROSNER and AARON E. GLATT

Abstract:

A rabbi is often consulted for advice by Jewish patients faced with a decision regarding medical treatments or operations that may pose serious health risks. Providing such advice carries a serious responsibility, and in order to optimize the likelihood of making the most appropriate decision possible, rabbis frequently consult with physicians to provide them with critical medical information. This paper discusses the potential role that an epidemiologist (a scientist and/or physician who studies the incidence, prevalence, spread, causes, prevention, and control of diseases in specified populations) might serve in addition to the rabbi's medical consultant panel.

Brenda Breuer, PhD, MPH (correspondence bbreuer@chpnet.org), is Director of Epidemiology in the Department of Pain Medicine and Palliative Care of Beth Israel Medical Center, and Associate Professor of Neurology at the Albert Einstein College of Medicine. She has published extensively in peer-reviewed medical journals and has written a book chapter on the epidemiology of pain.
Fred Rosner, MD, MACP, is Professor of Medicine at the Mount Sinai School of Medicine, and Visiting Professor of Medicine at the Albert Einstein College of Medicine of Yeshiva University. Dr. Rosner is an internationally renowned authority on Jewish medical ethics and the medical writings of Moses Maimonides, and has written and lectured extensively throughout the world.
Aaron E. Glatt, MD, FACP, FIDSA, FSHEA, is President and CEO of New Island Hospital, Assistant Rabbi at the Young Israel of Woodmere, and Professor of Medicine at New York Medical College. The author of two *seforim*, he has published extensively in peer-reviewed medical journals, and lectured extensively throughout the world on infectious diseases, medical ethics, and *halackhic* issues.

A rabbinic decisor (*posek, poskim* (pl.)) is often consulted to help a patient decide whether or not it is *halakhically* permissible to undertake a medical procedure. Some consult *poskim* who have a special reputation within the Orthodox Jewish community of being experienced in such consultations, and are widely sought out for their rabbinic knowledge. Frequently, the local synagogue rav / *posek* is consulted, who is more familiar with the patient and family situation. However, in both scenarios, the *posek* may not have the experience and or expertise to deal with a complex medical issue. This can present a significant dilemma for him, especially for unusual questions where appropriate medical consultation is not readily available.

The objective of this paper is to suggest an additional resource for this problem. Even in the best of circumstances, there is a critical need for improvement of the process of making the most complete, relevant medical information available to the *posek*, so that he can provide appropriate advice that is consistent with Jewish law (*halakhah).* The road toward an acceptable, easily available and logistically feasible methodology may be a long one, and perhaps it may be too complicated to actually develop and maintain a fully acceptable process. However, it behooves us to address the issue responsibly.

Some medical *halakhic* decisions are relatively simple (if there is even the need to ask a *shailah*), such as removal of a cataract that significantly affects a person's vision, or repair of a torn rotator cuff (shoulder injury) to relieve pain and restore mobility. The *halakhic* risk/benefit consideration is readily apparent and easy for the *posek* to decide with minimal if any medical consultation. However, decisions about other procedures, such as cardiac surgery, salvage cancer chemotherapy, or surgical treatment of back pain, may be more complicated *halakhically.* To provide the best *halakhic* advice, a *posek* should consult with expert, experienced physicians. While most procedures and operations have usually been thoroughly vetted and evaluated before they become common practice, and medical specialists can provide the *posek* with reliable opinions, there are cases that are not as clear, e.g., for recently introduced medical / surgical therapies and for controversial or less well-proven regimens. The fact that procedures or operations are widely accepted does not necessarily guarantee their effectiveness. The paper *When professional opinion is not enough*[(1)] discusses precisely that problem, as does the book *How doctors think,*[(2)] by Jerome Groopman, past Chairman of Medicine at Harvard Medical School.

Many *rabbonim* frequently rely upon clinicians in their community for practical medical advice regarding questions they receive, but a physician may be too busy or inadequately trained to comprehensively explore and critically evaluate a given treatment in areas that they do not regularly practice. Most medical schools require a course in research design, and throughout medical training physicians attend journal clubs where they are required to analyze medical papers and assess the validity of a study's conclusions in light of its research methods. Nevertheless, decades of working with physicians in the capacity of consultants for their research designs or as participants in their journal clubs have shown us that physicians often do not have the time or skills to critically evaluate medical research in areas outside their expertise. In contrast, epidemiologists (scientists and / or physicians who study the incidence, prevalence, spread, causes, prevention, and control of diseases in populations, and take courses in biostatistics and research methodology) are trained to critically evaluate literature reports about treatment and often themselves contribute to such literature. Therefore, a *posek* should be aware that expert epidemiologists can provide an important element of critical evaluation of the treatment literature.

We would like to clarify that *poskim* and their consulting physicians currently are committed to helping patients choose the best medical options in the most responsible way they know. The objective of this paper is a constructive one; i.e., to improve the quality of a *posek*'s options for the less common conditions where a clinical expert is not readily available or where there is a difference of opinion amongst the clinical experts. Further, the applicability of the points made in this paper may vary from *posek* to *posek*. For example, it may be less applicable to *poskim* who live in large metropolitan areas and consult with practicing physicians of high-caliber academic institutions, as compared to those who do not have access to these professionals. Nevertheless, this paper can be helpful to all *poskim*.

Let us present a hypothetical issue that might require a *posek*'s opinion, and then follow it with several actual problem issues in the areas of cancer and heart disease.

Suppose a *posek* is asked whether a patient should undergo a certain serious cardiac operation that is purported to extend life, and let us suppose that the operation has become accepted because investigators found that patients who underwent the operation lived longer than those who had only medical treatment. A clinician or epidemiologist trained to critically evaluate such reports would pose several questions about how study patients were chosen to undergo the operation: Did the surgeons choose the healthiest patients? Were patients who were especially frail and not expected to live much longer, no matter what, excluded from the study? If so, the observed beneficial effect of the operation might be an artifact, with the longer survival due to the better pre-op health of these patients, and not to the operation itself. More definitive and reliable evidence for the benefit of the operation could be demonstrated if the study patients were properly controlled and randomized *a priori* to undergo surgery or to be non-operated, medication-treated "controls," with the two groups having similar pre-operative health status and life expectancy assessments. Having a clinician or epidemiologist available to critically analyze a study to see whether or not it met those standards would enable a *posek* to get the best advice from physicians he may consult.

Could the need for obtaining the advice of an epidemiologist be obviated by consulting comprehensive review articles about outcomes, such as those in the Cochrane Database of Systematic Reviews, an electronic library that is available to the public and physicians, dedicated to providing accurate, up-to-date information about the effects of various aspects of healthcare? Such reviews can be very helpful, but one must recognize that the state of medical knowledge is dynamic—the best practice changes as a result of newer critical studies and evaluations. A review article, be it ever so comprehensive, is fixed at a point in time, whereas a living, critically trained advisor, such as an epidemiologist, is continuously current with the best available practices.

An example of this issue is provided by the history of surgical removal of pulmonary metastases from colon cancer. Over the past

10–15 years, numerous papers have addressed the advisability of this procedure.[3–15] While the results have been somewhat inconsistent, on balance the evidence, till very recently, indicated that the procedure could extend survival, and was so stated in a review in 2007.[3] However, a more recent study, in 2009,[16] reports that surgery was usually unsuccessful in female patients under 65, with less than one year between the diagnosis of colon cancer and the appearance of lung metastases, and/or with more than two metastases. No such patient was cured by the surgery. The investigators concluded that indeed routine surgery for these patients was not indicated, and that medical management should be the standard treatment for patients who have more than two metastases and less than one year between the diagnosis of the primary cancer and the lung metastases.

In order to further clarify which patients can benefit from surgical removal of lung tumors that have metastasized from a colon malignancy, a funded randomized clinical trial was launched in the United Kingdom in March 2010.[17] This example underscores the dynamic nature of medicine and that a physician who advises a patient or a *posek* must be completely *au courant* with the latest research studies of a procedure and capable of evaluating them critically.

Another example of the importance of keeping up with the latest developments in a critical area of medical or surgical treatment is provided by the history of the evolution of knowledge about hormone replacement therapy (HRT) for postmenopausal women. The earliest clinical observation in this area was that women in every country, whether the prevalence of coronary artery disease (CAD) was high or low, have much lower rates of fatal CAD than men.[18] This prompted “observational” (i.e., non-randomized and usually non-prospective) studies that compared the incidence of CAD in women who received HRT and those who did not. Many such investigations concluded that HRT provided cardiac protection. Here too, however, the issue was clouded by the non-comparability of women who did or did not take HRT. Women who take HRT are more likely to be white, educated, upper middle class, and lean, and often have a generally healthy lifestyle; *thus one could not separate the effects of HRT itself from effects of the low-risk profile of women who take it*. Nevertheless, it became conventional wisdom that

HRT greatly lowered the risk of CAD. The ongoing concern about the validity of this conclusion prompted several randomized, placebo-controlled, double-blind studies of the effects of HRT on CAD. One such study, the Women's Health Initiative (WHI), was supposed to last 8.5 years but was terminated prematurely when it became evident that women taking HRT had significantly poorer health outcomes than those who were not. They had higher rates of CAD and also higher rates of breast cancer, stroke, pulmonary emboli, and dementia. Another trial, the Heart and Estrogen/Progestin Replacement Study (HERS), demonstrated similar results. These findings are highly instructive: it is just not possible to substitute non-randomized "observational" studies for the gold-standard randomized, double-blind, placebo-controlled studies—the results may be completely wrong, as they were in this case.

We now describe a patient in whom clinical and epidemiological information interacted with a *posek*'s decision about heart surgery.

Judy (not her real name) had had a mitral-valve defect since childhood. When she came into menopause, her physician prescribed HRT to control her hot flashes. Judy was pleased to read that HRT was also cardio-protective. When the results of the WHI and HERS trials were reported, Judy was horrified and immediately stopped taking HRT. Thereafter, her cardiac function deteriorated severely, and her physicians recommended that she undergo surgical repair of her mitral valve. The thought of open-heart surgery was, if anything, not taken lightly. As Judy was smart and an Orthodox Jew, she tried to cover all her bases. Her research revealed that a surgeon from a heart clinic that is well recognized for its expertise in cardiac surgery was moving to a hospital very close to where she lived. This, she thought, was indeed welcome news (although she did not know the reasons for his leaving the clinic). She would not need to burden herself or her family by being treated in a clinic accessible only by an airplane trip. Since Judy was an Orthodox Jew, her family asked their *posek* whether she should undergo the surgery. He advised that she should. Judy had the surgery and at first seemed to have come through it well. However, it soon became apparent that her liver and kidneys were failing; after 11 weeks in the hospital's intensive-care unit, Judy succumbed to an infection.

It should be pointed out, that the quality of a surgeon explains only a small part of the better surgical outcomes of a highly regarded heart clinic. Such clinics have systems in place and multidisciplinary teams that play critical roles in preventing and rapidly addressing complications after surgery. It is this team's interventions that can reduce morbidity and mortality. The decision as to whether to choose the best physician or the best medical center varies from case to case, and is recognized as being both critically important and complex (19). In retrospect, an expert physician could have made this clear to the *posek* who advised Judy.

As an aside, we now have information that can be relevant for future cases that could be similar to that of Judy's. In 2008,[20] after reviewing the medical charts of 24,977 patients (49% women) who had undergone mitral valve surgery, investigators concluded that estrogen withdrawal during the perimenopausal period is associated with a substantially higher mortality after mitral-valve surgery. Once again the dynamism of medicine, and thus the need to have up-to-date information, is apparent.

Summary and Conclusions

When a *posek* gives advice to a patient about undergoing an operation or dangerous medical procedure, he bases that advice on the information that he received from his panel of medical advisors. In seeking the best possible advice, as demonstrated from the examples presented in this article, such a panel should include experienced clinicians and /or epidemiologists who, when deemed necessary, can critically assess the total medical evidence and provide a report that is custom-tailored for a specific patient and their unique set of risk characteristics. A recent article in the New England Journal of Medicine holds that such personalized assessments are at times essential.[21] Further, in *Dangerous disease & dangerous therapy in Jewish medical ethics*,[22] Rabbi Dr. Akiva Tatz expounds, and argues that in order to act appropriately according to *halakhah*, it is frequently critically important to undertake the complex endeavor of accounting for both personalized medical and *halakhic* factors simultaneously.

There may be potential gaps that need to be filled when arriving at the correct *halakhic* answer for selected complicated medical conditions, and we hope that this article will serve as motivation to seek appropriate advice from experts. First, a *posek* needs to obtain appropriate information from his consulting physicians to make the best *halakhic* decision. The physicians should feel confident that they have provided all the necessary accurate information. If they feel any uncertainty, they should recommend that another specialist be consulted in order to get the most updated and complete relevant information. Second, for *rabbonim* without easy access to qualified experts, we need to develop and adopt an appropriate method for identifying the most competent physicians to serve as consultants for these *rabbonim*. Perhaps we should have a "bank" of physician consultants and epidemiologists who can competently access, assess, and review the literature for various medical conditions. Along with the creation of this "bank" one would need to design a mechanism for its funding.

Our proposal has advantages over other systems, such as ECCO, that primarily recommend physicians. 1) Our proposal involves a team that is dedicated to getting the most current, in-depth, accurate information that is applicable to a particular individual patient; 2) We propose to form a team that includes physicians who are recognized by their peers for their competence, as well as scientists who are capable of compiling a custom-tailored report based on a critical evaluation of the available medical literature. 3) As there are clinical situations for which Orthodox Jews would not deem such reports to be sufficient for arriving at a final decision, our team is led by *rabbonim*, who can integrate all relevant information in an Orthodox Jewish context. This could be critical when, for example, final *halakhic* decisions might require risk/benefit considerations—what the individual considers to be a worthwhile risk might not be *halakhically* justified. Working through *rabbonim* ensures that *halakhic* factors, even when not apparent, are considered. Working through respected *rabbonim* who are objective and compassionate provides a humane setting that facilitates the processing of information by the patient.

As no other existing system incorporates all these essential components—i.e., clinical advice from recognized physicians, a further custom-tailored report based on a critical assessment of the current state of knowledge, and the assimilation of this information by a Rav into a decision that is optimal medically and *halakhically*—it is likely that our proposal would consistently provide better results than other existing systems. We would, however, explore the possibility of forming a consortium with other systems in order to produce an organized, non-fragmented service, whose parts are not wastefully replicated.

Thus, improving the process of making *halakhic* medical decisions may be complicated and take a long time. However, it is our obligation to start.

*VeCHAI BaHEM (*AND LIVE BY THEM*)*[23]

Acknowledgment: We thank Barnett Zumoff, MD, Emeritus Chief of the Division of Endocrinology and Metabolism (Beth Israel Medical Center, NYC) for his critical review and editorial suggestions.

ര

References

(1) Treasure T, Utley M, Hunt I. *When professional opinion is not enough.* BMJ 2007; 334(7598):831-832.

(2) Groopman J. *How doctors think.* New York: Houghton Mifflin Company, 2007.

(3) Pfannschmidt J, Dienemann H, Hoffmann H. *Surgical resection of pulmonary metastases from colorectal cancer: a systematic review of published series.* Ann Thorac Surg 2007; 84(1):324–338.

(4) Pfannschmidt J, Muley T, Hoffmann H, Dienemann H. *Prognostic factors and survival after complete resection of pulmonary metastases from colorectal carcinoma: experiences in 167 patients.* J Thorac Cardiovasc Surg 2003; 126(3):732–739.

(5) Shah SA, Haddad R, Al Sukhni W, Kim RD, Greig PD, Grant DR et al. *Surgical resection of hepatic and pulmonary metastases from colorectal carcinoma.* J Am Coll Surg 2006; 202(3):468–475.

(6) Miller G, Biernacki P, Kemeny NE, Gonen M, Downey R, Jarnagin WR et al. *Outcomes after resection of synchronous or metachronous hepatic and pulmonary colorectal metastases.* J Am Coll Surg 2007; 205(2):231–238.

(7) Okumura S, Kondo H, Tsuboi M, Nakayama H, Asamura H, Tsuchiya R et al. *Pulmonary resection for metastatic colorectal cancer: experiences with 159 patients.* J Thorac Cardiovasc Surg 1996; 112(4):867–874.

(8) Iizasa T, Suzuki M, Yoshida S, Motohashi S, Yasufuku K, Iyoda A et al. *Prediction of prognosis and surgical indications for pulmonary metastasectomy from colorectal cancer.* Ann Thorac Surg 2006; 82(1):254–260.

(9) Zink S, Kayser G, Gabius HJ, Kayser K. *Survival, disease-free interval, and associated tumor features in patients with co-*

lon/rectal carcinomas and their resected intra-pulmonary metastases. Eur J Cardiothorac Surg 2001; 19(6):908–913.

(10) Inoue M, Kotake Y, Nakagawa K, Fujiwara K, Fukuhara K, Yasumitsu T. *Surgery for pulmonary metastases from colorectal carcinoma.* Ann Thorac Surg 2000; 70(2):380–383.

(11) Saito Y, Omiya H, Kohno K, Kobayashi T, Itoi K, Teramachi M et al. *Pulmonary metastasectomy for 165 patients with colorectal carcinoma: A prognostic assessment.* J Thorac Cardiovasc Surg 2002; 124(5):1007–1013.

(12) Koga R, Yamamoto J, Saiura A, Yamaguchi T, Hata E, Sakamoto M. *Surgical resection of pulmonary metastases from colorectal cancer: Four favourable prognostic factors.* Jpn J Clin Oncol 2006; 36(10):643–648.

(13) Sakamoto T, Tsubota N, Iwanaga K, Yuki T, Matsuoka H, Yoshimura M. *Pulmonary resection for metastases from colorectal cancer.* Chest 2001; 119(4):1069–1072.

(14) Yedibela S, Klein P, Feuchter K, Hoffmann M, Meyer T, Papadopoulos T et al. *Surgical management of pulmonary metastases from colorectal cancer in 153 patients.* Ann Surg Oncol 2006; 13(11):1538–1544.

(15) Watanabe I, Arai T, Ono M, Sugito M, Kawashima K, Ito M et al. *Prognostic factors in resection of pulmonary metastasis from colorectal cancer.* Br J Surg 2003; 90(11):1436–1440.

(16) Onaitis MW, Petersen RP, Haney JC, Saltz L, Park B, Flores R et al. *Prognostic factors for recurrence after pulmonary resection of colorectal cancer metastases.* Ann Thorac Surg 2009; 87(6):1684–1688.

(17) Treasure T, Fallowfield L, Lees B. *Pulmonary metastasectomy in colorectal cancer: the PulMiCC trial.* Journal of Thoracic Oncology: Official Publication of the International Association for the Study of Lung Cancer 2010; 5(6 Suppl 2):S203–S206.

(18) Barrett-Connor E. *Clinical review 162: cardiovascular endocrinology 3: an epidemiologist looks at hormones and heart disease in women.* J Clin Endocrinol Metab 2003; 88(9):4031–4042.

(19) Reynolds E. *A 37-Year-Old Man Trying to Choose a High-Quality Hospital.* JAMA 2009;2009.

(20) Song HK, Grab JD, O'Brien SM, Welke KF, Edwards F, Ungerleider RM. *Gender differences in mortality after mitral valve operation: evidence for higher mortality in perimenopausal women.* Ann Thorac Surg 2008; 85(6):2040–2044.

(21) Swensen SJ, Meyer GS, Nelson EC, Hunt GC, Jr., Pryor DB, Weissberg JI et al. *Cottage industry to postindustrial care—the revolution in health care delivery.* N Engl J Med 2010; 362(5):e12(1)–e12(4).

(22) Tatz A. *Dangerous disease & dangerous therapy in Jewish medical ethics.* Israel: Targum Press, Inc., 2010.

(23) Leviticus chapter 18, verse 5 (see Nachmanides [Ramban]).

Responses to "A Proposal to Improve Rabbinic Decision Making for Serious Medical Problems"

Response: Shimon Glick, MD and Alan Jotkowitz, MD

Rabbi Immanuel Jakobovits Center for Jewish Medical Ethics,
Ben Gurion University of the Negev,
Beer Sheva, Israel

The authors bring the attention of the readers to an interesting and serious problem. But we have serious reservations about their approach.

If the paper were entitled "A proposal to improve physician decision-making for serious medical problems," we would consider the proposal to be appropriate and useful.

Decisions about whether to undergo medical treatments are rarely halakhic decisions and should not be the subject for *poskim,* any more than physicians should be consulted for halakhic dilemmas. The increasing tendency in Orthodox Jewish circles to consult rabbis for decisions in areas in which they have no training or competence is to be decried as a distortion of halakha as well as of common sense. Unfortunately all too many rabbis render medical opinions that are misinformed and misleading. The suggestion that the rabbis should now consult not only physicians but also epidemiologists is misguided. In the example provided about hormone replacement therapy, those *poskim* will find significant differences among epidemiologists no less than among physicians. If a rabbi is consulted about such treatment, he should explain to the inquirer that the subject is not a halakhic matter and should refer the individual to a competent physician.

There have been, and there still are, unique rabbinic figures, such as the late Rabbi Twersky in the US and Rav Firer in Israel who are widely consulted for advice, to whom to turn for complicated diseases. And these rabbis somehow have developed significant expertise in medical areas. But in this capacity they are not acting as *poskim,* but as sort of special social workers guiding patients to the appropriate professional in complicated cases. However, notwithstanding the holy work these individuals perform, there is danger in what they do. They are not regulated, have no formal training, and rely on word of mouth for many of their referrals. They are justly regarded as saintly individuals by patients and many physicians. Unfortunately there are others less skilled and less talented who are trying to emulate them. In addition, what will prevent less scrupulous individuals from trying to duplicate what they do and from being influenced improperly through financial incentives, coming either directly or through donations to their favorite charitable institutions? Perhaps even more disturbing, there are now rabbinic figures who are influencing the care of patients not based on scientific criteria but instead relying on mystical traditions. It is difficult for the public to distinguish between these different kinds of medical advice, all being given by rabbinic figures. We believe strongly that medical expertise should be left to physicians and halakhic and spiritual guidance to rabbis. It does not enhance the stature of rabbis to provide guidance outside their expertise, and it behooves rabbis to act in a way that is more likely to bring credit to Judaism.

Two of the leading rabbinic figures of the past century were frequently consulted about medical decisions. Rav Shlomo Zalman Auerbach *zt"l* generally did not agree to give a medical opinion but rather referred the inquirer to his/her physician. The late Rebbe of Lubavich, when consulted, usually advised the individual to seek out a physician who is a personal friend but has no vested interest in the decision, and to ask that physician's advice. Neither assumed the role of *posek* in medical areas.

There is, however, an area where rabbinic knowledge of new developments in medical decision making, particularly the use of evidence-based medicine, might be useful. Traditionally, rabbis when making halakhic decisions in medical areas have relied on expert opinion. At the end of the last century, medicine embarked on a revolution, in which expert opinion has been replaced, or at least supplemented, by reliance on sounder scientific data. The well-done randomized clinical trial or meta-analysis, rather than the expert, may have the "final word." A *posek*, for example, who is asked whether a pregnant woman may fast on Yom Kippur, should use as medical consultants physicians who base their opinions on medical data rather than on their personal expert opinion alone.

The authors would perform a much greater public service if they tried to educate both the patients and the rabbis about which questions are subjects for rabbinic opinion and which for medical opinion—a healthy and appropriate division of labor. ☙

Response: Kenneth Prager, M.D., F.A.C.P.

Professor of Clinical Medicine,
Division of Pulmonary, Allergy and Critical Care Medicine
Director, Clinical Ethics
Chairman, Medical Ethics Committee

I have a central question about your paper: what is the appropriate role of *poskim* in answering medical questions put to them?

If their role is to apply halacha to the medical query, then that is not referred to in your article. Someone reading the article would not see any difference between the *posek* and a physician to whom a patient comes for a second opinion.

In other words, I think your paper misses an essential point: it fails to relate to the reader what unique qualities and expertise a *posek* brings to a medical question. The examples you give in your paper seem to me to be straightforward medical questions: should this patient have cardiac surgery or not? How does halacha enter the equation? Most readers would assume that this is a strictly medical question. If the benefits of surgery significantly outweigh the risks, then the surgery should be performed, or at least the physician should discuss the pros and cons of the operation with the patient and her family and let them decide.

As for new procedures without a track record of success or failure: here again I don't see how a *posek* is preferable to several well-informed medical specialists in helping the patient to make a decision. Is the *posek* simply a substitute for a patient advocate who can help the patient sort out the choices and review the medical data? If so, how does halacha impact on this decision? Your paper fails to mention this critical point in my opinion.

Of course there is a role for an epidemiologist in all these questions, but one assumes that medical decisions are usually made on the basis of prevalent medical practice and on knowledge of the respected medical literature, in which the peer reviewers for the journals should have eliminated articles that do not stand up to critical epidemiologic analysis. In addition, decisions need to be made on the basis of good clinical judgment that takes into account issues that are not strictly medical, such as the patient's lifestyle, tolerance for risk, values, family situation, etc. It is unclear from the article how a *posek* would bring light to these questions.

It would be most unfortunate if one had to rely on rabbis, or any other clergy for that matter, to evaluate the correctness and accuracy of medical recommendations regarding strictly medical issues. It would imply a failure of the physicians dealing with the patient to have up-to-date and correct knowledge of the medical literature, including epidemiologic input into the question raised. If, in fact, there is a problem with physicians giving accurate medical advice, including sound epidemiologic evaluation, then I don't see why *poskim* are required to correct the problem. I would think that a panel of expert physicians would do a far better job.

You give the examples of medical decisions that have to be made regarding women taking HRT and when to remove colon cancer metastases from the lung in an attempt at cure. Do we need *poskim* to help patients with these decisions, or the right doctors? I believe the latter. Rabbis can be helpful in steering patients to the right physicians. I don't see the halachic expertise of the posek as entering into these decisions.

Is there a role for *poskim* in dealing with medical questions? Of course—but these are questions relating to halacha and not to the correct operation or drug to take. *Poskim* should be asked questions relating to whether a feeding tube should be placed; to whether life support should be withheld or withdrawn; to whether artificial insemination may be employed to enable a single woman to have a child, and from whom the sperm should be obtained, etc.

I am well aware of a number of rabbis who specialize in doctor referrals. They are quite good at this and have spent time winnowing out the good doctors from the mediocre. But these rabbis are not functioning in the capacity of a *posek*, but rather with the expertise of a top- notch referral service.

I hope that these comments have been helpful. ☙

Response: Anonymous

The author is a prominent medical halakhic authority.

General comments:

1. You did not define at all the halakhic parameters of rabbinic involvement in medical treatment. I suggest for your consideration the following insights:
   a) According to Jewish law:
   לא יתעסק ברפואה אלא אם כן הוא בקי, ולא יהא שם גדול ממנו, שאם לא כן, הרי זה שופך דמים [שולחן ערוך יורה דעה סימן שלו סעיף א].
   That means that only a qualified physician should deal with medical treatment.
   b) The role of Rabbis is stated in the following ways:
   חולה בתוך ביתו, ילך אצל החכם, ויבקש עליו רחמים [ב"ב קטז א]. יש מי שכתב, שהכוונה לחכם שבעירו [רמ"א יו"ד שלה יא. וראה בהסבר הדבר בשו"ת שבט הלוי ח"ג סי' קסג אות א]; ויש מי שכתב, שמי שיש לו חולה בביתו ילך אצל חכם, וילמד ממנו דרכי התפילות ויבקש רחמים, והיינו שמבקש הרחמים הוא הקרוב עצמו, אלא שלומד מהחכם דרכי הרחמים [מאירי ב"ב שם].
   That means the basic role of rabbis is to pray for and bless the patient prior to a medical procedure.
   c) Only in highly risky medical procedures, when a patient might die unless a very risky operation will be performed, is there an opinion that the חכם שבעיר has to give his approval to the procedure [שו"ת שבות יעקב ח"ג סי' עה].
   d) Certain medical procedures involve inherent halakhic problems, e.g., abortion for a fetal defect; cosmetic surgery; non-kosher product for illnesses, etc. In these situations the added important role of a rabbi is to act as a *posek*, by deciding whether or not the procedure should be done at all or in a modified way. In most instances there is no role of *psak* involved in the Rabbi's intervention.
   e) Accordingly, the term *posek* referred to in your article is, in my view, used inappropriately for the purposes of this article. All cases discussed in the article have nothing to do with a *psak*-halakhah as such, except for the issue of risks vs. benefits. Indeed, this is a halakhic question, but in most in-

stances it is viewed as a factual matter, as is also strongly stressed in this article. More importantly, in most instances patients turn to rabbis and rebbes who, with all due respect, are not *poskim* in the deep meaning of the word. Those rabbis and rebbes serve more in the capacity of advisers and giving blessings than of *poskim*. Hence, in my opinion you should not use the term *posek* in your article, and should stress that the rabbis and rebbes are commonly approached to help in medical decision-making as wise and righteous people, but their advice ought to be based on the best medical facts.

2) I understand the motivation of this article, yet I think there are two points to be made:

   a) Even before consulting with an epidemiologist, it should be stressed that rabbis ought to consult with the treating physician and with physicians who are experts in the specific field they are being asked about. Unfortunately there are rabbis and rebbes who listen to the family and give their advice based on inadequate and inaccurate information.
   b) I am not sure how practical your suggestion might be in the real world. The precious few medical epidemiologists around may be all but unavailable to consult with rabbis. Also, your proposal for a bank of information seems to be problematic, since this bank itself will undergo changes and modifications, and once again you may need an expert for each particular case.

3) It seems to me that additional examples may clarify your point even better. For example: How to relate to bilateral prophylactic mastectomy in BRCA positive women? When to insert a PEG in a terminally ill patient? These are examples of truly controversial issues, and perhaps a medical epidemiologist could make some sense and order in them. ☙

Response: Gedalia Dov Schwartz

Av Beth Din
Beth Din Zedek Ecclesiastical Judicature of the Chicago Rabbinical Council

I was astounded by your description of how some physicians are not fully up to date in their practice of medicine. I therefore fully and enthusiastically support your viewpoint that we need to improve the process of rabbinic decision-making for serious medical problems. It is critical that rabbis receive the most current information available, and that the information be presented accurately and with complete clarity.

It is pertinent to note, however, that patients who are faced with a serious medical problem—such as undergoing surgery that poses significant risks—rarely ask for my guidance. More frequently I am asked about issues that relate to end-of-life, and that do not require an updated review of the medical literature. I also wonder how your ideas would be implemented. For example, if a patient's physician recommends a certain procedure, it is likely that he will be offended if I tell him that in order to provide my input I first need to ask an epidemiologist for an analytical review of the relevant medical information.

In conclusion, your paper alerts us to a problem that many individuals are not aware of. I enthusiastically support your bringing it to the forefront. When a rabbi is asked for guidance in making a decision regarding a serious medical problem, he needs to have current, relevant information. I hope that your paper leads to a discussion that will ultimately raise the level of this decision-making process in a manner that is feasible and acceptable to all concerned parties. ☙

Response: Aaron Twerski, J.D.

Brooklyn Law School
Irwin and Jill Cohen Professor of Law

I find your paper interesting and challenging. I have developed considerable familiarity with epidemiological studies and have used them in several law review articles. You are correct that epidemiological studies are an important part of the mix in deciding whether to undertake a given medical procedure. There are several possibilities. One is to provide seminars for the *poskim* to raise their level of understanding as to their meaning. That will make them more savvy advisors by allowing them to question doctors about the studies. However, this supposes that they will have constant access to the studies. In New York, where the quality of medical care is very good among the top physicians, I would hope that the doctors are fully informed and include the studies in their calculus as to whether to recommend any given treatment. I must say that I am troubled somewhat by relying on the latest epidemiological study to guide medical decisions. My experience in looking at how even highly sophisticated judges with a pretty good grasp of epidemiology have struggled with the data gives me little confidence that rabbis will be successful.

In using the data, so much depends on the integrity of the study and the multitude of variables and confounders that affect results. My reservations notwithstanding, your suggestion that a team of physicians and epidemiologists could serve as a resource in helping halachic decision-making is worth pursuing. How the *poskim* will use the information is beyond my expertise. They may have to develop halachic norms for how to utilize them. But that can't happen until they are will informed. ☙

Response: Binyomin Weiss

Av Beth Din
Montreal, Canada

I have read your paper carefully. While you raise an important issue, I do feel that your proposal does not apply in most cases. There are three basic situations in which a *rav* is approached for a medical-related matter.

First, people approach a *rav* when there are *halachic* considerations associated with a medical procedure. Examples can be whether a gynecological procedure would render a woman *niddah*, or whether a urologic procedure involves the *issurim* of *sirrus* or *ptzua daka*. A similar situation would be with treatments that are performed on *Shabbos* and *Yom Tov*. Often, the *Rav* will need to consult an expert physician in order to obtain all the facts needed for the *halachic* determination; e.g., for gynecologic procedures, it would be essential to have a description of the instruments that would be used, and to know exactly how they would be used. In such cases there is no need for an epidemiologist to undertake a medical literature search in order to update the status of the field.

Second, patients may ask a *rav* for a *bracha* or to say *tehilim* for them when they are about to undergo a clinical procedure that has significantly serious health risks. Clearly there is no role for an epidemiologist in such cases.

The third situation is the least common: i.e., when patients approach a *rav* for guidance in deciding among various possible options of treatment for a serious medical condition. In cases where the *rav* does not have the required training or experience, he needs to seek expert opinions. It is in such rare cases, I believe, that the skills of an epidemiologist to critically read, review and assess the medical literature could complement and enhance the information provided by a physician—so that critical decisions are based on the most up-to-date data regarding the procedure's risks and benefits that are relevant to a particular patient.

While having a "bank" of experts could greatly facilitate and improve the current process of making decisions regarding the third situation described above, the logistics of establishing such a "bank" seems problematic. It is also important to note that the need for a credible assessment of the various medical options also applies to the public at large and should not be limited to *rabbinic* consultations. Often the only option available to patients who are faced with these fateful decisions is to search the Web and then to hope that the information they find is accurate. Your suggestion, if implemented, would be extremely helpful whether or not *rabbinic* consultations are involved, but I doubt that the medical establishment would welcome it. ☙

The Authors Reply

We appreciate the thoughtful and comprehensive feedback, which greatly enhances the description of the problem this paper addresses.

Our paper's main objective had been to raise awareness of the problems that can be associated with medical decisions made within a *halakhic* context, and to propose one possible approach for addressing these problems. We specifically address situations when a *rav* is asked for his *halakhic* opinion regarding the treatment that a physician has recommended. We do not recommend that the rav replace the physician, but address those situations where the patient would like the rav's *psak* regarding whether the proposed therapeutic recommendation (or non-recommendation) is in line with *halakhah*.

The physicians' responses express deep concern about decisions often made by *rabbonim*—decisions that they hold would most appropriately be handled by physicians. We do not disagree with this—that is not the purpose or suggestion of our paper. While responding *rabbonim* do not express this concern in their feedback about our paper, they acknowledge that they often consult physicians. *This is a subject that our article addresses.* Ultimately, as recommended by those who provided feedback to our proposal, the role of the *rav* in medical decision making needs to be more clearly defined. Of note, when acting within his role, each *morah horo'a* needs to weigh the facts according to his own understanding. Therefore, given similar circumstances, heterogeneity in the *psakim* of different *rabbonim* is expected and appropriate.

The feedback to the paper shows that we have a fragmented and less-than-optimal process to address medical problems, and this has motivated us to take another step forward. We now present an idea that would begin to integrate all the fragments into one cohesive system. This process of developing an effective system for handling medical decisions within the *halakhic* framework must be an evolving one; and because we are dealing within a *halakhic* framework, this particular proposal is limited to the Orthodox Jewish community. *Halakhic* and secular criteria for medical decisions differ. As an example, the medical concept of autonomy may lead secular physicians to allow, or even to vigorously try to persuade, end-of-life actions, such as withholding a feeding tube, which a *rav* might hold to be inconsistent with *halakhah*. Another conflict between secular opinions and *halakhah* might arise in the case of women with first degree relatives (e.g., mother or sister) who have had breast cancer, and who themselves have a genetic marker, such as the BRCA gene, placing them at increased risk. Secular vs. *halakhic* approaches may or may not differ greatly regarding reproductive issues, appropriate risk taking, *chavalah* (damaging oneself) and *sirus* (removal of reproductive organs).

As a potential first step in addressing some of the concerns for the *rav* that we have raised, a rabbinical organization might wish to assemble a panel of clinical and scientific experts with various areas of expertise that could be available to its membership as consultants as needed. The objective would be to create a system that could easily be navigated and readily accessible. A cohesive organization of experts would maximize the likelihood of providing the *rav* with the correct medical input to provide expert *halakhic pesak*.

We acknowledge that putting these ideas on paper is simple; executing them is challenging. There are many practical challenges that need to be addressed in order to pursue the development of a consistent, comprehensive, unified, methodical system to deal with *halakhic* medical problems faced by Orthodox rabbonim. Some challenges were highlighted by those who provided feedback to our proposal. For example, Professor Twerski expressed concerns regarding cases of conflicting epidemiologic findings. Such cases are not uncommon, and when they do occur, epidemiologists and physicians need to assess all the available evidence and, to the best of their ability, clarify the possible sources of these differences, and how these differences might be relevant for a particular patient facing a decision. Often, the verdict may not yet be in. While striving for perfection is the goal, it cannot always be realized. Decisions must be made, and deciding not to explore the evidence because it could be inconsistent is unacceptable.

We would also like to comment on Dr. Prager's assertion that"...one assumes that medical decisions are usually made on the basis of prevalent medical practice and on knowledge of the respected medical literature, in which the peer reviewers for the journals should have eliminated articles that do not stand up to critical epidemiologic analysis." Prevalent medical practice is not always optimal, and peer reviewers may miss important points and paper weaknesses. The weaknesses of many papers, in spite of peer review, frequently become evident during journal clubs; not all peer-reviewers are equally competent. Where definitive medical advice is not available, the *rav* needs a resource to help him *pasken* for the patients.

In summary, it is our impression that *rabbonim* are sometimes faced with critical questions from their community, many of which might be life-threatening, and they do not always have a reliable expert clinician or epidemiologist on hand to help them ascertain what the facts are so that they can *pasken* appropriately. Certainly, the treating physician is the most appropriate place for the *rav* to turn to base his *pesak*, but there are times when that is insufficient or impossible, in which cases the *rav* will likely turn to colleagues or other clinical friends for assistance. Having a central source of reliable expert clinicians and epidemiologists would facilitate correct *pesak halakhah* in these difficult situations. ꙮ

On Reading Rambam in Brooklyn and in Haifa

By: MENACHEM KELLNER

In his article "Israel's Inheritance: *Olam Haba*," Rabbi Asher Benzion Buchman presents an interpretation of Rambam's views on *olam ha-ba* at variance with the understanding of Rambam widely accepted in the world of Maimonidean scholarship. According to this latter view the *only* key for achieving a share in the World to Come is a minimal level intellectual perfection of a special (Aristotelian) type. Such perfection depends upon antecedently achieving a high level of moral perfection, without which (for reasons Plato and Aristotle made clear) one cannot hope to achieve the understanding of God and the universe which is our perfection and felicity as human beings and which, as noted, is the only key for opening the door to *olam ha-ba*. This state of affairs gives Jews a dramatic advantage over Gentiles since, for Rambam, the Torah is the best (but not only) guide to achieving both moral perfection and intellectual perfection. This advantage is relative, and has everything to do with what Jews do and learn, and nothing to do with any innate characteristic they may be thought to have by non-Maimonidean interpreters of Torah.[1]

---

1 For studies of what Rambam actually wrote about the question of human perfection, see Menachem Kellner, *Maimonides on Human Perfection* (Atlanta: Scholars Press, 1990), esp. pp. 1-5 and "Is Maimonides' Ideal Person

---

Menachem Kellner, Professor of Jewish Thought at the University of Haifa, earned his Ph.D. from Washington University in St Louis. At Haifa University he served as Chair of the Department of Maritime Civilizations (1988-91), as Dean of Students (1994-97) and from 1990-2005 he held the Sir Isaac and Lady Edith Wolfson Chair of Jewish Religious Thought. Over the years he has published nineteen books and more than one hundred articles in the areas of medieval Jewish philosophy and modern Jewish thought.

Rabbi Buchman is not the first person to (mis)read Rambam as he does. There is a long history of Jews looking at what Rambam wrote and responding: "This is Greek to me! It is not possible that Rambam actually believed these things." Taking the Orthodoxy of their day as determining what Rambam must have meant, these interpreters have forced Rambam's text to mean whatever they think Judaism (as they claim to understand it) teaches. There are two widely accepted ways of viewing Rambam. One may be called vertical, the other horizontal. In the first view, Rambam is situated in a chain of Jewish tradition stretching back to Moses, and is seen primarily as a halakhic decisor. It is primarily in this tradition that Rambam's views are studied and understood. In the second view, Rambam is located in the context of contemporary or near-contemporary Muslim philosophy, and it is in relation to thinkers like al-Farabi that his views are studied and understood. The correct interpretation, in my opinion, is that Rambam must be understood as standing at the intersection of both arrows, the vertical one stretching back to Moses and the horizontal one encompassing his philosophical contemporaries and near contemporaries. Rambam was convinced that one could and must live simultaneously in both these worlds. It is that understanding of Rambam which Rabbi Buchman seeks to overturn in his article.

Rabbi Buchman chose to use one of my books[2] as a platform for rejecting this (correct) interpretation of Rambam: I guess it is easier to argue with Kellner than with Rambam. His criticisms of some of my scholarship reminded me of several experiences I have had. Some years ago, I had the privilege of participating in a Jewish-Christian-Shi'ite religious "conversation" outside of Lucerne, Switzerland. Many of the Muslim participants in the event were leading Ayatollahs from Iran. They proved themselves to be far more cultured, urbane, and sophisticated than one would expect from the image of Iranian ayatollahs to which we are usually exposed. I found it both striking and amusing that they saw themselves, not as

---

Austerely Rationalist" in Kellner, *Science in the Bet Midrash: Studies in Maimonides* (Boston: Academic Studies Press, 2009), pp. 63-80.

2 *Must a Jew Believe Anything?*, 2nd ed. (Oxford: Littman Library of Jewish Civilization, 2006).

the intellectual *descendants* of medieval rationalist Muslim theologians known as Muatazilites (known to readers of *Hakirah* from *Guide of the Perplexed* III.17), but as still engaged in their debates, as if 800 years had not passed. They were still angry with the Asherites (doctrinaire orthodox opponents of the Muatazilites) for misrepresenting Islam. Unlike Islam, Judaism has developed a linear tradition of interpretation (such as *geonim, rishonim, aḥaronim*) and a sense of its own history. Muslims are still in the original period. Some Haredi thinkers treat Judaism in much the same fashion as the Muslim theologians whom I met (while also insisting on *yeridat ha-dorot*[3]). Opposed to this is the historical approach which characterizes the academic study of Judaism and about which Modern Orthodoxy seems to me to be somewhat schizophrenic. Instead of asking: what could Rambam have known in his own day, what did he actually read, by whom did he claim to be influenced,[4] the approach I am criticizing here assumes that Rambam has to fit well into the interpreter's version of Judaism, and is forced to do so.

A second experience concerns one of the most embarrassing things that ever happened to me: I found what I thought was a mistake in the late Rav Kafih's wonderful Arabic-Hebrew edition of Rambam's Commentary on the Mishnah. I rushed to write to him about it and after a few days received a very polite letter suggesting that I look at the footnotes of the page in question. I will note below how this is relevant to Rabbi Buchman's criticisms of my work.

The third experience occurred in connection with my book, *Maimonides on Judaism and the Jewish People* (SUNY Press, 1991). But first, a word of explanation on how I came to write the book.

---

3 I wrote a book on the subject which Rabbi Buchman would most likely hate: *Maimonides on 'The Decline of the Generations' and the Nature of Rabbinic Authority* (Albany: SUNY Press, 1996).

4 In this connection see: Steven Harvey, "Did Maimonides' Letter to Samuel Ibn Tibbon Determine Which Philosophers Would Be Studied by Later Jewish Thinkers?" *Jewish Quarterly Review* 83 (1992): 51-70 and Shlomo Pines' introduction to his translation of the *Guide of the Perplexed* (Chicago: University of Chicago Press, 1963), pp. lvii-cxxxiv.

In one of my first Hebrew articles[5] I argued that for Rambam the difference between Jew and Gentile would disappear by the time the messianic era reached fruition and that, in effect, his Thirteen Principles are a messianic definition of who is a Jew.[6] I gave a copy of the article to a gentleman in my shul in Haifa who told me that he could not possibly accept the thesis for which I argued in my article. I told him I would write an article in his honor, explaining why Rambam could not avoid the conclusion I attributed to him. Well, I sat down to write the article, and it became the book I just mentioned, *Maimonides on Judaism and the Jewish People*. When the book appeared, I gave a copy to my friend from shul who duly read it, and then, with great intellectual honesty told me that he found my arguments convincing and that in consequence his admiration for Rambam had been seriously diminished. Anyway, to get to the point, my older sister (who then lived in Kew Gardens) arranged for the book to be read by a reading group in her shul, one of whose members wanted to talk to me about it. He said he could not accept the views I attributed to Rambam. I asked how he could not, seeing that in the first half of the book I had laid the philosophical groundwork (Rambam's adoption of the theory of the acquired intellect, and his adoption of Aristotle's definition of human beings as rational animals) from which flowed all of the universalist Jewish positions in the second half of the book. My sister's friend replied: "Oh, I skipped all that philosophical stuff and went straight to the Jewish issues." As I will note below, Rabbi Buchman's rejection of my readings of Rambam is a consequence of "skipping all the philosophical stuff."

Rabbi Buchman seems to be fighting battles originally fought 800 years ago, battles that led to the burning of Rambam's books in 1232. If Rambam were really as uncomplicatedly '*farfrumt*' as Rabbi

---

5 "A Suggestion Concerning Maimonides' Thirteen Principles and the Status of Gentiles in the Messianic Era," *Tura: Oranim Studies in Jewish Thought* (Tel Aviv: Ha-Kibbutz Ha-Meuḥad, 1988): 249-260 (Hebrew).

6 For a recent restatement of that thesis, in English, and in much greater depth, see my discussion with Rav Chaim Rappoport: "Maimonides' *True Religion* – for Jews, or All Humanity?" *Me'orot* [=*Edah Journal*] 7.1 [2008] [http://www.yctorah.org/content/view/436/10/].

Buchman would like him to be, why were his books burned? Why did the ba'alei ha-Tosafot seek to place the *Guide of the Perplexed* and *Sefer Madda* on the index of forbidden books? Why did his 15th century commentator Shem Tov open his commentary to *Guide of the Perplexed* III:51 as follows:

> Shem Tov said: Many rabbinic scholars said that Maimonides did not write this chapter and if he did write it, it ought to be hidden away or, most appropriately, burned. For how could he say that those who know physics are on a higher level than those who engage in religion, and even more that they are with the ruler in the inner chamber, for on this basis the scholars who are engaged with physics and metaphysics have achieved a higher level than those engaged with Torah!?[7]

Why did the Rivash write that Rambam wrote things "that it is forbidden to hear" (responsum 45)? Why did R. Ḥasdai Crescas (d. 1412) devote a whole book (*Or ha-Shem*) to showing how Rambam had been (in his words) seduced by the beauty of Greece at the expense of remaining faithful to true Judaism? The examples are endless, but apparently of little interest to Rabbi Buchman.

Now to some details. Rabbi Buchman maintains that, according to Rambam, in the words of M. Sanhedrin X.1, all Jews have a share in the World to Come and that upon conversion a proselyte "immediately gains *olam haba*." He is clearly upset by the fact that according to Kellner Rambam could not possibly hold these positions since Rambam "required absolute certainty, perhaps rising to the level of clear knowledge, rather than mere faith, to acquire *olam haba*." In order to "refute" my interpretations he writes, among other things, that Kellner

> "'quotes' Rambam as writing (after listing the 13 *ikkarim*), 'anyone who doubts any one of these basics has no part in the

7 I actually think that Rambam makes a much less radical claim in the parable of the palace; see *Maimonides on Human Perfection*, pp. 13-40. The point for our purposes here is that Shem Tov and the rabbinic scholars (*rabani'im* in the original) to whom he refers may not have liked the views they found in Rambam, but did not deny that they found them there.

World to Come.' This 'quote' is based on an understanding of *Perush haMishnah* that is obviously inaccurate."

Rabbi Buchman then goes on to cite a variety of Hebrew translations of Rambam's text, as if that proves the meaning of the original Arabic. Attention to footnotes, which Rav Kafih, z"l, gently suggested to me was important, would have led Rabbi Buchman to Menachem Kellner, *Dogma in Medieval Jewish Thought* (Oxford, 1986) and from there to the original Arabic text of the 'Thirteen Principles.' He could then have consulted with an Arabist who would have told him that the Arabic ואד'א אכ'תלת ללשכ'ץ means precisely 'one who doubts.' A competent Hebraist would also have told him that the terms מפקפק and מערער do not mean "actively arguing against..." in contemporary Hebrew, but rather "casting doubt upon."[8]

In a footnote to this passage Rabbi Buchman claims that

> Dr. Kellner also misrepresents Rambam's position on the issue of error and on what qualities are necessary to earn *olam haba*. On p. 138 of his book, he does note that 'in not a few places Maimonides speaks as if he accepted a traditionalist account of reward and punishment.' But he chooses not to try to resolve the sources he uses with the many sources that show that his interpretations are impossible. He instead explains that Rambam was merely conning us. He justifies this approach with yet another misreading of the *Moreh Nevukhim*, perhaps his most offensive. (When Rambam speaks of 'necessary' beliefs be certainly does not mean that they are not true as Dr. Kellner claims.)

That parenthetical sentence really made me scratch my head in amazement. But before that: what to do? Rambam himself tells us in the introduction of the *Guide of the Perplexed* that he "cons" his

---

[8] The Arabic is found in Rav Sheilat's edition of *Hakdamot ha-Rambam la-Mishnah* (Ma'aleh Adumim: Ma'aliyot, 1992), p. 375. Rabbi Buchman ignores Rav Sheilat's Hebrew translation (p. 146): ואם יתקלקל לאדם.

audience, to adopt Rabbi Buchman's inappropriate expression.[9] As to necessary beliefs, I invite the readers of *Ḥakirah* to study *Guide of the Perplexed* III.28 (in which the issue is introduced), and then *Guide of the Perplexed* III.32 and then decide who offensively misrepresents Rambam: Kellner or Rabbi Buchman. Rambam is not much given to humor, but there is a sort of joke in *Guide of the Perplexed* I:36, where Rambam implies that God gets angry at anyone who thinks that He actually gets angry. Rabbi Buchman's claim that for Rambam "necessary" beliefs are true would probably earn God's ire—I have no doubt that it would earn Rambam's.

Rabbi Buchman continues the footnote under discussion by sending the reader to my friend David Berger's highly critical but respectful review of *Must a Jew Believe Anything?*[10] He mentions my reply to David in the second edition of the book[11] without further comment. I urge readers of this note to read the review and my reply; here I would like to make one comment about the debate. If David's interpretation of Rambam and of the history of Jewish thought is correct, and my interpretation of them is incorrect, then his campaign against Ḥabad is absolutely on the mark,[12] since there can be no doubt that attributing divinity to the Rebbe is out-and-out heresy according to Rambam. If Rabbi Buchman is so convinced by David Berger, he had better stop all contact with Ḥabadniks, stop eating Lubavitch *sheḥitah*, and take no advantage of Ḥabad *shliḥim* when he travels, otherwise he endangers his own share in the World to Come (although, from my perspective, misrepresenting Rambam is a bigger sin).

I was amused by another issue raised by Rabbi Buchman since he (silently) adopts a *ḥiddush* of mine and misapplies it to the Rambam. In arguing (against Rambam) that Ḥazal did not intend M. Sanhedrin as a statement of dogma I note that the mishnah speaks

---

9 A friend suggested that there is room to judge Rabbi Buchman לכף זכות: perhaps all he is trying to do is to fulfill Rambam's wishes by keeping his true views hidden from the masses.

10 *Tradition* 33 (1999), pp. 81-89.

11 This second edition appeared in 2006; the "afterword" is on pp. 127-147.

12 David Berger, *The Rebbe, the Messiah, and the Scandal of Orthodox Indifference* (London: Littman Library of Jewish Civilization, 2001).

of actions, not beliefs. The Mishnah is interested in socially disruptive behavior, and not in what people think. That is why it writes of האומר[13] and why the Mishnah speaks primarily of forbidden behavior and nowhere speaks of forbidden thought.[14] This admittedly new interpretation of M. Sanhedrein X.1 is a key element of my argument about the nature of אמונה in classical Judaism and is developed and defended in chapter two of *Must a Jew Believe Anything?* and is central to my disagreement with David Berger. Rabbi Buchman "borrows" this reading of mine and misapplies it to Rambam.

Rambam does not, as Rabbi Buchman thinks, use the expression "he who says" in his statement of the principles in his commentary on the Mishnah. Rabbi Buchman may have not wanted to bother to hunt up my *Dogma in Medieval Jewish Thought*, but he could have found an accurate English translation of the principles in an appendix to *Must a Jew Believe Anything?* and saved himself this mistake. It is true that Rambam says האומר in his restatement of the principles in the *Mishneh Torah*, but given "all that philosophical stuff" which forms the basis for his positions (and which Rabbi Buchman resolutely ignores, even though it is explicated at length in *Dogma* and cited in *Must a Jew*), I do not attach much importance to this—Rambam was simply using the language of the Mishnah. Moreover, as Rambam himself tells us in an important responsum (# 264 in Blau's edition), his interest in the *Mishneh Torah* discussion is on the social consequences of heresy; in that context, his use of the term האומר makes perfect sense.[15]

I have largely restricted myself here in this note to a discussion of the places where Rabbi Buchman explicitly targets my interpretations of Rambam. A full-fledged discussion of his article would involve much more time and effort than I am willing to invest.[16] I

---

13 As opposed to locutions such as "*ḥoshev*," "*meharher*," "*omer el libbo*," etc.

14 See the discussion in *Must a Jew*..., pp. 33-38.

15 For details, see Menachem Kellner, "Must We Have Heretics?" *Conversations* 1 (2008): 6-10.

16 But one of Rabbi Buchman's strangest claims cries out for even a brief reply. He is the author of a work called *Rambam and Redemption*. As such, I find it amazing that he could believe, as he apparently does, that according to Rambam there is a judgment day which precedes *olam ha-ba*. It is beyond doubt (and this is affirmed by the many medieval authorities

invite the interested reader to compare what I have written about Rambam to Rabbi Buchman's interpretations and judge between us. In addition to my books and articles cited above, I would also like to direct the reader's attention to *Maimonides' Confrontation with Mysticism* (Littman Library of Jewish Civilization, 2006), esp. ch. 7.

Jews have responded in many ways to the challenge implicit in Rambam's writings. At first, an attempt was made to throw him out of the dormitory. When that failed, the next step was basically to ignore what he said.[17] Given the plethora of editions and translations of his works in the modern world, not to mention the literally thousands of articles and books written about him, that has grown ever more difficult. One option is to decide that since he is obviously still in the dormitory, he must agree with what all the other denizens of that dormitory think—that is Asher Benzion Buchman's approach, an approach that involves forcing Rambam's square peg into round holes. Another approach, truer to Rambam, is to acknowledge that the dormitory has more rooms than is often thought. ☙

who were upset by Rambam) that according to Rambam *olam ha-ba* is the name given to the status achieved by those (apparently few) individuals whose souls survive the death of their bodies. There is no *yom ha-din* on which all human beings are judged at one and the same time.

17 It is striking that the "yeshiva world" has yet to produce a single translation of or commentary on the *Guide of the Perplexed*. There is not even a "yeshivish" edition of Samuel ibn Tibbon's medieval translation of the *Guide of the Perplexed*.

Reading Rambam in Haifa and Studying Rambam in Brooklyn

By: ASHER BENZION BUCHMAN

I wish to thank Dr. Kellner for taking the time to share his interesting anecdotes with the *Ḥakirah* audience and for explaining to us how Rambam should be read. With regard to what is actually relevant to my essay, however, Dr. Kellner has little to say. In his claim that Rambam, in describing a heretic in *Perush HaMishnah,* says it refers to one who "doubts" rather than "casts doubt"[1] or "argues," Dr. Kellner seems to miss the point that I make—that the choice between the possible translations must be decided by studying other statements of Rambam. The sometimes dramatic differences in meaning that exist in different translations of the *Perush HaMishnah* and especially the *Moreh Nevuchim* make it necessary for one studying these texts to use his judgment in deciding between them. In our case we must take into account: 1) That one of the thirteen principles is an act, actually worshipping *avodah zara*, rather than thought or speech, demonstrates that it is not beliefs that we are speaking of—but means of commitment to a position that are done outwardly,[2] and 2) Rambam's lengthy explanation of the concept of לא תתורו demonstrates that doubt with regard to the thirteen *ikkarim* does not constitute heresy. And whereas Dr. Kellner claims that he learned his lesson from Rav Kappach, that attention must be

1 "Casts doubt" that Dr. Kellner accepts as valid generally means "voices doubt," which supports my position, and yet Dr. Kellner seems oblivious to this.

2 Thus when I write that Rambam in *Perush HaMishnah* refers to stating denial, I am explaining his intent, and I proceed to prove that when he says מפקפק he means stating his denial.

Asher Benzion Buchman is the author of *Encountering the Creator: Divine Providence and Prayer in the Works of Rambam* (Targum, 2004), and *Rambam and Redemption* (Targum, 2005).

given to footnotes, it seems he missed note 21[3] where I quote the Arabic that he implies is unknown to me. I explain there that "no other reading" than mine is possible, based on the arguments that I present later.

His lack of attention to the above point is minor, when compared to the fact that in his opening paragraph Dr. Kellner states, with regard to the advantage that a Jew has in gaining *olam haba*, "This advantage is relative, and has everything to do with what Jews do and learn, and nothing to do with any innate characteristic which they may be thought to have by non-Maimonidean interpreters of Torah." He clearly thinks that I disagree with this statement, thus demonstrating that he actually did not read the essay but merely skimmed it and assumed he knew what my position was, fitting it into one of his preconceived categories. To restate my position: My essay explains that while it is not something innate in being Jewish that earns *olam haba*, nevertheless, the minimal requirement is reached by the simple commitment of faith to the principles of our religion. This constitutes sufficient knowledge. If this commitment is reflected in the person's exterior speech and actions, his inner turmoil, whatever it might be, will not cause him to lose his share. As is often noted, there are no atheists in a foxhole. People are not certain about their own beliefs and may change their mind internally at any instant, even about issues of great moment. It is the commitment to an idea that a person states to the world that defines him and that is relevant to *olam haba.*

As for Dr. Kellner's accusation that I expropriated the "*hiddush*" of his interpretation of האומר in the Mishnah, he must forgive me, for in Brooklyn we do not believe that translating a Mishnah to mean what it is obviously saying is a "*hiddush.*"[4] But what should be

3 And checking the reference to the Rabinowitz translation in note 20 would find the same translation as Sheilat's that I am faulted for overlooking.

4 The mere fact that he thinks I took this from him demonstrates how far Brooklyn is from Haifa. In Brooklyn one does not sit down to write an article until he has developed all the significant points that will be presented in his article. He writes to present what he has previously learned. Only when one writes for the sake of publishing and with an agenda does he look to accumulate data for his presentation in the midst of his writ-

of interest to the *Ḥakirah* readers is that, while realizing that the Mishnah refers to speech and that Rambam quotes the Mishnah, Dr. Kellner is certain that Rambam cannot take it to refer to speech. Why is this so? Because Dr. Kellner has only three choices about how to view Rambam and the mesorah. In his opinion Rambam transmitted two independent mesorahs to Israel, one Jewish and one Greek. He leaves out a fourth way of looking at Rambam and the mesorah, which is what Rambam himself says on the matter. Rambam is the bearer of the mesorah from Sinai, but since much had been lost by his time, he set out to reconstruct what was missing. He did this in both the areas of halacha and hashkafa.[5] The reason Rambam uses the language of the Mishnah is because he is expressing the conceptualizations of the Mishnah.[6]

The crux of most academic reasoning on this subject is that *Chazal* were not the sophisticated thinkers the Greeks were and thus any philosophical idea that Rambam expresses is due to Greek influence. Dr. Kellner refuses to accept Rambam's own claim that he is explicating the words of *Chazal*. Rambam read not only everything available of the thought of the Greek philosophers but everything available in the writings of the idol-worshippers. He was no more influenced by the Greeks than he was by the idolaters—he accepted what he felt was proven and it helped him understand the deep thoughts of *Chazal* expressed in their *aggodos*. My essay in this volume is an example of how Rambam in *Moreh Nevuchim* explains the deeper meaning of an *Aggadic* Mishnah. As I quote there, Rambam says that those who take Midrashim literally are fools, while those who scoff at them are much worse. Those who refuse to ac-

---

ing. My article was formulated long before I heard of Dr. Kellner's book, and only a *Ḥakirah* author's claim that Rambam's position was as stated in the book, led me to consult his work. I read every word of his book carefully and found no Rambam that I was not aware of nor any evidence to back his contentions.

5 Rambam says this quite clearly in the *Moreh* and elsewhere and I discuss this at length in *Ḥakirah* 8 "*Tradition! Tradition?*"

6 See *Ḥakirah* 9 "Mishneh Torah Science and Art," and *Ḥakirah* 7 "A Hagiographer's Review."

cept that *Chazal* spoke at a deeper level are in this second category.[7] The Moreh Nevuchim was written for the third group, who realize that Chazal spoke words of great depth and are willing to apply themselves to understanding them.[8] Rambam explains that the central feature of the work is to explain the metaphors of Tanach. The key to understanding the Torah and the *Moreh Nevuchim* is to understand the philosophical truths couched in simple language.[9]

We all agree that Rambam writes many times that all of Israel will acquire *olam haba*, but some[10] academics claim that Rambam cannot be trusted to write what he believes in Mishneh Torah. Thus, according to Dr. Kellner, the sufficient and necessary qualification for *olam haba* is (Aristotelian) knowledge of the first five of Rambam's principles. What about the other eight principles that Rambam claims are necessary? According to Dr. Kellner, it seems that these are just rhetoric. What about the other categories of sinners who lose their share, listed by Rambam in *Hilchos Teshuvah* 3:7? These are apparently just rhetoric too. What about Rambam's definition of the righteous gentile in *Hilchos Melachim* 8:11, who

---

7 The reason I referred to Dr. Berger's criticism was to point out that not all academics share Dr. Kellner's viewpoint on this matter and not all should be lumped together in one category. I then referred to Dr. Kellner's response as a matter of courtesy. With regard to what attitude we should have to Lubavitchers, only those Lubavitchers who are *magshimim* are relevant to this issue and they are a very small minority.

8 See introduction to *Moreh*.

9 See Introduction to Chelek cited above and brought completely in my essay *Completing Creation.*

10 Dr. Kellner claims he is left "scratching his head in amazement" by the "assertion" that necessary beliefs are not untrue beliefs. Yet this is also stated by the late Marvin Fox in a book that was reviewed (rather favorably) by Dr. Kellner. See Marvin M. Fox, *Interpreting Maimonides: Studies in Methodology, Metaphysics, and Moral Philosophy* (Chicago and London: University of Chicago Press, 1990) p. 320 and M. Kellner, "Reading Rambam: Approaches to the Interpretation of Maimonides" *Jewish History*, Vol. 5, No. 2 (Fall, 1991), pp. 73–93. (My thanks to Eliyahu Krakowski for this reference.) Shem Tov is cited by some as the originator of the opinion that necessary beliefs are untrue because he uses the word שקר, but he goes on to clarify "והחכם יבין כי זה נאמר בלשון דברה תורה כלשון בני אדם".

gains *olam haba* by accepting and keeping the *mitzvos* he is commanded? Apparently, according to Dr. Kellner, that is rhetoric too.

The claim that what Rambam writes in *Mishneh Torah* can be ignored at times, is based on two passages in *Moreh Nevuchim* 3:28.[11]

> "Scripture further demands **belief in certain truths,** the belief in which is indispensable in regulating our social relations: **such is the belief that God is angry with those who disobey Him,** for it leads us to the fear and dread of disobedience [to the will of G-d]. ....in some cases the law contains a truth which is itself the only object of that law, as e.g., the truth of the Unity, Eternity, and Incorporeality of G-d; in other cases, that truth is only the means of securing the removal of injustice, or the acquisition of good morals; such is **the belief that G-d is angry with those who oppress their fellow-men, as it is said, "Mine anger will be kindled, and I will slay," etc. (Exod. xxii. 23); or the belief that G-d hears the crying of the oppressed and vexed, to deliver them out of the hands of the oppressor and tyrant**, as it is written, "And it shall come to pass, when he will cry unto me, that I will hear, for I am gracious" (Exod. xxii. 25)."

In order to interpret this as Dr. Kellner wishes, we must say that Rambam believes that the Torah (*chas v'shalom*) is also lying when it says G-d listens to the crying of the oppressed or gets angry with sinners. Of course the whole point of the Moreh is that G-d does not get angry and we cannot translate these words literally; however, when the Torah says such a thing it refers to some phenomenon within Creation that demonstrates anger and G-d's *hashgacha.*[12] Were we to interpret this passage as Dr. Kellner says, we would then conclude that Rambam did not believe in *Schar V'Onesh* and that G-d does not listen to prayers and deliver the oppressed

---

11 I think I can guess why Dr. Kellner quotes *Moreh* 3:32, but it is certainly irrelevant.

12 People have a tendency to deal lightly with how Rambam explains the meanings of Biblical anthropomorphisms in the first part of the *Moreh*—they suffice with the understanding that the terms are not literal but do not dwell on why the terminology was used and the profound meanings that must be drawn from it.

from their oppressors. One would have to assume that Rambam does not believe in *hashgacha.*[13] This interpretation would render much of what Rambam explains in the *Moreh* as meaningless and unnecessary. If one studies this passage, considers all the translations, and understands how Rambam views *hashgacha,*[14] he will understand that of course these things are "truths,"[15] and man must know it is true so that he will have the proper fear instilled within himself, for only if man understands G-d's ways will man purge himself of evil, otherwise evil will destroy him.[16]

Once we do not interpret this passage as some academics would have us do, their ability to dismiss anything they wish in Mishneh Torah evaporates. (In fact, one might argue that, for the academy's masses, their understanding of 'necessary beliefs' as false beliefs that are necessary for the masses is their own necessary belief—a false belief that is necessary for their agenda.)[17] Their methodology of

---

13 *Hashgacha pratis* on the individual.

14 The introduction to my book *Encountering the Creator: Divine Providence and Prayer in the Works of Rambam* gives a brief description of Rambam's views on *hashgacha* and *Tefillah,* and the entire book is dedicated to understanding Rambam's views on *hashgacha* and *tefillah* and explicating *Sefer Breishis* and *Medrashei Chazal* based on this understanding.

15 Rambam differentiates between beliefs about G-d in which the knowledge itself improves the person, and beliefs in things such as *schar v'onesh* where the improvement comes based on the subsequent actions that these beliefs lead one to take. Since knowledge of *schar v'onesh* is knowledge of a creation of G-d and not about G-d Himself, the belief itself does not bring the ultimate improvement.

16 This is not the place for explaining this idea fully. Rambam's words must be studied and large parts understood, before one understands how this comes about. Reading "Is Reward And Punishment A True or A Necessary Belief? Musings on MN 3:28" <http://yediah.blogspot.com/2010/09/is-reward-and-punishment-true-or.html> will give the interested reader a start on this issue.

17 Rambam tells us that he does conceal within *Moreh* Nevuchim, as Chazal insisted that we not teach *Maaseh Merkava* except to those who are capable of understanding it. This is irrelevant to what is explained in Mishneh Torah. Dr. Kellner seems actually to claim that the *ikkar* of *schar v'onesh* is not true, thus overturning any understanding on why the *ikkarim* should be relevant to *olam haba.*

reading *Moreh Nevuchim* requires that *Mishneh Torah* be ignored whenever it contradicts what they perceive the Moreh to be saying.

There are some misreadings of Rambam in *Must A Jew Believe* but little of what qualifies as *"hiddush."* Yet one thing is worth discussing here since it is a major issue in Dr. Kellner's work and aptly demonstrates how he builds castles on sand. As I quoted in my essay, Rambam calls for the execution of those who are מגשימים even if this is caused by error, and yet of the *Karaim* he expresses tolerance.

> אבל בני אותן הטועים ובני בניהם, שהדיחו אותם אבותם ונולדו במינות, וגידלו אותן עליו--הרי הן כתינוק שנשבה לבין הגויים וגידלוהו הגויים על דתם, שהוא אנוס; ואף על פי ששמע אחר כך שהיה יהודי, וראה היהודיים ודתם--הרי הוא כאנוס, שהרי גידלוהו על טעותם. כך אלו האוחזים בדרכי אבותיהם שתעו. לפיכך ראוי להחזירן בתשובה, ולמשוך אותם בדרכי שלום, עד שיחזרו לאיתן התורה; **ולא ימהר אדם להורגן**. (ממרים ג:ג)

Thus, Dr. Kellner is *mechadesh* that there is a difference between denial of the first five principles and of the last eight, and he claims this strengthens his position. In fact there is no contradiction at all. The only reason Dr. Kellner could make this argument is that he left out the last four words in *Hilchos Mamrim* **ולא ימהר אדם להורגן**. With these words in place, there is no evidence that Rambam distinguishes among various heretics. What Rambam says in the *Moreh* about those who have been misled is clarified in *Hilchos Mamrim*. When the Jewish Kingdom and Sanhedrin will be reestablished, the Torah leaders will accost those who are members of sects that reject the 13 *ikkarim*, and will try to convince them of the error of their ways—as Rambam says, ולא ימהר אדם להורגן. But should they insist on sticking to their beliefs and wish to die for what they consider קדוש השם, they will be accommodated.[18] Why did Dr. Kellner leave out these last four important words?[19] This is merely the way of some academics not to be bothered by phrases that do not "fit in." They don't accept that every word Rambam writes is chosen with

18 Will those who argue for rejecting the *ikkarim* be מוסר נפש? I doubt it. I don't believe the "orthodoxy" they hope to form will have that type of devotion to the Torah.

19 It exists in Kappach's version and Frankel's and most manuscripts and was the text before the early *acharonim*.

the greatest of care, and it is because of this that they don't understand him.

I originally had no intention of mentioning Dr. Kellner's work.[20] He writes for other academics, people who work with the same premises—who share a common theology, who "read" Rambam and who, when they have a question, are faced with a contradiction, produce a superficial answer that does not require Rambam to be consistent and certainly not "frum." But *Must A Jew Believe* has made its way into our community,[21] and the pain of seeing Rambam misrepresented led me to attempt to point out that adopting Rambam's rationalism does not mean accepting unquestioningly the musings of a self-proclaimed intellectual elite—often academic scholars who are not orthodox.[22] Rambam puts up a red light in the second chapter of the *Moreh* to bar those he wishes to advance no further. He describes a "learned man"[23] who had posed a question to him. "You appear to have studied the matter superficially, and nevertheless you imagine that you can understand a book[24] that has been the guide of past and present generations, when you for a moment withdraw from your lusts and appetites, and glance over its contents as if you were reading a historical work or some poetical composition. Collect your thoughts and examine the matter carefully, for it is not to be understood as you at first sight think, but as you will find after due deliberation." Rambam cannot be read; he has to be studied, he has to be learned—every word weighed carefully.

20 His book is mentioned in one paragraph and one footnote.

21 See note 4.

22 Rambam writes in the introduction to the *Moreh* that it is written for the observant Jew who accepts the principles of our faith—others cannot be expected to understand it. He writes in *Hil. Yesodei HaTorah* (4) that the preparatory study for *maaseh breshis* and *maaseh merkava* dealt with in the *Moreh* is the Talmudic discussions of Rava and Abaye. Only those expert in those discussions will appreciate the *Moreh*.

23 This term is one of Rambam's jokes. They are more plentiful than Dr. Kellner intimates.

24 Rambam is talking about the Torah but it applies to studying the Torah's teachings based on the *Moreh*.

Dr. Kellner is right when he says that misinterpreting Rambam endangers one's *olam haba*. In the introduction Rambam implores us, "I adjure any reader of my book, in the name of the Most High, not to add any explanation even to a single word, nor to explain to another any portion of it except in conformity to what has been explained by previous theological authorities, nor may he teach others anything of his deductions that are not in conformity.[25] The reader must, moreover, beware of raising objections to any of my statements, because it is very probable that he may understand my words to mean the exact opposite to what I intended to say. He will injure me, while I endeavored to benefit him. 'He will requite me evil for good.'" Rambam's rule is to interpret him conservatively when there is any doubt about his meaning. I have interpreted Maimonides in the *Moreh* to be consistent with another known famous *mechaber,* Rambam of *Mishneh Torah*.

As Dr. Kellner notes, there is a stream within traditionalist Judaism that from the very beginning opposed Rambam's rationalist understanding of the Torah, and it is today perhaps as strong as it ever has been. Many articles have been written in Hakirah in opposition to this stream,[26] but it is important to understand that rationalism does not lead to what one stream of Modern Orthodoxy is calling for—a Judaism defined as humanism plus meaningless acts of halachic compliance that can be manipulated whenever apparent need arises, coupled with lip-service allegiance to a few of the *ikkarim.* The schizophrenia that Dr. Kellner feels he encounters in Modern Orthodoxy is a split within the movement between those who turn to Rambam as their guide and those who wish to use him as a stepping stone to something better of their own making. Those within the movement must decide where they stand.

---

25 While most of the translation is from Friedlander's edition, I modified the last sentence according to Kappach's translation—the reader should research the various editions to ascertain what he thinks is the exact meaning. The serious reader should not believe anything I say or that Dr. Kellner says, but use our essays as a starting point to investigate these issues for themselves.

26 In *Ḥakirah* 2 "*U'Madua Lo Yeresem*" we explained how magic and astrology were viewed as sciences, and thus Rambam's views were reasonably rejected. Ramban called the view *chassidus.*

Rambam was indeed *farfrumt.* [27] Rav Meir Simchah of Dvinsk was a student of both Maimonides of *Moreh Nevuchim* and Rambam of *Mishneh Torah*. He would answer questions in *Mishneh Torah* based on insights from the *Moreh* and it was his reading during the month of Ellul.[28] He stated כי דברי רבינו בכל ספריו...רוח אחת להם, "one spirit informed all the works of our teacher." No person as *"frum"* as Rambam has lived since the *siyyum hashas.*[29] In the midst of the condemnation of Rambam's works, his opponent in thought, Ramban,[30] said it best:

> הלא שאלתם עוברי דרך ..בתהלת הרב הגדול במעלת חסידותו בתוקף אמונתו בעוצם ענותנותו בגדלות יחוסו בנדבת כיסו במעשיו הנפלאים במליו הנוראים בהיותו ביראת אלקיו דבק וחושק ובתלמודנו נושק.

---

27 While *Shem Tov* may quote those who had problems with *Moreh* 3:51, it is quoted often in my essay as support to my "farfrumt" position, and in my Flatbush Shabbos morning pre-shacharis shiur on *Sefer HaMada* we read from it (as well as from many other sections) often and discuss it in depth to the delight and inspiration of the entire group. Those whom Dr. Kellner has exposed to this material to their dismay must read in a different way.

28 See *Imrei Rebbe Shefatiah* p. 18.

29 I will always remember my discussion twenty-five years ago with one of the last of the surviving *Alter Mirrer*. He spoke of how he would read *Hilchos Yesodei Hatorah* and understood that Rambam was the genius philosopher, and he also read a *teshuva* by Rambam of how he had accepted upon himself the *chumra* of *tevilas Ezra,* which he never missed except in case of illness. Rav Finkelstein *shlita* was in awe of how these different qualities coexisted.

30 See *Ḥakirah* 2, "*U' madua Lo Yeresem.*"

כשיטת אביי[כד]) לשיטת אביי בנושא לחי. בצירוף העובדה שכל הקשיים בסוגיא הם לשיטת רבא – כך נתקבלה תשתית הלכתית שהובילה לפסיקת הלכה כאביי[כה] – כנגד הכלל להלכה: "אביי ורבא – הלכה כרבא"[כו] – וזו אחת מסוגיות: "יע"ל קג"ם" – ל' = לחי - שנפסקה הלכה כאביי.

האם כל הפוסקים תמימי דעים? כלומר, האם כולם התרשמו מהתשתית ההלכתית הזאת בסוגיא – לצורך קביעת הלכה – כאביי?

מסתבר שרובם – כן, אך - לא כולם. לדוגמה: רבינו תם[כז] - סבור - ל' - של יע"ל קג"ם – הוא לידה – ולא - לחי העומד מאליו. רבינו תם פסק כך, מפני שיש הסבורים: "רבא לא איתותב, ולמה הלכתא כאביי".[כח]

סיכום

בסוגיא הראשונה, הצליחו עורכי הסוגיא האחרונים להטביע את חותמם בסיומה של הסוגיא, בכך שהתוו את הדרך לשינוי הלכתי והכרעה במחלוקת בין רב פפא ורב הונא בריה דרב יהושע, וכך פסקו רוב הפוסקים להלכה.

בסוגיא השניה הפוסקים חלוקים ביניהם. הרמב"ם והמגיד משנה פסקו להלכה בהתאם למתווה ההלכתי של עורכי הסוגיא. אך בעל השו"ע לא הושפע מהמתווה ההלכתי בסוגיא ולא פסק כפי שמשתמע ממנה.

בסוגיא השלישית נטו רוב הפוסקים לפסוק את ההלכה בהתאם למתווה ההלכתי שהציגו עורכי הסוגיא. אך לא כולם ולא תמיד, מקבלים הפוסקים את הדרך לקביעת ההלכה – כפי שהיא מוצגת בסוגיא – על-ידי עורכי הסוגיא. ✿

כד ראה עירובין, יב ע"ב. רב יהודה ורבה סבורים לחי משום מחיצה, ומן הסתם רב יהודה למדה מרב שהיה רבו.

כה רמב"ם , הל' שבת פי"ז הכ"ב; טוש"ע, הל' שבת, סי' שסג סע' יא.

כו יד מלאכי, סי' קנג, קנו-קס.

כז תוס', נדה, לז ע"א, ד"ה: "אביי".

כח ראה דורש לציון, דרוש שלוש עשר, עמ' 96, 103.

בהמשך הסוגיא היו נסיונות להוכיח שמחלוקת אביי ורבא היא גם במחיצה – כלומר, מחיצה שעומדת מאיליה, ולא הועמדה על-ידי אדם, האם היא נחשבת מחיצה או לא – וכל הנסיונות הללו אינן צריכות והן מיותרות בסוגיא - שעוסקת בדיני לחי בנושא עירובין, ולא במחיצה – נושא שקשור לענייני סוכה במסכת סוכה – ושם גם דנו בכך.

כל מטרת עריכת הנסיונות הללו כאן בסוגיא, נועדו להרחיב ולהאריך את מסגרת הסוגיא .

מה-גם, שלעורכי הסוגיא לא הייתה בעיה מיוחדת להציג את כל הנסיונות הללו כקשיים על שיטת רבא – מפני שהיה להם תירוץ חוזר ומוכן לכל הקשיים הללו: "שעשאן מלכתחילה לכך", או "שנטעו מלכתחילה לכך", או "שבנאן מלכתחילה לכך". בדיוק כמו שעשו שימוש בתירוץ חוזר במסכת סוכה (כד ע"ב – כה ע"א): "דעביד לה בהוצא ודפנא" לאותם בעיות במסכת סוכה.

במילים אחרות, עורכי הסוגיא כאן עשו שימוש בתירוץ חוזר כפתרון למספר בעיות, כאותם בעיות המצויות במסכת סוכה, וכמו שבמסכת סוכה השתמשו בתירוץ חוזר למספר בעיות, כך גם כאן בעירובין השתמשו בתירוץ חוזר - אחר – לאותם בעיות.

רק לאחר שהרחיבו את הסוגיא בנושא: "מחיצה" חזרו לדון בנושא: "לחי", וערכו בנושא לחי שתי בעיות נוספות ופשוטות - מפני שגם הן ניתנות לפתרון באותו תירוץ החוזר: "ש(בנאן/עשאן) מתחילה לכך". הבעיה הראשונה: "ת"ש, אבני גדר היוצאות מן הבניין". הבעיה השנייה: "ת"ש, דתני ר' חייא: כותל שצידו אחד כנוס מחבירו". שלא כמו בתלמוד הירושלמי – שם הן אינן מופיעות כבעיות.[כא]

אך לא מן הנמנע הוא, ששתי הבעיות האחרונות הללו עם התירוץ החוזר - קדמו לכל אותם בעיות בנושא מחיצה ממסכת סוכה (כד ע"ב כה ע"א). כך שלמעשה, היו בסוגיא רק שתי הבעיות הללו בנושא לחי, ואת כל הבעיות מן המקבילה במסכת סוכה (בנושא מחיצה) – צירפו כאן לסוגיא (בנושא לחי) – אך ורק מפני שהיה לגביהן פתרון שהיה כבר מצוי וקיים : "ש (בנאן/ עשאן) מלכתחילה לכך". כך שאפילו לא נזקקו לתירוץ החוזר – הקיים במסכת סוכה: "דעביד לה בהוצא ודפנא". (יש מחלוקת - היכן הוא מקורן של הבעיות הללו ממסכת סוכה – האם במסכת סוכה, או כאן - בעירובין. לפי דברי הלבני:[כב] "מקור הסוגיא בעירובין ומשם הובאה לכאן" [לסוכה]. לפי דברי עמינח[כג] – סבור ההיפך – שכל הבעיות כאן בסוגיא בעירובין בנושא מחיצה – הובאו ממסכת סוכה לעירובין).

הואיל ועד כה, לא הייתה הוכחה חותכת לשיטת אביי, נאלצו עורכי הסוגיא להסתפק בעריכת סיפור "מעשה דרב" - שנדחה לסוף הסוגיא כהוכחה (לכאורה) (רב סבור

[כא] ירושלמי, עירובין, פ"א ה"ו, יט ע"ב.

[כב] הלבני, מקורות ומסורות, סוכה, עמ' קצח-קצט.

[כג] עמינח, עריכת מסכתות סוכה ומועד קטן בתלמוד הבבלי, עמ' 179.

ר' יהודה בן בבא – הרי שאין אפשרות לבצע צריכותא - מפני שלא מדובר בשני עניינים אלא בעניין אחד בלבד.

כך באמצעות ה"צריכותא" (המדומה)– יצרו עורכי הסוגיא – את ההנמקה לשיטת ר' יהודה בן בבא - החסירה כל נימוק, וכך גם סימנו את שיטת ר' יהודה בן בבא - לצורך קביעת הלכה.

ואכן, כך גם פסק הרמב"ם:[כ]

> "לא התירו הפסים האלו אלא בארץ ישראל ולבהמת עולי רגלים בלבד שיהיה באר מים חיים של רבים" וכו'. שם, הל' לא: "וכן בור הרבים ובאר היחיד אפילו בארץ ישראל אין ממלאין מהן אלא אם כן עשו להן מחיצה גבוהה עשרה טפחים".

המגיד משנה, שם, הביא את דברי ר' יהודה בן בבא מן המשנה, וכתב: "ומפורש בגמרא (דף כג) הלכה כריב"ב. עוד שם אמרו: לא הותרו פסי ביראות אלא לבאר מים חיים בלבד" – מדבריו משמע, שהוא מסתמך על שתי המימרות הללו (שהן למעשה אחת, ושמא אף על הצריכותא המדומה ביניהן) לקביעת ההלכה.

אבל השו"ע - לא התייחס לכך –ולא פסק כרמב"ם - ואולי מפני שלא נקט או לא הושפע מהמתווה לקביעת הלכה שהציגו עורכי הסוגיא.

הסוגיא השלישית: איתמר לחי העומד מאיליו – כולי שנייהו (טו ע"א)

אחד מדרכי תיקון המבוי על-מנת שיהיה אפשר לטלטל בו בשבת הוא העמדת לחי או קורה בכדי שיהא ניכר בינו לבין רשות הרבים כרשות נפרדת לעצמה.

קורה – היא לוח עץ ששמים על גבי פתח המבוי.
לחי – הוא אותו פס צר שמצמידים לפתח המבוי הפונה לרשות הרבים.

הסוגיא עוסקת במחלוקת אביי ורבא בנושא: "לחי העומד מאיליו". המחלוקת ביניהם נסובה על לחי המצוי בפתח המבוי שלא העמידו אותו מלכתחילה לשם לחי, אלא הוא עומד במקום כזה שהוא יכול לשמש כלחי לצורך היתר טלטול במבוי. לפי אביי - הוא נחשב כלחי, ולפי רבא – אינו נחשב כלחי.

במהלך הסוגיא צמצמו את המחלוקת ביניהם רק לאפשרות: כשסומכים על הלחי הזה לפני כניסת השבת (ואם לא סמכו על הלחי הזה לפני כניסת השבת – אין מחלוקת – שהוא לא מהווה לחי) – ולא מן הנמנע, שאת האפשרות הזאת ערכו בתחילת הסוגיא לאור המסקנה בסוף הסוגיא.

[כ] רמב"ם, הל' שבת, פי"ז ה"ל- הל"א.

לעומת זאת, לשיטת ר' יהודה בן בבא - עושים פסים רק לבאר הרבים בלבד, ולבור הרבים ובאר היחיד עושים חגורה (=מקיפים בחבלים – רש"י,[טז] מחיצה – תוס'[יז]; וכן משמע לגבי בור הרבים ממסכת שבת צט ע"א –ע"ב), וכל שכן –לבור היחיד.

רש"י מבאר את ההבדל בדין באר של רבים ביחס לבור הרבים ובאר היחיד, בשתי תכונות חיוביות המצויות בו. האחד, באר – שמימיה נובעים. השני, באר המיועדת לרבים – לכן מסתפקים בפסים.

הסוגיא נפתחת בקביעה הלכתית משמו של "רב יוסף אמר רב יהודה אמר שמואל הלכה כר' יהודה בן בבא" (כג ע"א), והשאלה היא מדוע פסק שמואל הלכה כר' יהודה בן בבא? הרי אין שום ראיה כר' יהודה בן בבא כנגד ר' עקיבא.

יתירה מזו, המשנה הבאה (כג ע"א) מציגה מחלוקת נוספת בין כר' יהודה בן בבא לר' עקיבא בנושא: "הגינה והקרפף" ושם נפסקה הלכה כר"ע : "קמ"ל הלכה כר' עקיבא" (כג ע"ב).

ולמעשה, מן הראוי היה לפסוק גם כאן בסוגיא - כשיטת ר' עקיבא[יח] ולא כשיטת כר' יהודה בן בבא.

לבסוף, מיד לאחר הקביעה שהלכה כר' יהודה בן בבא בתחילת הסוגיא, הובאה מימרה נוספת משמו של "רב יוסף אמר רב יהודה אמר שמואל: לא הותרו פסי ביראות אלא לבאר מים חיים בלבד". המימרה, למעשה, היא חזרה נוספת בנוסח אחר על דברי ר' יהודה בן בבא מן המשנה, והשאלה היא מדוע הובאה בסוגיא?

אפשר לנסות להסביר את ייתורה של המימרה השנייה מההיבט של עריכת המתווה להלכה בסוגיא. שהרי כאמור אין ראיה לשיטת ר' יהודה בן בבא כנגד ר' עקיבא – בסוגיא,[יט] ואדרבה, ראוי היה לנקוט בשיטת ר"ע.

אלא שאפשר להסביר את עריכת המימרה השנייה המיותרת לכאורה, כמימרה שנועדה לבאר את הקביעה: שהלכה כר' יהודה בן בבא - בתחילת הסוגיא - בדרך של "צריכותא".

במבוא התלמוד המיוחס לר"ש הנגיד, כתב: "וההצרכה היא הבאה לקיים שני עניינים והסי'[מן] צריכא". לפי דברים אלו, בצריכותא - מימרה אחת צריכה לגלות על המימרה השנייה – וזהו לכאורה המצב שנוצר כאן בסוגיא – שתי מימרות משמו של "רב יוסף אמר רב יהודה אמר שמואל" שצריכות לגלות אחת על השנייה. אבל בפועל, הואיל ותוכן שתי המימרות הללו אחד הוא: אין עושים פסין אלא לבאר הרבים בלבד – כשיטת

טז רש"י, עירובין, כב ע"ב, ד"ה:"חגורה".

יז תוס', שם, כב ע"ב, ד"ה: "חגורה".

יח ראה דרוש וחדוש, עירובין, עמ' יח, ד"ה: "ולפ"ז".

יט הלבני, עירובין, עמ' נד: "אין לדעת כלל אם הלכה כר"ע או כר' יהודה בן בבא".

אך ישנה גם אפשרות אחרת: לשיטתם של אותם עורכי סוגיא מאוחרים, אפשר שהם מתבססים (גם) על ההנחה שיש יותר קשיים על שיטת רב הונא בריה דרב מלשיטת רב פפא. זאת, אם נניח שהם מתייחסים לקושיה: "והא אפשר לצמצם" (טו ע"ב) כקושיה נוספת לשיטת רב הונא בריה דר"י.[יד] כך שמאזן הקשיים והתירוצים אינו שווה. יש חמישה קשיים לרב הונא בריה דר"י, וארבעה קשיים לשיטת רב פפא, ולכן אותם עורכי סוגיא מאוחרים הכריעו לשיטת רב פפא.

אכן, עמדתם להלכה של עורכי הסוגיא המאוחרים הללו כשיטת רב פפא, באה לידי ביטוי בפסיקת ההלכה. הפוסקים, כמו רמב"ם ושו"ע,[טו] ראשונים ואחרונים, פסקו להלכה: "פרוץ כעומד – מותר" כשיטת רב פפא.

הסוגיא השניה: אמר רב יוסף אמר רב יהודה אמר שמואל – הלכה כר' יהודה בן בבא (כג ע"א)

המשנה בקשר לסוגיא זו מציינת מחלוקת בין ר' עקיבא לר' יהודה בן בבא בנושא: לאילו סוגי ביראות עושין פסין כדי לטלטל בתוך ההיקף שלהם (כב ע"ב). יש ארבעה סוגי ביראות: בור היחיד ובור הרבים , באר היחיד ובאר הרבים.

מטרת הפסין, לפי פירוש רש"י (יז ע"ב) היא, הצורך להכין תיחום סביב הבור או הבאר כדי שהאיזור מסביב לבור או הבאר יהיה רשות היחיד, ואז אפשר למלא מהם מים, להוציאם ולהניחם שם ליד הבאר, כדי שהבהמות יכנסו לשם להשקות אותם .

יש לציין, שההבדל בין בור לבאר הוא: בור - מימיו מכונסין ואינם נובעים. באר – מימיו נובעים.

לשיטת ר' עקיבא - עושים פסין לבור הרבים, לבאר הרבים ולבאר היחיד, אבל בור של יחיד – עושים לו מחיצה גבוהה של עשרה טפחים. מדברי רש"י שם משתמע, שההבדל בדין של בור היחיד ביחס לבור הרבים באר הרבים ובאר היחיד - נובע משתי תכונות גורעות המצויות בו. האחד – מדובר בבור שמימיו מכונסין ולא נובעים. השני, מדובר בבור של יחיד, אדם פרטי (ולכן לפי ר' עקיבא עושים לו מחיצה גבוה עשרה טפחים בהשוואה לשאר שמסתפקים רק בפסים בלבד).

הנימוק לשיטת ר' עקיבא, לעשיית פסים לבור הרבים – מפני שהרבים משתמשים בו וגם אם יפסקו מימיו – יזכרו מספר אנשים מציבור הרבים לא לטלטל שם ויודיעו על כך לשאר הציבור.

והנימוק לעשיית הפסים לבאר הרבים ובאר היחיד - מפני שמימיהם תמיד נובעים ולא יפסקו .

[יד] חידושי הרשב"א, עירובין, מהד' י"ד אילן, ירושלים 1989, עמ' קיד, ד"ה: "ה"ג רש"י".

[טו] רמב"ם, הל' שבת פט"ז הט"ז; טוש"ע, הל' שבת, סי' שסב סע' ט.

עורכי סוגיא מסויימים שצידדו כשיטת רב הונא בריה דרב יהושע וכנגד רב פפא הם שסיימו את הסוגיא ב"תיובתא דרב פפא" וחתמו במונח: " תיובתא" לשם הכרעה נגד רב פפא.

אך עורכי סוגיא מאוחרים יותר,[יא] צידדו להלכה כרב פפא וקבעו: " והלכתא כוותיה דרב פפא" נגד רב הונא בריה דרב יהושע, מפני שהם סבורים, שהקביעה: "הילכתא כמאן דאיתותב" , גם אם נאמר בסוגיא "תיובתא דפלוני תיובתא" - יכולה להתממש רק כאשר ישנה ראיה ברורה וחד-משמעית ל"תיובתא".[יב]

אם אין ראיה ברורה וחד משמעית ל"תיובתא" במהלך הסוגיא - ה"תיובתא" אינה מוכרחת, ולכן אין לדחות את שיטת רב פפא.

הואיל ולדידם של אותם עורכי סוגיא המאוחרים הללו, הדיוק מן המשנה בתחילת הסוגיא בנושא: "פרוץ כעומד" הוא ראיה ברורה כשיטת רב פפא - דווקא. לכן, הם ערכו את המשך הסוגיא וקבעו: "והילכתא כוותיה דרב פפא, תיובתא והילכתא, אין, משום דדיקא מתניתין כוותיה, דתנן לא יהיו פרצות יתירות על הבנין, הא כבנין - מותר" – וכל זאת לצורך הנמקת דעתם לקביעת הלכה כשיטת רב פפא דווקא: "פרוץ כעומד – מותר" .

ההבדל בדרך קביעת ההלכה בין שתי אסכולות העורכים הללו נובע מתפיסות שונות.

אם נניח ששתי אסכולות העריכה הללו מתבססות על העובדה - שמספר הקושיות והתירוצים לרב פפא ולרב הונא בריה דרב יהושע הוא שווה (ארבע קושיות לכל אחד מהצדדים).

הרי שלנגד עורכי הסוגיא הראשונים שפסקו כרב הונא בריה דרב יהושע סייעה העובדה, שמהברייתא האחרונה: "ת"ש, דפנות הללו" (טז ע"ב) יש ראיה לרב הונא בריה דרב יהושע, ולכן הכריעו ב"תיובתא" כנגד רב פפא: "פרוץ כעומד –אסור".[יג]

לעומתם, אותם עורכי סוגיא מאוחרים שפסקו כרב פפא מנמקים את דעתם: "דדייקא מתניתין כוותיה" . כלומר, המשנה מדוייקת כמותו (של רב פפא) אע"פ שמהברייתא האחרונה יש סתירה לשיטת רב פפא, והיא מסתיימת ב"תיובתא" על רב פפא.

ויש לכך תקדים, לדוגמה, בספר "הליכות עולם", בכללי הג"מ למוהר"י קארו, הביא דוגמה מסנהדרין כז ע"א: "תיובתא דאביי תיובתא, ואפילו הכי מסיק כאביי".

לפיכך, לשיטתם, יש להעדיף במחלוקת האמוראים את השיטה התואמת את דברי המשנה (שיטת רב פפא), יותר משיטה התואמת את דברי הברייתא (שיטת רב הונא בריה דרב יהושע) – ולכן אמרו: "תיובתא והילכתא – אין".

[יא] ראה ש"מ רובינשטיין, לחקר סדור התלמוד, בתוך: מחקרים ומבואות בתלמוד, ירושלים תשל"א, עמ' 20 ; הלבני, מקורות ומסורות, ביאורים בתלמוד לסדר מועד, מיומא עד חגיגה, ירושלים תשל"ה, עמ' קלד הע' 3*.

[יב] ראה ש' אסף, תשובות הגאונים מן הגניזה, נדפס מחדש, ירושלים תשל"א, עמ' 32-33.

[יג] ראה שארית יוסף, הנתיב השני, נתיב הקושיה, כלל כד, עמ' 34-35 , על תיובתא וקשיא.

יהושע, אך הוא הוגדר ע"י הפרשנים "כשינויא דחיקא",[ז] שמשמעותו הפשוטה היא – דיוק שלכשעצמו – מיותר וחסר צורך, אך הוא היה נחוץ לצורך פיתוח הסוגיא. מפני שרק באמצעות הדיוק הדחוק הזה יכלו עורכי הסוגיא לפתח את הסוגיא על ידי הצגת קושיה על הדיוק, הבאה כנגד רב הונא בריה דרב יהושע: "אי הכי ליתני : לא יהו פירצות כבנין".

כלומר, לו דיוק זה היה נכון לשיטת רב הונא בריה דרב יהושע, המשנה היתה יכולה לומר: "לא יהו פירצות כבנין" , ומכאן היה משתמע בבירור ש"פרוץ כעומד – אסור" כשיטתו של רב הונא בריה דרב יהושע, וכל שכן אם הפרוץ מרובה על העומד.

כאן, כאמור, סיימו עורכי הסוגיא את המשא-ומתן הזה ב"קשיא" ולא ב"תיובתא",[ח] כדי שהם יוכלו להמשיך את המשא-ומתן בסוגיא[ט] שיתווה את הדרך להכרעה[י] במחלוקת ביניהם.

אכן בהמשך הסוגיא, העלו שלושה קשיים ותירוצים רק לרב פפא:

1. "ת"ש, שיירא שחנתה בבקעה" (טו ע"ב).
2. "נמצאת אתה אומר... קתני מיהת... תיובתא דרב פפא" (טז ע"א).
3. "ת"ש, דפנות הללו" (טז ע"ב).

ושלושה קשיים ותירוצים רק לרב הונא בריה דרב יהושע :

1. " אי הכי ליתני: לא יהו פירצות כבנין, קשיא" (טו ע"ב).
2. "ת"ש, המקרה סוכתו בשיפודין" (טו ע"ב).
3. "בשלמא לרב פפא... אלא לרב הונא בריה דרב יהושע ליערבינהו ולתנינהו" (טז ע"א).

ועוד קושיה ותירוץ לכל אחד מהם מברייתא: "סיפא קשיא לרב פפא, רישא קשיא לרב הונא בריה דרה יהושע"... סיפא לרב פפא – לא קשיא... רישא לרב הונא בריה דרב יהושע - לא קשיא".

בסך הכל, ארבעה קשיים ותירוצים לכל אחד מהם.

בסיומה של הסוגיא, ביקשו העורכים להתוות דרך להכרעה במחלוקת בין רב פפא לרב הונא בריה דרב יהושע בנושא שבו פתחו את הדיון בסוגיא: "פרוץ כעומד".

ז יד דוד, שם.

ח חידושי הריטב"א, שם.

ט הלבני, שם.

י גאון יעקב, שם.

סוכה (טו ע"א) – נאמר שם עם המונח: "דאתמר", ומהסוגיא בסוכה הועבר לגירסת הסוגיא בעירובין.[א]

אולם לגופו של ענין, כל הנושא הזה: "פרוץ כעומד" ומחלוקת האמוראים: רב פפא ורב הונא בריה דרב יהושע לכאורה מיותרים,[ב] מפני שאפשר היה לפתוח את הסוגיא בדיון עם התייחסות ישירה לדברי המשנה הנידונה: "תנן ולא יהו פרצות יתירות על הבנין" ועם כל הדיוקים המצויים שם בסוגיא: "הא כבנין מותר... אבל כבנין מאי אסור" – ללא מחלוקת האמוראים.

יתירה מזו, גם אם כבר נוספה מחלוקת האמוראים – הרי שהיא יכלה להסתיים ב"תיובתא" על רב הונא בריה דרב יהושע וכשיטת רב פפא - פרוץ כעומד - כבר בתחילת הסוגיא, לאור הדיוק מן המשנה: " תנן ולא יהו פרצות יתירות על הבנין, הא כבנין - מותר".

אבל עורכי הסוגיא לא רצו לסיים כאן את הסוגיא, ולבטל את דברי רב הונא בריה דרב יהושע ב"תיובתא",[ג] ולכן סיימו ב"קשיא"[ד] - מהסיבות הבאות:

1. כדי שלא יווצר מצב שבו לכאורה רב הונא בריה דרב יהושע טועה בדבר משנה, משא"כ ביחס ל"תיובתא" על רב פפא מברייתא ("ת"ש: דפנות הללו") בסוף הסוגיא– הואיל והיא ברייתא- לא חששו מכך עורכי הסוגיא.[ה]
2. עורכי הסוגיא בקשו להתוות את הדרך להלכה בסוגיא כשיטת אחד מהצדדים במחלוקת (רב הונא בריה דרב יהושע או רב פפא) באופן אובייקטיבי ומשכנע יותר.
3. כך מתאפשר לעורכי הסוגיא להמשיך ולפתח את המו"מ בסוגיא.[ו]

לו היו מסיימים כבר בתחילת הסוגיא ב"תיובתא" על דברי רב הונא בריה דרב יהושע – לא היו יכולים להמשיך ולפתח את הסוגיא, וכך היתה מתקבלת סוגיא קצרה על דברי המשנה, ומזה רצו עורכי הסוגיא להימנע.

לאור כל האמור, דחו את הקושי: "תנן: ולא יהו פרצות יתרות על הבנין - הא כבנין מותר" - על דברי רב הונא בריה דרב יהושע בדיוק הבא: "אלא אימא אם בנין יתר על הפירצה - מותר, אבל כבנין מאי? – אסור?" דיוק זה שמתאים לשיטת רב הונא בריה דרב

[א] ראה נ' עמינח, עריכת מסכתות סוכה ומועד קטן בתלמוד הבבלי, תל אביב תשמ"ט, עמ' 176-177.

[ב] ראה יד דוד, עירובין, טו ע"ב, ד"ה: "ע"ב, איתמר".

[ג] ראה חידושי הריטב"א, עירובין, מה' מ' גולדשטיין, עמ' קכב, ד"ה: "קשיא".

[ד] ראה ד' הלבני, מקורות ומסורות, ביאורים בתלמוד, מסכתות עירובין ופסחים, ירושלים תשמ"ב, עמ' לח הע' 7 על יישוב לקשיא של בעל דברי למנצח לדוד.

[ה] ראה גאון יעקב, עירובין, עמ' מד, ד"ה:"קשיא".

[ו] ראה חידושי הריטב"א, שם; הלבני, שם.

שיקולים בעריכת המתווה לקביעת הלכה, בסוגיות מסכת עירובין והשפעתם על הפוסקים

מאת: אורי צור

ברוב סוגיות התלמוד הבבלי השונות ישנו משא-ומתן הנוגע לענייני הלכה. אך אין מטרת הסוגיא לקבוע את ההלכה כספרי הפסיקה אלא להציג ולשקף את השתלשלות פני הדברים בנושא הנדון. הקורא (הפוסק) צריך לקבל הכרעה לאור המצוי בסוגיא.

אך האם הסוגיא אובייקטיבית? האם עורכי הסוגיא מציגים את כל החומר הרלוונטי לסוגיא? האם יש לעורכים שיקולים מסויימים בעלי השפעה להלכה? ואם כן, מהם?

מטרת המאמר להציג לדוגמה שלוש סוגיות ממסכת עירובין בתלמוד הבבלי, שיש בהן שיקולים מצד עורכי הסוגיא שהשפיעו על הדרך לקביעת ההלכה באותן סוגיות, ואת מתווה העריכה בסוגיא שהובילו לדרך קביעת ההלכה בסוגיא. במקביל, לבחון את דברי הפוסקים בהכרעתם את ההלכה, ואופי נימוקיהם, קרי, האם הכרעתם אכן מבוססת על המתווה להלכה של העורכים לאור שיקוליהם השונים או מנימוקים אחרים שאינם מתחשבים בעריכת המתווה להלכה של העורכים.

הסוגיא הראשונה: פרוץ כעומד (טו ע"ב – טז ע"ב)

עורכי הסוגיא פתחו את הדיון על משנתינו בסוגיא בנושא: "פרוץ כעומד". כלומר, מה דין היקף מקום מסוים שחלקו הפרוץ שווה לחלקו הקיים לעניין עירוב, האם הוא ייחשב כפרוץ או כעומד וקיים?

כהערת אגב, יש לציין את השתלשלות המונח: "איתמר" בתחילת הסוגיא. עורכי הסוגיא כאן בבבלי גרסו בלי המונח: "איתמר" אלא רק: "פרוץ כעומד" ואת מחלוקת האמוראים רב פפא ורב הונא בריה דרב יהושע, ורק אח"כ כשהסוגיא הועברה למסכת

אורי צור - ראש המחלקה למורשת ישראל במרכז האוניברסיטאי אריאל בשומרון. חוקר ומרצה בכיר לתלמוד במחלקה למורשת ישראל. קיבל תואר דוקטור בשנת 1996 מטעם אוניברסיטת תל-אביב בנושא: "שיקול הדעת בעריכת סוגיות במסכת עירובין בתלמוד הבבלי, פרקים א-ג". המחקר נתפרסם כספר: "אור ישראל", מטעם מכון הברמן למחקרי ספרות, לוד 1999.

סיכום:

נראה שבנד"ד יש כמה ספיקות אם יש לפדות גלעד שליט נ"י שלתמורת פדיונו משחררים אלף מחבלים.

א) יש לדון משום שהוא יותר מכדי דמיהם, [שלכאורה חייל אחד תמורת אלף מחבלים נראה כיתר מכדי דמיהם לפי מה שנהוג בין שאר האומות כשמחליפים חייליהם] ואף שיש בו סכנת נפשות לא שנא.

ב) נראה שבכה"ג שיש סכנה לאחרים ליכא מצות פדיון שבויים כלל.

ג) יש לדון כיון שבשחרור המחבלים יש חשש גדול שחוזרים לסורם בכה"ג אדרבה יש לאסור מטעם שכל המשתדל בזה חשוב כרודף.

כמובן, כל זה לא כתבנו לדינא אלא לפלפולא כדרכו של תורה, ויה"ר שלא נצטרך לדון בכגון זה למעשה. והמקום ירחם עליהם ולכל אחינו בית ישראל הנתונים בצרה ובשביה ויוציאם מצרה לרווחה בזמן קרוב, אכי"ר. ☙

ענף ב: אם יש חשש בשחרור המחבלים משום שחוזרים לסורם ועוד

א) והנה היה אפשר לדון מטעם אחר שאין לפדותו תמורת אלף מחבלים, כיון שבשחרורם כידוע יש הסתברות גדולה שהרבה מהם חוזרים לסורם לחבל ולהרוג שוב, וא"כ בשחרורם גורם עוד חשש פקוח נפשות.

ונראה שיש לדמות לזה מש"כ בש"ך (חו"מ סימן קס"ג ס"ק י"ח), וז"ל: המלך או שר שמטיל איזה דבר על עשיר א' או ב', ויש ליהודי א' כח בהיכל המלך והשר להשתדל לפוטרם, אם הדבר ברור וודאי שאם יפטרם לאלו יטיל על אחרים אי רשאי להצילם לאלו או לא. פסק בתשובת מהריב"ל (ח"ב סימן מ) דאם כבר הטיל המלך על אנשים ידועים ופרט אותם ונלכדו ברשתו אזי אין יהודי רשאי להשתדל לפוטרן בשום ענין שיזיק לאחרים בודאי, אבל אם יצא גזרה להטיל על ב' אנשים בסתם יכול יהודי להשתדל על איזה אנשים שרוצה שלא יהיו בכלל הגזירה אף שבודאי יכנסו אחרים, עכ"ל, וע"ש עוד.

ונראה שכן הוא בנד"ד, כיון שכבר תפסו אחד א"כ אי תמורת שחרורו גורם שאחרים הם בפקוח נפשות הרי מזיק לאחרים, ואף שאינו ברי היזיקא מ"מ כיון שיש הסתברות גדולה שחוזרים לסורם י"ל שוא"ת עדיף, וצ"ע.

ב) ועוד יש לדון לענ"ד, דהנה בעיקר חובת פדיון שבויים שהוא מצוה רבה שמוטל על הציבור להשתדל לפדותם, הרי לא מצינו אלא שמחוייבים הציבור לפדותם בממון וגם לעסוק בגופם שהוא בכלל חיוב צדקה והחסד, אבל לא מצינו שמחוייבים הציבור לסכן עצמם כדי לפדותם.

ואשר על כן נראה שבאופן שגורם לסכנת נפשות אצל הציבור או אחרים באופן זה אינו בכלל החיוב של פדיון שבויים.

ג) יש להוסיף עוד שכיון שלאחר שחרורם אותם המחבלים רובם חוזרים לסורם להרוג ח"ו מאחינו בנ"י, א"כ מי שמשתדל לשחררם יש לו גם דין רודף.

ונראה שגם הגורם ליהרג יש לו גם דין רודף מהא דמצינו לענין מוסר שחשוב רודף, עי' רמב"ם בהלכות חובל ומזיק (פ"ח ה"י), וז"ל: מותר להרוג המוסר בכל מקום ואפילו בזמן הזה שאין דנין דיני נפשות, ומותר להרגו קודם שימסור אלא כשאמר הריני מוסר פלוני בגופו או בממונו ואפילו ממון קל הרי התיר עצמו למיתה, ומתרין בו ואומרין לו אל תמסור, אם העיז פניו ואמר לא כי אלא אמסרנו מצוה להרגו וכל הקודם להרגו זכה, עכ"ל. וכן מובא בשו"ע (חו"מ סימן שפ"ח סעיף י') והטעם משום שחשוב כרודף, ע"ש ברמ"א עוד פרטים בזה.

והנה במוסר לעכו"ם אינו אלא גרמא בעלמא [ע' ביאור הגר"א שם ס"ק ע"ד] ומ"מ חשוב כרודף, וא"כ ה"ה בנד"ד מי שמשתדל בשחרור אותו השבוי תמורת מחבלים הרי ע"י שחרורם הוא גורם לעוד פקוח נפשות ויש לו דין רודף לכאורה.

האסורים, אמר: (ישעיהו מב:) "מי נתן למשיסה יעקב וישראל לבוזזים" ענה אותו תינוק ואמר "הלא ה' זו חטאנו לו ולא אבו בדרכיו הלוך ולא שמעו בתורתו". אמר מובטחני בו שמורה הוראה בישראל, העבודה! שאיני זז מכאן עד שאפדנו בכל ממון שפוסקין עליו. אמרו לא זז משם עד שפדאו בממון הרבה, ולא היו ימים מועטין עד שהורה הוראה בישראל. ומנו רבי ישמעאל בן אלישע, ע"כ.

ובתוס' שם (ד"ה כל ממון שפוסקין עליו) הקשו, וז"ל תירוצם: כי איכא סכנת נפשות פודין שבויין יותר על כדי דמיהן כדאמרינן בפרק השולח (לעיל דף מד.) גבי מוכר עצמו ואת בניו לעובדי כוכבים כ"ש הכא דאיכא קטלא. אי נמי משום דמופלג בחכמה היה, עכ"ל. וכן מובא תירוץ זו ברמב"ן (גיטין מה.) בשם י"א, וכן במאירי (שם).

והנה כבר הארכנו לעיל (פרק א' ענף א' אותיות ג'-ה') בביאור השיטה הנ"ל אי דוקא באופן שיש ודאי סכנה פודים יותר מכדי דמיהם או גם בספק סכנה. אלא שנראה שאצל הערבים הללו ימ"ש נוטה שהוא ודאי סכנה, ולכן לשיטת התוס' ודעימיה הרי פודים אותם גם ביותר מכדי דמיהם.

ג) אלא שיש לדון אי קי"ל לדינא כתירוץ הנ"ל.

ע' בפתחי תשובה (שו"ע שם סימן רנ"ב ס"ק ד') שהביא בשם כמה תשובות מגדולי אחרונים דלא קי"ל כתירוץ הראשון שבתוס'.[יא]

ועוד הביא משו"ת כנסת יחזקאל (סימן ל"ח) שכתב שאותו תירוץ של תוס' לא שייך אלא לפי הטעם משום דוחקא דצבורא שבכה"ג שיש סכנת נפשות צריך הציבור לדחוק יותר, אבל לפי הטעם דלא לגרבי ולייתו טפי הסברא הוא להיפך דאם בסכנת נפשות פודין יותר מכדי דמיהן א"כ ירצו להרוג את השבוים כדי שיפדו יותר מכדי דמיהם, וגם יגרבו וירצו להרוג עוד. וא"כ כיון שהרמב"ם והשו"ע פסקו כטעם הנ"ל א"כ על כרחך לא קי"ל כתירוץ התוס',[יב] וע"ש עוד.

ונראה שבנד"ד יש לצדד שמותר לפדות יותר מכדי דמיהם, דידוע שכל חיל יוצא לצבא בידיעה ובהבטחה שאם יתפס ח"ו יעשו בעבורו כל המאמצים כדי לשחררו, ובלא זה לא יתעסק למלאות תפקידו כראוי, כגון לסכן את עצמו בשביל להציל חבירו שנפל ביד האויב וכדומה. ונמצא שאם פודים אותם רק בכדי דמיהם הוא מפריע גדול באופן שיש חשש שעל ידי זה מרתיע החיילים מלעשות תפקידם כראוי. ולפ"ז יש כעין הטעם של "דלא לגרבי ולייתו" שאדרבה אם אין פודין יותר מכדי דמיהם מרבה עוד סכנה.

יא וכן משמע בשו"ע שם שהביא לדינא תירוץ הב' של התוס', וז"ל: וכן לת"ח, או אפילו אינו ת"ח אלא שהוא תלמיד חריף ואפשר שיהיה אדם גדול, פודים אותו בדמים מרובים, עכ"ל.

יב ולפי זה צ"ל שהתוס' פסקו כאותו הטעם של דוחקא דציבורא. ובאמת במסקנת הגמ' שם בגיטין הוא בעיא דלא איפשטא, וע"ש בר"ן על הרי"ף (דף כג. ד"ה או דילמא) מש"כ בזה. וע' בביאור הגר"א (ס"ק ו') שביאר הוכחת השו"ע לפסוק כהטעם של דלא לגרבו. אלא שיש להעיר מדברי המאירי, שפסק כטעמא דלא לגרבו ומ"מ הביא תירוץ של התוס' הנ"ל שכשיש חשש מיתה אין לדבר קצבה, וצ"ע.

פרק ב'
בענין פדיון שבויים על ידי תמורת שחרור של מחבלים

כידוע תפסו הערבים המחבלים ימ"ש כמה חיילים וביניהם גלעד שלית נ"י ולאחר משא ומתן הסכימו לשחררם תמורת שחרור של אלף ערבים שהם במאסר אצל מדינת ישראל. וכידוע אותם הערבים התעסקו בחבלנות בעבר וידיהם מלאים דם של אחינו בני ישראל ל"ע.

ויש לדון בו ע"פ דין תורתינו הק' בכמה אופנים:

א) ע"פ המבואר במתני' (גיטין מה.) שאין פודין את השבויין יתר על כדי דמיהן, מפני תיקון העולם, יש לדון אם שייך זה לנד"ד שלכאורה הוא ביותר מכדי דמיהם.

ב) יש לחוש שיצא שכרו בהפסדו שהרי אותם הערבים שידועים למחבלים ורוצחים הרי יש הסתברות גדולה שהרבה מהם חוזרים לסורם וא"כ בשחרורם גורם עוד חשש פקוח נפשות, ואפשר אפילו שהמשחררם חשוב כרודף.

ענף א: בדין אין פודין את השבויין יותר מכדי דמיהן

א) תנן בגיטין (דף מה.) אין פודין את השבויין יתר על כדי דמיהן, מפני תיקון העולם, ע"כ. ובסוגיא שם איתא: איבעיא להו: האי מפני תיקון העולם משום דוחקא דצבורא הוא, או דילמא משום דלא לגרבו ולייתו טפי. ת"ש: דלוי בר דרגא פרקא לברתיה בתליסר אלפי דינרי זהב. אמר אביי, ומאן לימא לן דברצון חכמים עבד דילמא שלא ברצון חכמים עבד, ע"כ.

ופירש"י, וז"ל: מפני דוחקא דציבורא הוא: אין לנו לדחוק הצבור ולהביאו לידי עניות בשביל אלו. או דילמא: דלא ימסרו עובדי כוכבים נפשייהו וליגרבו ולייתו טפי מפני שמוכרין אותן ביוקר. ונפקא מינה בתליסר אלפי דינרי: אלמא משום דוחקא דציבורא הוא, עכ"ל.

והנה הרמב"ם כתב בהלכות מתנות עניים (פ"ח הי"ב) וז"ל: אין פודין את השבויים ביתר על דמיהן מפני תקון העולם, שלא יהיו האויבים רודפין אחריהם לשבותם, עכ"ל. וכן הובא בשו"ע (יו"ד סימן רנ"ב סעיף ד').

ולפ"ז אף אם יש לו אב עשיר או קרוב שרוצה לפדותו בדמים הרבה ולא יפילהו על הצבור מ"מ אסור לפדות ביתר מכדי דמיהם מדינא דמתני' משום תיקון העולם.

ב) והנה יש לדון עוד ע"פ מה שחדשו מקצת ראשונים שבמקום סכנה פודין יותר מכדי דמיהם.

יעויין בסוגיא בפרק הנזקין שהבאנו למעלה (גיטין נח.), דאיתא שם: ת"ר: מעשה ברבי יהושע בן חנניה שהלך לכרך גדול שברומי, אמרו לו: תינוק אחד יש בבית האסורים, יפה עינים וטוב רואי וקווצותיו: סדורות לו תלתלים. הלך ועמד על פתח בית

סיכום:

ז) ונראה לנידון הנ"ל במי שנתחייב במשפט כדין [ולא מתוך עלילות ובהגזמה וכדומה] בערכאות של המדינה בעבור עוונות שעשה ולדיניהם מחוייב מאסר, נראה שלפי הראשונים הנ"ל שיש כח למלכות לענוש כן בעונש הגוף, אין בו משום מצות פדיון שבויים.

ואף לפי מש"כ בשו"ת אגרות משה שגנב ומזיק יש בו איסור מסירה אם המלכות מענישין יותר מדין תורה, אבל מ"מ חיוב פדיון שבויים לא מצינו [והראיה שהרי מי שהוא ממונה מהמלך מותר למסור בכה"ג, וכמו שנתבאר], וצ"ע בזה.

וכן ראיתי מובא בספר עלהו לא יבול שהביא שאחד ששאל להגרש"ז אורבאך זצ"ל אודות מי שנתפס במאסר שגנב סכומי כסף גדולים ונידון לכמה שנים במאסר ונשאל אם ראוי לאסוף כסף לפדותו משום מצות פדיון שבויים. והשיב: פדיון שבויים?! - מה זה פדיון שבויים, פדיון שבויים הוא כאשר תופסים בלא טעם מוצדקת אבל מי שגנב והתורה אמרה "לא תגנוב" והוא גנב, אדרבה טוב שישב קצת בכלא וילמד שאסור לגנוב, עכ"ד.[י]

אלא שיש להעיר מדברי הרדב"ז (הלכות מתנות עניים פ"ח הי"ג) שכתב, וז"ל: וכבר נשאלתי על היהודים הרגילים לגנוב ממון עכו"ם אם אנו מחוייבים לפדותם אי מדמינן להו למי שלוה מהם ואסרוהו או למי שהמיר דמה לי אוכל נבלות, ומה לי לא תגנוב. והעליתי דלעולם פודין אותו כדין מי שלוה מן העכו"ם שהרי אינו גונב להכעיס אלא לתאבון שאם היה מוצא ממון בהיתר לא היה גונב. ומזה הטעם אפילו הוא רגיל לגנוב ממון של ישראל ותפסוהו העכו"ם פודין אותו ואפילו לפי דעת האומרים דמומר אוכל נבלות לתאבון אין ישראל חייבין לפדותו הכא איכא טעמא אחרינא, שכל הגונבין ממון העכו"ם טועין וסוברין דקרא ד"לא תגנוב" בישראל קאי וסומכין על קרא ד"ראה ויתר" כו' (חבקוק ג:ו) וכיון שהם טועין בדין אינם נקראים מומרים וכל שכן שהורגים על הגניבה הילכך חייבים לפדותם אפילו כמה פעמים, עכ"ל.

הרי מבואר שאף שתפסוהו על גניבה ולכאורה תפסוהו כדין מ"מ יש מצוה לפדותו, וצ"ע.

י וכן שמעתי מעשה במי שביקש מאת הגאון הסטייפלער זצ"ל ברכה להצלחה למי שהיה עובר משפט בערכאות של מדינת ארצה"ב עבור גניבה, וענה לו: "אם באמת גנב מגיע לו ואם לאו ה' יעזור", עכ"ד.

שהם דנים ביסורי הגוף במאסר הרבה שנים, הנה לכאורה פשוט שאין שייך להתיר. אף אם לא היה כלל איסור לידון בדיני המדינות לפני שופטי המדינה, אבל הא אין לנו למוסרו לדונו בדברים שלא שייך בדיני התורה, שהוא ממון כפי שומת הבקיאין, והם דנים ביסורים שזה לא חייבה תורה. וע' במו"ק (דף יז.) וכו'.[ט] חזינן דאף על גנבא אסור להחמיר יותר מדינו שחייבה תורה. וא"כ פשוט שגם מכות וישיבה במאסר וכל יסורי הגוף, שאסור וכו', וממילא לא שייך להתיר למסור את הגנב לערכאות, לדונו במאסר ובשאר עונשי הגוף, עכ"ל.

ובסוף התשובה הקשה מסוגיא דב"מ הנ"ל, וז"ל: ולא קשה מעובדא דר"א בר"ש ור' ישמעאל בר' יוסי בב"מ (דף פג:), כדתירץ הב"י בסוף סימן שפ"ח, דכיון שנתמנו ע"ז מהמלכות שאני, והביא זה מתשובת הרשב"א, עכ"ל.

הנה מבואר בדבריו שכל שהמלכות עונשים יותר מדברי תורה יש בו איסור מסירה, וישיבה במאסר הוא ג"כ בכלל, שהרי מדין תורה אין על הגנב והגזלן אלא חיוב תשלומין ולא עונש ויסורי הגוף, וא"כ מטעם זה הוא בכלל מסירה.

ולכאורה יש להעיר מדברי שו"ת הרשב"א והריטב"א הנ"ל שמבואר שיש כח למלכות לענוש כן אפילו יותר מדיני תורה.

ועל כרחך צ"ל כמש"כ לעיל דאיסור מסירה שאני והוא אף באופן שיש כח למלכות לענוש כן. אמנם כיון שעכ"פ יש למלכות רשות לעשות כן מי שהוא שליח של המלכות יכול למסור וכמש"כ גם האגרות משה להדיא, והדברים מחודשים מאד.

ו) ויל"ע בגוונא הנ"ל שיש בו איסור מסירה כיון שהוא יותר מדיני תורה אם יש בו עכ"פ משום מצות פדיון שבויים.

ולכאורה אי נימא שיש בו מצות פדיון שוב יקשה שא"כ איך מותר אפילו מי שהוא שליח המלך למוסרו למלכות. וכי נימא שאחר מחוייב לפדותו והוא מותר למוסרו - הרי גם על השליח מוטל עליו לפדותו וכש"כ שלא למוסרו, וצ"ע בזה.

ט וז"ל: ועיין במו"ק דף י"ז ע"א, בעובדא דר"ל הוה מנטר פרדיסא, אתא ההוא גברא וקאכיל תאיני, רמא ביה קלא ולא אשגח ביה, ושמתיה ר"ל, וא"ל ההוא גברא אדרבה ליהוי ההוא גברא בשמתא, אם ממון נתחייבתי לך נידוי מי נתחייבתי לך, ושאל ר"ל בבי מדרשא ואמרו שלו נידוי שלך אינו נידוי, והוצרך ר"ל להתיר נידויו. חזינן וכו', עכ"ל.

ולכאורה צ"ל שהם ב' דינים נפרדים, שכל שהוא שליח המלך יכול למסור ואין בו איסור מסירה, אמנם מי שהוא יחיד ואינו שליח המלך אסור למוסרו למלכות [ואף בכה"ג שיש למלכות כח ורשות לענוש כן].

ג) וע"ע בשו"ת שבט הלוי (ח"ב סימן נ"ח) שנשאל באחד שעובד במשרד המכס וכשהוא רואה מי שרימה את הממשלה וצריך למסור אותו לבית המשפט אם זה בגדר מלשין או דינא דמלכותא דינא.[ו]

והשיב, וז"ל: הנה בעצם דין מכס לית דין ולית דיין שזה נכנס בגדר דינא דמלכותא דינא וכו'.[ז] ולענין למסור למלכות הנה מש"ס ב"מ (דף פג:) בעובדא דר"א בר"ש דהוי מחר וורא למלכות מוכח דהוא מותר משום הורמנא דמלכא, ואף על גב דאמרו לי' עד מתי אתה מוסר עמו של אלקינו להריגה, היינו משום שנוגע לסכנת נפשות של ישראל, וכן מש"כ אליהו הנביא זל"ט שם (דף פד.) לר' ישמעאל ב"ר יוסי, אבל מעיקר הדין משמע דגם בכזה איכא דין מלכות עיין היטב בריטב"א שבשטמ"ק, עכ"ל.

וע"ש שכתב שכיון שהוא מחויב מן הדין א"כ אין לו דין מוסר (ע' חו"מ סימן שפ"ח סעיף י"ב), ואף שעכ"פ אסור מטעם אחר משום שהוי כמשיב אבידה לעכו"ם, מ"מ מי שממונה על כך מהמלכות אין בזה איסור וכמבואר בסוגיא הנ"ל.[ח]

ונראה שזה כמו שכתבנו לעיל ששליח המלך שאני, אלא שלדברינו מוכח שאף בכה"ג שיש ליחיד שאינו שליח המלך דין מוסר מ"מ לשליח המלך מותר והוא חידוש [וכן מוכח בדברי שו"ת אגרות משה שמובא להלן אות ה'].

ד) והנה ניחזי אנן באופן שיש כח ורשות למלכות לענוש אם יש בו משום מצות פדיון שבויים.

ולכאורה הסברא נותנת שכיון שעכ"פ מי שהוא שליח המלך יכול למסור והטעם משום שיש רשות להמלכות לענוש כן וכדמבואר בדברי הרשב"א והריטב"א, ואף להריגה, א"כ אין בו מצות פדיון. והגה בעצמך - אם היה בו מצות פדיון א"כ איך היה מותר לרבי אלעזר ב"ר שמעון למוסרו למלכות גם להריגה, אלא על כרחך כיון שהוא נענש כדין אין מחוייב לפדותו.

ונראה שאף דלגבי היחיד שאינו שליח המלך יש לו דין מוסר מ"מ נראה שכל זה רק שאסור למסור להם בידים, אבל שיהא מחוייב לפדותו לא מצינו.

ה) ויש להעיר ע"פ מש"כ בשו"ת אגרות משה (או"ח ח"ה סימן ט' אות י"א) שנשאל אם מותר למסור גנב שגנב ס"ת וכלי כסף מביהכ"נ לערכאות המדינה, והשיב וז"ל: שידוע

ו וע"ע בשו"ת אגרות משה (חו"מ ח"א סימן צ"ב) שנשאל ג"כ בענין זה.

ז ז"ל: גם לדעת החולקים בחו"מ סימן שס"ט ס"ח ברמ"א, ועיין בש"ך חו"מ סי' ע"ג ס"ק ל"ט ובלבוש סוף סימן שס"ט שם ובתשובת השיב משה סימן צ' בזה, עכ"ל.

ח ומסיק שם דמ"מ לכתחלה כדאי שלא לקבל משרה כזאת שיהיה צריך למסור אפילו בהיתר דלאו משנת חסידים הוא.

שמם שירבו הרצחנים וחבריהם, וכדר' עקיבא אלו הייתי בסנהדרין לא היה אדם נהרג מעולם. ואמרו כל הסנהדרין שהרגו שני פעמים נקרא קטלנית, עכ"ל.

ועוד הביא הרשב"א מסוגיא בב"מ (דף פג:) דאיתא שרבי אלעזר ב"ר שמעון היה ממונה ממלך והיה תופס גנבים והיה המלכות עונשים וממיתים אותם, וכן רבי ישמעאל ב"ר יוסי (שם פד.). ואף על גב דא"ל רבי יהושע בן קרחה חומץ בן יין וכו' וכן אמר ליה אליהו לרבי ישמעאל ב"ר יוסי, לא היו טועים גמורים בדינים מפורשים אלא שמחמת חסידותן טענו להם שהיה להם להמנע מלהרוג על מה שלא חייבה תורה מיתה, אבל מעיקר הדין כל שהוא ממונה על כך מהמלך דן ועושה במשפטי המלוכה כי מלך במשפטים אלו יעמיד ארץ, עכתו"ד.

וכ"כ שם הריטב"א (ד"ה אמר להם תפסוהו), וז"ל: והא דדאין בלא עדים והתראה ושלא בזמן סנהדרין, שאני הכא דשליחא דמלכא הוא ומדיני המלכות להרוג בלא עדים והתראה לייסר העולם, כמו שראינו בדוד שהרג גר עמלקי ושלוחו של מלך כמותו. ומ"מ במקום שאין כח למלך לעשות כן מחוקי המלכות אף הממונה שלו אינו רשאי ואם אמר לו המלך לעשות כן יהרג ואל יעבור, עכ"ל.

ומבואר בדבריהם שיש למלכות כח להעניש אף ישראל בעונשי הגוף ומיתה, וגם באופן שלא כדין תורה [כגון בלא עדים ובלא התראה וכו']. וכל שהוא מחקי המלכות גם רשאי ישראל שהוא בשליח המלכות למסרו להם להנך עונשים ואף למיתה.

וע' שו"ת מהר"ם שי"ק (חו"מ סימן נ') שנשאל בישראל שנחשד שהרג, וכתב שלפי הריטב"א הנ"ל מי שמשתדל להביאו במשפט כדין עושה שיש למלכות עכו"ם כח לענוש ביסורים ומיתה. [ומסיק שלמעשה אין לגדולי ישראל להתאמץ ולהשתדל בזה אלא שב ואל תעשה עדיף, ע"ש עוד, ועי' להלן].

אמנם בשו"ת הנ"ל (ד"ה אבל) מדייק מדברי הרמב"ם בהלכות רוצח (פ"ב ה"ד) שחולק על הריטב"א הנ"ל, וס"ל שרק למלך ישראל יש כח לענוש כן שלא בעדים והתראה, ע"ש [ויש לדחות].

ויש להעיר עוד בשיטת הרמב"ם, דהנה מש"כ הרשב"א הנ"ל דלא קי"ל כרבי יהושע בן קרחה ואליהו הנביא שם שכנראה חולקים וס"ל שאין למסור לעכו"ם, שכוונתם רק למדת חסידות אבל מעיקר הדין קי"ל כשיטת רבי אלעזר ב"ר שמעון שיכולין למסור.

אמנם בעין משפט (שם דף פג: אות ד'-ה') ציין על דברי רבי יהושע בן קרחה למש"כ הרמב"ם בהלכות חובל ומזיק (פ"ח ה"ט), וז"ל: אסור למסור ישראל ביד גוים בין בגופו בין בממונו, ואפילו היה רשע ובעל עבירות ואפילו היה מיצר לו ומצערו, וכל המוסר ישראל ביד גוים בין בגופו בין בממונו אין לו חלק לעולם הבא, עכ"ל. וכן ציין למש"כ בשו"ע (חו"מ סימן שפ"ח סעיף ט') שהעתיק דברי הרמב"ם הנ"ל. ומשמע שהבין שלהרמב"ם קי"ל כרבי יהושע בן קרחה.

אמנם מדברי הב"י לא משמע כן, שהעתיק דברי שו"ת הרשב"א הנ"ל, ומ"מ בשו"ע הביא דברי הרמב"ם הנ"ל.

לשיטתם בעי סכנת נפשות וכדמבואר להדיא בסוגיא דב"ב שהטעם שהוא מצוה רבה הוא משום דכולהו איתנהו ביה, שיש בו סכנה או עכ"פ ספק סכנה.

אלא שיש לתמוה שבשו"ת ויאמר יצחק הנ"ל ביאר לדעת הש"ך הנ"ל שאף בליכא סכנה מצות פדיון שבויים הוא קודם לפרנסת עניים ולכסותן ומצוה גדולה היא וכו'. ויש להעיר דזה סותר את הסוגיא דב"ב, וצע"ג.

ט) ולפי הנ"ל, אותם יהודים הנתפסים באותם מאסרים שאין בהם חשש סכנת נפשות, לכו"ע יש חיוב ומצוה על הציבור לפדותם מצרה לרוחה. ולאידך ראשונים אפשר שגם הוא בכלל עיקר מצות פדיון שבויים שהרבה הפליגו בה חז"ל שהוא מצוה רבה וקודם לרל הצדקות וכו'.

ענף ב: אם ע"פ דין תורה יש כח למלכות עכו"ם לענוש עונש הגוף אף לישראל

א) והנה בעיקר הדין של דינא דמלכותא דינא, יעויין ברשב"ם ב"ב (דף נד: ד"ה והאמר שמואל דינא דמלכותא דינא), וז"ל: כל מסים וארנוניות ומנהגות של משפטי מלכים שרגילים להנהיג במלכותם דינא הוא, שכל בני המלכות מקבלים עליהם מרצונם חוקי המלך ומשפטיו והלכך דין גמור הוא ואין למחזיק בממון חבירו ע"פ חוק המלך הנהוג בעיר משום גזל, עכ"ל.

ומבואר בדבריו שהטעם משום שכל בני המלכות מקבלים עליהם,[ה] ולכן דינא דמלכותא דינא אף לענין דיני תורה. ויל"ע במש"כ הרשב"ם "ומנהגות של משפטי מלכים" ו"חוקי המלך ומשפטיו" אם זה כולל גם לענין שאר עונשין של יסורי הגוף כגון הכאה ומאסר וכדומה שזה גם בכלל קבלתם כיון שהוא בכלל חקי ומשפטי המלך, או רק לענין דיני ממונות הוא כן, וצ"ע.

ב) אמנם הדבר מפורש בדברי הרשב"א (החדשות מכתב יד סימן שמ"ה, מובא בב"י חו"מ סימן שפ"ח אות ט"ז), וז"ל: וגדולה מכל אלו בנדון שלפנינו, שאנו לא דננו, אלא נשאל נשאלנו מאת המלך יר"ה לראות בעינינו ולהגיד לו עצתנו לפי מה שעשה [והנידון על מסור אחד שנשאלו הרשב"א ועוד מהמלך אם להרגו, והורו לו שהוא חייב מיתה וצוה המלך להרגו], ואמרנו שהוא יכול להמיתו, לפי שלא נאמרו כל הדברים הללו אלא בדיני סנהדרין מגזרת הכתוב, **אבל בדינא דמלכותא אין משגיחין בכל אלו, שאין דינם אלא אחר ידיעת האמת, ונהרג בדיני המלכות אפילו על פי קרובים ואפילו על פי עצמו ושלא בהתראה ושלא בעשרים ושלשה**, שאין דין המלכות אלא אחר ידיעת האמת. כי אם אין אתה אומר כן אלא שאתה מעמיד הכל על דין תורה כדין סנהדרין, היה העולם

ה ואף במי שעומד וצווח שאינו מקבל עליו לכאורה בטלה דעתו, וצ"ע. וע"ע בר"ן בנדרים (דף כח. ד"ה במוכס) בשם תוס' שדוקא במלכי עובדי כוכבים אמר דדינא דמלכותא דינא מפני שהארץ שלו ויכול לומר להם אם לא תעשו מצותי אגרש אתכם מן הארץ וכו', ע"ש.

וכן מצאתי בשו"ת ויאמר יצחק (בן וואליד, יו"ד סימן ס"ז) שכתב לפרש כן דברי הש"ך, שאף בליכא אפילו ספק סכנת נפשות יש חיוב לפדות, ובהמשך דבריו ביאר שאף באופן שלא יטמע בין גויים ורק משום צערא דגופא לחוד[ד] יש מצוה לפדותו, ע"ש.

ז) וכן משמע בדברי הרדב"ז (הלכות מתנות עניים פ"ח הי"ג), שכתב וז"ל: וכבר נשאלתי על היהודים הרגילים לגנוב ממון עכו"ם אם אנו מחוייבים לפדותם או מדמינן להו למי שלוה מהם ואסרוהו, או למי שהמיר, דמה לי אוכל נבלות ומה לי לא תגנוב. והעליתי דלעולם פודין אותו כדין מי שלוה מן העכו"ם, שהרי אינו גונב להכעיס אלא לתאבון, שאם היה מוצא ממון בהיתר לא היה גונב וכו', וכל שכן שהורגים על הגניבה. הילכך חייבים לפדותם אפילו כמה פעמים, עכ"ל.

ולכאורה משמע שאפילו ליכא סכנה מחוייבים לפדות, ורק לבסוף מסיק שכש"כ שיש מצוה משום שיש סכנה, אבל משמע שגם בלא סכנה איכא מצוה, [ואולי יש לדחות שכוונתו דכש"כ משום שאיכא ודאי סכנה, וצ"ע].

סיכום:

ח) המורם מכל הנ"ל, לדעת הרמב"ן מצות פדיון שבויים הוא רק באופן שיש בו סכנת נפשות. ולהשדי חמד גם דעת התוס' כשיטת הרמב"ן, אלא שלשיטתם יש חילוק בין ודאי סכנה לספק סכנה שבודאי סכנה פודין אף ביותר מכדי דמיהם, וכן בארנו בדעת הרמב"ם.

אמנם דעת המאירי וכן נראה שהוא שיטת הי"א המובא ברמב"ן [וכן י"ל שהוא שיטת התוס'] שגם כשליכא אפילו חשש ספק נפשות הוא בכלל מצות פדיון שבויים, וכן משמע שהוא דעת הש"ך והרדב"ז.

אלא שנראה לומר בעיקר פלוגתתם, שאף לשיטת הרמב"ן ודעימיה שנקטו שסתם שבי הוא במצב של סכנת נפשות, היינו דוקא לענין המצוה הרבה המיוחדת של פדיון שבויים שהוא קודם לכל הצדקות וכו', וכן שמוכרין ס"ת בעבורו, אבל גם בלא סכנת נפשות יש מצוה לפדותם.

והטעם פשוט, שהרי הרמב"ם מנה הרבה מצות שהם בכלל מצות פדיון שבויים, ואמר שהוא בכלל צדקה ומצות ואהבת לרעך כמוך וכו', וזה שייך אף במקום שליכא חשש סכנה, ומשו"ה מחוייבין הציבור לפדות אף בשבי שעיקרו משום ממון אף שאין בו סכנת נפשות לפדותו.

וכן י"ל שמש"כ המאירי ודעימיה שאף בליכא סכנת נפשת מחוייב לפדותם היינו רק לענין שיש עכ"פ מצוה ומוטל על הציבור כן [כדמוכרח ממתני' ששבוי שעיקרו משום ממון פודין כדי דמיהם] אבל לענין שפדיון שבויים הוא מצוה רבה וקודם לכל הצדקות גם

ד ומפרש הא שבמוכר עצמו בקשו להרגו פודים אותו אף לאחר ג' פעמים, היינו בספק סכנת נפשות, אבל זה שמן הסתם פודים עד פעם שלישית הוא גם בליכא סכנה כלל, ע"ש.

היה סכנה יותר מסתם שבוי] ולפיכך הקשה עליו הרמב"ן מהסוגיא דב"ב הנ"ל דכל שבי יש חשש מיתה.

והאמנם כדי לתרץ קושיית הרמב"ן צ"ל כמש"כ השדי חמד שכוונתם היא, שהמעשה של אותו תינוק ברומי היה בו ודאי סכנה, וכמו שנתבאר שיש לחלק בין ודאי סכנה לספק.

ה) והמאירי (גיטין דף מה.) כתב ליישב קושיית הרמב"ן הנ"ל, וז"ל: ויש שואלים בה [על מתני' שאין פודין יותר מכדי דמיהם] שהרי בפרק הניזקין אמרו העבודה לא אזוז מכאן עד שאפדנו בכל ממון שפוסקין עלי ולא זזו משם עד שפדאו בממון הרבה וכו'. או שמא כל שיש **חשש** מיתה אין לדבר קיצבא, ואע"פ שאמרו ב"ב (דף ח:) דרך כלל שבי כולהו איתנהו ביה, **מכל** מקום שבי שעיקרו לממון אין בו חשש מיתה (ובו אמרו הכלל, שאין פודין השבוין יותר על כדי דמיהן), עכ"ל.

מבואר מדבריו שסוגיא דפרק הנזקין איירי באופן של ספק סכנה, ואז פודין יותר מכדי דמיו, והא דתנן שפודין רק כדי דמיו איירי בפדיון שבויים באופן שאין בו אפילו חשש מיתה כגון שעיקרו משום ממון.

ושיטת המאירי מבואר, שאיכא מצות פדיון גם באופן שאין בו משום סכנת נפשות, רק שסתם פדיון שבויים שאין עיקרו משום ממון איכא פקוח נפשות ובזה איירי הסוגיא בב"ב הנ"ל.

וכד אתינא להכא י"ל שגם התוס' הנ"ל נתכוונו כשיטת המאירי [אלא שדבריהם סתומים קצת] ולפ"ז אין צריך לתירוץ השדי חמד הנ"ל.

ו) ונראה שכשיטת המאירי מבואר עוד בדברי הש"ך.

דיעויין בשו"ע (יו"ד סימן רנ"ב סעיף ט'), שכתב וז"ל: הוא ואביו ורבו בשבי, הוא קודם לרבו, ורבו קודם לאביו, אמו קודמת לכולם, עכ"ל. ועי"ש בש"ך (ס"ק י') שכתב, וז"ל: קודמת לכולן. פירוש, אפילו לדידיה, אף על גב דחייו קודמים לחיי אביו ורבו וכו', אפ"ה להוציא מבית השבי אמו קודמת לכולן, משום דלמא עבדי בה איסורא וכו'. ומשמע דאין בשביה זו משום סכנת נפשות, אבל אם יש סכנת נפשות חייו קודמין לשל אמו, עכ"ל.

ולכאורה כוונת הש"ך שאיירי שליכא סכנת נפשות, היינו אפילו בליכא אפילו ספק, שהרי גם בספק סכנה חייו קודמים.[ב]

ולפ"ז הא דאיתא בשו"ע שאמו קודמת הוא באופן שליכא סכנה כלל, ומ"מ יש בו משום מצות פדיון שבויים.[ג]

ב וכ"כ בברכי יוסף שמדוקדק מדברי הש"ך שמיירי בידוע שאין בשביה זו סכנת נפשות, ואינה כסתם שביה ד"כולהו איתנהו ביה". אלא שהעיר דסתמא קתני היה הוא וכו' בשבי אמו קודמת לכולם, ומשמע דמיירי בסתם שבי דכולהו איתנהו ביה שיש חשש סכנה, ונשאר בצ"ע, וע"ש עוד.

ג ודוחק לומר שאין בו מצוה, ורק כשבא לפדות בתורת רשות יש דין סדר שאמו קודמת.

ג) ולכאורה היה אפשר לחלק בין ספק סכנת נפשות לודאי סכנה, שכוונת הסוגיא בגיטין שמבקשין להרגו, היינו שהוא באופן שיש ודאי [או קרוב לודאי] סכנת נפשות, ובכה"ג הוא דפודין אפילו אחר כמה פעמים. והא דתנן שבמוכר עצמו פודים רק עד שלשה פעמים, זהו בסתם פדיון שבויים שאינו מצב של ודאי סכנה ורק ספק סכנה. וזו כוונת הגמ' בסוגיא דב"ב שכולהו איתנהו ביה - היינו שיש חשש ספק סכנת נפשות, וגם בספק סכנת נפשות יש בו אזהרה משום "לא תעמוד על דם רעך", ומשו"ה בכל פדיון שבויים מצוה רבה היא דכולן אתנהו ביה וכמו שנתבאר.

ד) וחילוק הנ"ל כבר נמצא בדברי הראשונים, כאשר יתבאר. דהנה כבר עמדו הראשונים על הא דתנן בגיטין בפרק השולח (דף מה.) "אין פודין את השבויין יתר על כדי דמיהן מפני תיקון העולם", דקשה מהא דאיתא בפרק הנזקין (שם דף נח.): תנו רבנן מעשה ברבי יהושע בן חנניה שהלך לכרך גדול שברומי, אמרו לו תינוק אחד יש בבית האסורים יפה עינים וטוב רואי וקווצותיו סדורות לו תלתלים הלך ועמד על פתח בית האסורים, אמר (ישעיה מב:כד) "מי נתן למשיסה יעקב וישראל לבוזזים", ענה אותו תינוק ואמר "הלא ה' זו חטאנו לו ולא אבו בדרכיו הלוך ולא שמעו בתורתו", אמר מובטחני בו שמורה הוראה בישראל, העבודה שאיני זז מכאן עד שאפדנו בכל ממון שפוסקין עליו, אמרו לא זז משם עד שפדאו בממון הרבה, ולא היו ימים מועטין עד שהורה הוראה בישראל ומנו רבי ישמעאל בן אלישע, ע"כ. ומבואר שפדהו רבי יהושע בן חנניה לאותו תינוק ביותר מכדי דמיו, ולכאורה הוא נגד משנה מפורשת הנ"ל.

וע' תוס' שם (ד"ה כל ממון שפוסקין עליו) שתירצו, וז"ל: כי איכא סכנת נפשות פודין שבויין יותר על כדי דמיהן, כדאמרינן בפרק השולח לעיל (דף מז.) גבי מוכר עצמו ואת בניו לעובדי כוכבים, כ"ש הכא דאיכא קטלא, עכ"ל.

ובחידושי הרמב"ן (שם דף מה.) שהביא תירוץ הנ"ל, וז"ל: ואי קשיא הא דאמרינן בפ' הניזקין העבודה לא אזוז מכאן עד שאפדנו בכל ממון שפוסקים עלי, אמרו לא זזו משום עד שפדאו בממון הרבה, וי"ל וכו'. וי"א דכל היכא דאיכא **חששא דמיתה** פודין אותן בכל ממון שיכולין לפדותן. ולא מסתבר, דכל שבי כולהו איתנהו ביה, עכ"ל.

וע' בשדי חמד (ח"ה שו"ת דברי חכמים סימן ע"ז ד"ה מה שדחה) שהביא קושית הרמב"ן מספר בן אברהם (עה"ת פרשת ראה דף קט"ו ע"ג), ותירץ שכוונתם שרק באופן שהוא ודאי סכנה[א] אז פודין יתר על כדי דמיהם, משא"כ בסתם שבויים שהוא רק בחזקת סכנה ולא ודאי, באופן זה הוא שתקנו שאין פודין יותר מכדי דמיהם, וע"ש עוד.

אמנם מדברי הרמב"ן מבואר שהתירוץ הנ"ל לא נתכוון שהסוגיא בהנזיקין איירי בודאי סכנה אלא רק **חששא דמיתה** [וכנראה כוונתו דמהיכי תיתי לומר שבאותו מעשה

א וכן משמע ממה שהוכיחו התוס' מהא דמוכר עצמו "דאיכא קטלא" והיינו במבקשים להרגו והוא באופן של ודאי סכנה וכמו שכתבנו לעיל.

מחבירו. חרב קשה ממות וכו' רעב קשה מחרב וכו', שבי קשה מכולם דכולהו איתנהו ביה, ע"כ. ופירש"י, וז"ל: שבי כולהו איתנהו ביה: שהוא ביד העכומ"ז לעשות בו כל חפצו אם למות אם לחרב אם לרעב, עכ"ל.

ומבואר דהא שפדיון שבויים הוא מצוה רבה מכל הצדקות, הוא באופן שכולם איתנייהו ביה שיש בו משום מות חרב ורעב. וכן מובא ברמב"ם בהלכות מתנת עניים (פ"ח ה"י), וז"ל: פדיון שבויים קודם לפרנסת עניים ולכסותן, ואין לך מצוה גדולה כפדיון שבויים, שהשבוי הרי הוא בכלל הרעבים והצמאים והערומים ועומד בסכנת נפשות. והמעלים עיניו מפדיונו הרי זה עובר על "לא תאמץ את לבבך" "ולא תקפוץ את ידך" ושל "לא תעמוד על דם רעך" ושל "לא ירדנו בפרך לעיניך", וביטל מצות "פתח תפתח את ידך לו", ומצות "וחי אחיך עמך", "ואהבת לרעך כמוך", ו"הצל לקוחים למות" והרבה דברים כאלו. ואין לך מצוה רבה כפדיון שבויים, עכ"ל.

ומדנקט הרמב"ם שבכלל מצות פדיון שבויים הוא הלאו של "לא תעמוד על דם רעך" וכן המצוה מדברי קבלה של "הצל לקוחים למות" על כרחך דמיירי היכא שיש בו סכנת נפשות, [או עכ"פ ספק סכנת נפשות].

וכן העתיק בשו"ע (יו"ד סימן רנ"ב סעיף ב') והוסיף עוד (שם סעיף ג'), וז"ל: כל רגע שמאחר לפדות השבויים, היכא דאפשר להקדים, הוי כאילו שופך דמים, עכ"ל. ומקורו משו"ת מהרי"ק (שורש ז').

ב) ויש לעיין טובא מסוגיא דגיטין (דף מו:-מז.) דתנן: "המוכר את עצמו ואת בניו לעובדי כוכבים אין פודין אותו, אבל פודין את הבנים לאחר מיתת אביהן". ובגמ': "אמר רב אסי והוא שמכר ושנה ושילש". ועוד שם: "ההוא גברא דזבין נפשיה ללודאי (פירש"י: אומה שאוכלין בני אדם) אתא לקמיה דרבי אמי, אמר ליה, פירקן, אמר ליה, תנן: המוכר עצמו ואת בניו לעובדי כוכבים אין פודין אותו, אבל פודין את הבנים משום קלקולא, וכ"ש הכא דאיכא קטלא", ע"כ.

והנה משמע דפעם ראשונה ושנייה מצוה לפדותן אף בכה"ג שליכא חשש מיתה, שהרי באופן שמבקשים להרגו פודין אף פעם שלישית.

ולכאורה צ"ע, הא מבואר בסוגיא בב"ב הנ"ל שמצות פדיון שבויים היא בכה"ג ד"כולהו איתנהו ביה" ואיך אומר כאן שבפעם ראשונה ושניה יש מצוה אפילו כשאין חשש מיתה, וצ"ע.

ואין לומר שהוא מחלוקת הסוגיות, שהרי הרמב"ם בהלכות מתנות עניים (פ"ח הי"ג) הביא להלכה גם את הסוגיא דגיטין הנ"ל, וז"ל: מי שמכר עצמו ובניו לעכו"ם או שלוה מהן ושבו אותן או אסרוהו בהלואתן, פעם ראשונה ושנייה מצוה לפדותן, שלישית אין פודין אותן, אבל פודין את הבנים לאחר מיתת אביהן. ואם בקשוהו להורגו פודין אותו מידם אפילו אחר כמה פעמים, עכ"ל.

וכל זה צריך פירוש וביאור ליישב ב' סוגיות הנ"ל.

בענין מצות פדיון שבויים

מאת: דוד ליכטנשטיין

פרק א

לאחרונה ל"ע נתפסו כמה יהודים למאסר לכמה שנים, ביניהם ר' שלום מרדכי רובשקין נ"י שנתפס על עניני גזל ומרמה, וג' בחורים מא"י שנתפסו במדינת יאפאן על העברת המכס, ובתוך הדברים מצאו גם סמים. וכן מר יונתן פאללארד נ"י, שנתפס בגלל שהיה מרגל למדינת ישראל. המקום ירחם עליהם ולכל אחינו בית ישראל הנתונים בצרה ובשביה ויוציאם מצרה לרוחה בזמן קרוב, אכי"ר.

ויש לדון לפי דין תורה באנשים שנאסרו ע"פ המלכות ובאופן שלפי דיניהם של המלכות נענשו כדין, שאכן פשעו באותם העוונות שבהם נתפסו ונאסרו במאסר אי חל עליהם וכיוצא בהם המצוה הגדולה של פדיון שבויים [אבל באופן שגם במשפטם נענשו שלא כדין מתוך עלילות ובהגזמה וכדומה, באופן שלית דין ולית דיין, בודאי הדין משתנה אז, ומקרה זה אינו מענין המאמר שלפנינו]. ויש לדון בזה בכמה ספיקות:

א) אם מצות פדיון שבויים היא דוקא במצב של סכנת נפשות, ואת"ל שבכה"ג שאין סכנת נפשות אין בו משום מצות פדיון שבויים האם עכ"פ חייבים לפדותו מצד מצוה אחרת.

ב) אם על פי דין תורה יש כח למלכות עכו"ם לענוש עונש הגוף אף לישראל, כגון מאסר כשעוברים על חוקי המדינה. ואם על פי דין יש להם כח כנ"ל, האם גם באופן זה יש עליו שם שבוי לענין מצות פדיון שבויים.

ענף א: בגדר מצות פדיון שבויים אם צריך סכנת נפשות דוקא

א) גרסינן בפ"ק דב"ב (דף ח:): פדיון שבוים מצוה רבה היא. אמר ליה רבא לרבה בר מרי מנא הא מילתא דאמור רבנן דפדיון שבוים מצוה רבה היא, א"ל, דכתיב: (ירמיהו טו:ב) "והיה כי יאמרו אליך אנה נצא ואמרת אליהם כה אמר ה' אשר למות למות ואשר לחרב לחרב ואשר לרעב לרעב ואשר לשבי לשבי", ואמר רבי יוחנן כל המאוחר בפסוק זה קשה

דוד ליכטנשטיין למד בישיבת מיר בירושלים עיה"ק, וזכה לשמוע שיעוריו הבהירים של רבו הגדול הרה"ג ר' נחום זצ"ל ארבע שנים. עוסק במלאכה ונהנה מיגיעת כפיו, עכשיו הוא גר בשכונת וועסלי הילס בראקלאנד קאונטי ניו יורק, ושם קובע מקום תפלתו בק"ק בית ברוך. שם הוא מרצה שיעורים מדי שבת בשבתו בעניני הלכה, על דברים העומדים על הפרק בעולם היהדות. המאמר לפנינו הוא משיעוריו הנ"ל ובזה רואה אור הדפוס לראשונה להגדיל תורה ולהאדירה.

חקירה

כרך י"א – שנת תשע"א

תוכן עניינים

הלכה

חקירה

כרך י"א – שנת תשע"א